OPEN RANGE

STEAKS, CHOPS & MORE FROM BIG SKY COUNTRY

JAY BENTLEY AND PATRICK DILLON

RUNNING PRESS
PHILADELPHIA · LONDON

Text © 2012 by Jay Bentley and Patrick Dillon
Photography © 2012 by Lynn Donaldson
Published by Running Press,
A Member of the Perseus Books Group

Printed in China

Books published by Running Press are available at special discounts
for bulk purchases in the United States by corporations, institutions,
and other organizations. For more information, please contact the
Special Markets Department at the Perseus Books Group, 2300 Chestnut Street, Suite 200, Philadelphia, PA 19103, or call (800) 810-4145,
ext. 5000, or e-mail special.markets@perseusbooks.com.

ISBN 978-0-7624-4153-2
Library of Congress Control Number: 2011938606

E-book ISBN 978-0-7624- 4706-0

9 8 7 6 5 4 3 2 1
Digit on the right indicates the number of this printing

Cover and interior design by Amanda Richmond
Edited by Kristen Green Wiewora
Food styling by Ricardo Jattan
Prop styling by Amanda Richmond
Photography assistant Jeff Hawe
Typography: Archer, Archive, and Rosewood

Special thanks to Montana Camp Antiques

Running Press Book Publishers
2300 Chestnut Street
Philadelphia, PA 19103-4371

Visit us on the web!
www.runningpresscooks.com

TO THE LATE A.J.McLANE
SPORTSMAN, AUTHOR, MASTER CHEF, AND GENTLEMAN.

And remember, plants and animals have died for this book. Use it.

CONTENTS

INTRODUCTION

TO OUTSIDERS, MONTANA HAS ALWAYS seemed to be a beautiful expanse of misty mountains, crystalline rivers, and endless emerald green prairies. That's how I found it when I arrived from Washington, DC in 1971, a fresh young civil servant on loan from the federal government to advise Montana's government on fledgling housing projects. I was supposed to stay six months, but, hooked on the beauty, western lifestyle, and my addiction to fly-fishing, I refused to leave.

For all its beauty, let's not forget that Montana, in the beginning, was a hard land populated by hard people who wrested ore from the bowels of the earth, or cattlemen who braved the scorching summers searching for grass and outlived the long winters with sudden freezing "northers" that always seemed to hit at calving time. The farmers, who every spring planted wheat and barley, gambled on rain and market prices, in essence rolling their dice, their gaming tables being the vast flat windblown and empty spaces along the highline.

The old mining town of Butte, just 75 miles up the road from our restaurant in Belgrade (Montanans think nothing of driving 100 miles for a good meal), had during the nineteenth century a population of over 100,000 and more millionaires than any city in America. It was also home to an international mix of Irish, German, Welsh, Chinese, Slovaks and a host of other nationalities with their own neighborhoods, music, customs, and yes, the best part from my viewpoint, their own food! At one time in Butte, you could walk into a place serving just about any kind of cuisine you desired, from Chinese to German.

Montana was, and still is, a home for people who do things with their hands, working people who like their steaks big and their drinks dark brown. But things have turned upside down in the last 25 years. The great mines have closed and Butte's fortunes have folded.

Still, I believe most things in Montana are changing for the better. Due to creative and farsighted management by the state and federal agencies, Montana hosts a higher game population today than at any other time in the twentieth century. Elk, deer, antelope, and moose have all rebounded from the low population levels of the early 1900s and can now be found in large numbers; people come from all over the world to fish the pristine rivers for wild trout and to hunt big game in the fall. Fortunately for my staff and me, both the fish and game and those in pursuit arrive regularly for open range-style cooking at The Mint. I'm proud to say that luminaries such as President Jimmy Carter, Buzz Aldrin, Ted Turner, Tour de France champion Greg Lamont, legendary basketball coach Bobby Knight, broadcast personalities Tom Brokaw and Judy Woodruff, actors Michael Keaton, Ali McGraw, Jane Fonda, Sam Elliott, Kevin Costner, Chris Cooper and Steven Seagal, and CEOs and entrepreneurs ranging from Chuck Schwab to Liz Claiborne have all enjoyed my cooking. With this cookbook you can join them.

—**JAY BENTLEY** *Belgrade, Montana*

THE AUGUST SUN RAN BLOOD ORANGE as it slung low toward the far western horizon, casting an incandescent, brassy glow over the windshields of the requisite Chevy pickups as they stood parked along the old main street. The towering granary, a dull white landmark by day, now glowed with antiquity standing over the timeworn town of Belgrade, just off I-90 in southwest Montana. Once, the Northern Pacific ran through it. Once, agriculture and farming ruled. As in a lyric by Lyle Lovett: "Once, this old town meant to be really something, once." Today, it is a few-block jangle of low-slung, worn brick buildings resembling a set from the television series *Deadwood*, but only after the cast and crew had long decamped. Belgrade remains a kind of period-piece town and, I suppose, the term "venerable" might be applied if one were inclined to be sentimental. But at the time of our arrival we were not in a sentimental mood. We were famished.

My companions, living in an upscale hillside enclave in Bozeman, ten miles down the road, and I had just come off the river. That would be the East Gallatin, coursing near Belgrade's backyard, where we had fly-fished the evening hatch for big rainbow and brown trout. This form of sport involves catch and release, meaning each prize is returned to the water, an exercise that bait fishermen deride as "playing with your food."

As we eased out of our boots and waders and climbed into the pickup, I had lamented that it would be a good hour before we got home, showered, changed, and hit a restaurant in downtown Bozeman. My hosts looked at me blankly, and one said, self assuredly, "We'll just hop over to The Mint."

Within minutes, our vehicle joined the other trucks, at least half of them covered in field dust, strung out along Main Street, where the only neon sign exclaimed: The Mint Café & Bar. We entered and I immediately found myself to be within one of those fabled places where everyone seems to know one another and if you don't, you probably will by the end of the evening. The patrons, an eclectic mixture of New West elegance, big-buckle, blue-jeans chic, casual and neighborly, and some wearing Stetsons and starched shirts but keeping the country look about them, mingled at the long bar and at the booths and tables. Sepia-toned photos depicting iconic scenes of the True West covered the walls. A country band, Montana Rose, which I learned was nationally renowned, but local, was setting up in the front. Dancing—appropriately, the two-step, as I was also about to experience—was encouraged. It was as though Steven Sondheim had suddenly alighted to create an out-west rendition of *Sunday in the Park with George*.

Presiding over this mélange was a twinkly-eyed, bearded, bearish, delightful gruff by the name of Jay Bentley, an East Coast transplant, with a deceptively bemused look about him, whom I guessed got most of his exercise at the bar. He immediately sized me up and pronounced himself, in a booming, gravelly voice to be "probably the only liberal Democrat in all of this part of Gallatin County." This was more of a friendly barb, a spark tendered to dry grass, for my more right-of-center-leaning Bozeman companions, also his longtime friends, with whom he loves to spar. If I have inadvertently planted a vision of *Cheers*, Montana-style, in the reader's mind, I only partly apologize. At The Mint, nearly everyone does want to know your name. But the comparison does not do justice to Jay Bentley, who trained in the classically inspired kitchens from Tampa to New Orleans, nor to Linda, the sure-handed, irrepressibly direct governess of the bar, nor to Jordon Boutry and his recent succesor Michael Phillips and the rest of his gifted kitchen crew. They could just as easily have been steeped in *Le Guide Culinaire*, or the *Art of Eating Well*; as it is how to turn a hunk of bison into a filet with maître d'hôtel butter that has refined my definition of oral sex. Incidentally, the menu offers a gentle caveat:

WE DO NOT GUARANTEE THE FLAVOR OF MEAT COOKED MEDIUM-WELL OR MORE.

The sensation of my first of more than a dozen meals here lingers. The pop of garlic roasted in olive oil, served with crusty bread, the ambrosial smoked mountain trout served with sautéed sweet peppers and onions on crisp crostini, the double cut pork chop brined for two days, and enhanced by rosemary, thyme, oregano, and garlic, seared over a hot, hot, cast-iron grill, that comes off equally earthy and delicate, accompanied by grilled but still slightly snappy local asparagus and creamed spinach baked in a ramekin. This came with an iceberg lettuce wedge with sesame vinaigrette, and a touch of balsamic to give it some boot. For wine we went with the recommended Three Valleys Zinfandel, a bold varietal from the famed Ridge winemakers of Northern California.

As they say, there is only one first time and yet with every meal and upon every occasion that I have stopped by The Mint over the years, that first experience is redoubled. Whether it's buffalo tenderloin or rib-eye, a flat iron or tenderloin, or a marinated, cast-iron roasted half chicken, the experience is routinely sublime. The meal arrives, the small talk ceases, the knives and forks get brandished and serious eating commences.

Jay and I have become friends, sharing our love and hatred of politics, joshing, story-telling, fly-fishing, and various alimentary endeavors, including combing our respective countryside's back roads searching serendipitously for meals to be treasured, deconstructed, and repeated. We share recipes by phone, and when our coordinates cross, we like to stand together at the stove or over the grill. Invariably, I allow that this is a great honor. He mumbles something to the effect that I seem to know my way around the kitchen. The mutual rejoinder has morphed into a kind of comedy routine. "Above all," he reminds all of us, "cooking should be fun."

With that we offer *Open Range*. The recipes and anecdotes are mostly his, although he has bestowed upon me the ultimate honor of allowing my thoughts and fingerprints on these pages as an editor and occasional commentator, mostly to share my enthusiasm for his cooking and thus bestow my approbation upon him in return. We're confident that in these pages we have achieved the perfect amalgam of western humor, veneration for what we've inherited as cooks and food lovers, and, most important, recipes whose outcomes speak for themselves. We want *Open Range* to be among your indispensible kitchen tools, as trusted as your well-seasoned grill or favorite spatula. We encourage you to do as we westerners do, learn and adhere to the basics for your own security, and then explore, innovate, and explore some more.

—**PATRICK DILLON** *San Francisco and Sebastopol, California, and sometimes but not nearly enough, Bozeman, Montana*

WELCOME TO THE MINT

WHEN I OPENED THE MINT BAR & CAFÉ in the little town of Belgrade on the outskirts of Bozeman in 1994, it was a case of a location looking for a concept.

There has been a bar and sometimes a restaurant, even a bowling alley, at this location since 1904, its relative antiquity reinforced by the old sepia-toned photographs hanging in the bar showing the dusty town in its youthful years—a time of a dirt main street, hitching posts, and a jumble of brick and wooden storefronts, most of which have disappeared. In short, a classic portrait of early western Americana, a time and place that exists mostly in memory and myths, except here.

I was conflicted. On the one hand here was a classic Montana roadhouse, a sort of dying breed in a business where upscale, fusion, and cutting edge was the mantra of the time. My own experience and background in the food industry (my New Orleans apprenticeship at the then-fashionable Louis XVI with its acclaimed chef Daniel Bonnot, as well as several other stints under various French chefs) was leading me to go au courant, but my instincts said, "Wait a minute. This place has been here for almost a hundred years. You can't just throw all of this tradition away."

In the end I decided to do both. We tore down the existing building and rebuilt, restoring the look and feel of a classic old Montana roadhouse. We had a great local architect who went about creating a saloon by incorporating used brick and a timeless design that has everyone convinced it's an original. That skillful blend of old and new is also reflected in our menu. At The Mint, basic red-meat roadhouse fare meets Cajun, Creole, French, and Italian, classic and nouveaux. This amalgam also reflects and appeals to our diverse range of customers—ranchers, ranch hands, business tycoons, artists, musicians, writers, and people passing through on the way to Yellowstone or the Big Sky resort. We must be doing something right because The Mint is considered a "destination," by leading travel and gourmet magazines, and we recently celebrated our fifteenth anniversary.

We get a lot of Butte folks now in The Mint. We also get a lot of people from Bozeman, just down the road, and from places like Atlanta, Sarasota, Orange County, California, Dallas, and even Miami: refugees searching for authenticity but still demanding products and services the average Montanan would have never dreamed of a decade ago.

The Mint's menu served as a template for this cookbook. I envisioned *Open Range* as an edgy, red-meat cookbook. But my thinking evolved from roadhouse classics, like T-bone and Angus burgers, to a wider array of fare ranging from free-range lamb to boldly augmented pastas, local veggies and experimental side dishes reaped from the incredible

diversity of fresh ingredients available in our little part of paradise. If you are looking for upscale, Asian-influenced fusion, or other esoteric, off-the-wall concepts that seem to dominate the cookbook market today, then our fare is not for you. But if you're looking for great, honest, and authentically hearty chow that you can prepare at home, then keep reading.

Grease stains, wine spots, and dog ears will make us happy. Use this book, enjoy it, and remember that it makes us happy to be able to share a little of the fun we've had over a common stove, grill, or in our respective kitchens.

Lest we forget your purpose for picking up this book, Patrick and I promise you that regardless of your level of confidence or expertise, if you follow the directions you'll put out a meal that will turn idle table chatter into hosannas for the chef, followed by one of the sweetest sounds of all: mostly silence punctuated by the tinkle of knives and forks delivering the goods to appreciative mouths.

These are recipes that result from a seat-of-the-pants kind of cooking style. I try to give you quantities and measurements, but remember: recipes are only general guidelines to point you in the right direction. What I really want to do is give you a feel for cooking. Experiment with your own ideas. Over the years I've found that I learn a lot more from my mistakes than my successes.

A BRIEF HISTORY OF MEAT IN MONTANA

MONTANA IS A PLACE WITH A LOT OF grass, and a lot of grass means red meat and wild game. Historians tell us the first residents were Native American tribes who followed the woolly mammoth across the frozen expanse of the Bering Straits. Today, their descendants, the Crow, Blackfoot, Gros Ventre, Cheyenne, Arapaho, Shoshone, Sioux, and Flathead comprise the principle Montana nations. Their ancestors were big meat eaters! Their diets relied mainly on bison, elk, and antelope that roamed the region's immense grasslands in huge numbers. When the Lewis and Clark expedition passed through on its journey to the Pacific, the explorers' journals were filled with passages exalting the incredible variety of game they encountered. Unfortunately for the tribes and the animals, the stories in those journals spelled the beginning of the end for plentiful wild game. Grass was gold and there were fortunes to be made. In less than a life span, the bison were virtually exterminated. The native tribes were subdued and "relocated" to reservations, where, once out of the way, they could begin the process of becoming "civilized." The age of cultivated, grass-fed beef had begun.

Hunting Camp, Gallatin Canyon, Montana, 1915

Packing in Camp Supplies, Mill Creek, Montana, 1940

Picnic, Caldwell Ranch, Cherry Creek, July 4, 1900

The opening of the range happened in a few short years as cattlemen and sheep men arrived from all over to get rich in the livestock business. At first, the longhorn was the steer of choice because of its heartiness and ability to survive the cruel climate. In those days there was nothing but open range and these tough critters would graze over thousands of square miles like the bison they replaced. One problem was that longhorns tended to taste as tough as the landscape they roamed. Soon, they were replaced by more delectable Angus and Herefords, and like the bison before them, the longhorn all but disappeared.

Blizzards, drought, range wars, and fluctuating prices took their toll on the original cattle and sheep empires and most of the old ranches were broken up and sectioned off as the days of the open range drew to an end. Some cattle and sheep men got rich but most faded away, their era over.

Today, cattle and, to a smaller extent, sheep, still account for most of the ranching industry in Montana, but since nothing stays the same, a new beast is gaining popularity. Although they presently account for only a small share of the total livestock, bison are making a widely heralded return to the marketplace. Because of their low fat content, heartiness, and just plain romantic appeal, a lot of Montana ranches are switching from cattle to buffalo production. The acknowledged king of the buffalo movement is Ted Turner, who has dedicated his 1.5 million acres in Montana, New Mexico, and

Cooking Breakfast, Tom Minor Basin, Montana, September 1925

Twilight View of Lambing Camp, Strickland Creek, Paradise Valley, Montana, July 1939

Norris Spangler and Lamb, Harvat Flats, near Livingston, Montana, May 4, 1939

Nebraska to return bison to the land and to dinner tables.

Sheep ranching still lives, and in many areas of the state you can glimpse the occasional old sheep wagon in use. Every summer as the sheep go onto the grass in the high country, a shepherd with his dogs guards them. To this day, these men still stand as solitary sentinels over their flocks through the long summer twilights much as their Basque and Spanish ancestors have done in the American West for the last hundred and fifty years. I don't know if there is anything better than a marinated, roasted leg of lamb from an animal that has spent the summer eating the rich, sweet grasses of the upper Big Hole Valley, accompanied by a great Merlot or Pinot Noir.

EQUIPMENT AND ESSENTIALS

EVERY TRADE HAS ITS TOOLS AND COOKING IS CERTAINLY NO EXCEPTION. OBVIOUSLY, AT A minimum, you could get by like our ancestors did, with an open fire and a sharp stick, but here is a list of the tools, spices, and odds and ends that will make your cooking experience easier and more consistent. Most of these items can be found at good cooking stores or restaurant suppliers. Costco is high on my list for all kinds of herbs, spices, and equipment. You don't have to go crazy like I have (a collection of equipment, herbs, spices, and tools like mine takes years), but here are some basics to get you started turning out great food.

CAST-IRON SKILLET: A 12-inch pan is the ideal size for searing and blackening.

CAST-IRON GRIDDLE: (Also referred to in this book as a plancha), A standard-sized griddle is great for blackening and searing. You can use it indoors if you have a good kitchen exhaust fan, and outside on your grill.

NONSTICK PANS: For all-around use I like to have two nonstick pans: 10 inches and 14 inches. I buy medium weight, lower-cost pans because when the nonstick surface wears out, which is inevitable despite the manufacturer's claims, I simply buy a new one. They are also called omelet pans because their gently sloped sides are designed to slide an omelet on to the plate. This shape is the most versatile, being suitable for all kinds of cooking. Usually I can find a set of pans at Costco for around $20.

MEAT THERMOMETER: My favorite is a Thermapen—very fast, but also very expensive. There are a lot of choices but do get something, preferably a digital instant-read. It's absolutely essential for thicker cuts of meat.

COOKING TONGS: Use the spring-driven kind found in most restaurant supply stores: normally 8 to 10 inches in length. Use 10-inch tongs for barbecuing and big jobs.

COOKING SPOONS: Heavy-duty, restaurant quality is best here. You should have at least two regular spoons, one wood, one metal, and two slotted spoons, one wood and one metal.

COOKING FORKS: I use a heavy-duty cooking fork along with a heavy cooking spoon or tongs for lifting and moving heavy roasts, chickens, and turkeys.

ROASTING PAN: A good heavy-duty roasting pan will last a lifetime. Buy the largest that will fit in your oven (and be sure to get one with a raised lid that fits well).

POTS AND PANS: Good heavy-duty pots and pans, as opposed to nonstick ones, are an investment. Start with two good-quality saucepans, a small (2-quart), a medium (8-quart), and a large (16- to 20-quart) stockpot for pasta or soups and all-around use. Be sure to get matching lids and add more pots as needed. I also have an old cast-iron Dutch oven as my go-to for just about any kind of braising.

KNIVES: Always purchase the best-quality knives you can afford. If you have only one knife, make it an 8-inch chef's knife. I like German steel, but there are a number of other great choices available. To round out a collection, I would buy them in this order: 2-inch paring knife, 6-inch boning knife, 8-inch fillet knife, and 12-inch slicer. Also, be sure to include a good steel sharpener to maintain your knives.

PEPPER MILL: Spend some money and get a good pepper mill that you can adjust to regulate the size of the grind. Very coarse pepper is good for meats and finer ground pepper works for table use. I like a large Peugeot.

STORAGE: We marinate frequently and for long times, so leak-proof, resealable plastic bags are essential. Go with either Hefty® or Ziploc®. Plastic wrap is also an essential for marinating large pieces of meat and for all-around storage needs.

HERBS, SPICES, AND CONDIMENTS

WHEN I REFER TO DRIED HERBS I ALMOST ALWAYS USE WHOLE, RATHER THAN GROUND. I BUY MY chicken and beef base in a concentrated paste: Better Than Bouillon is, in my opinion, the best brand available. (Of course, being the Costco devotee that I am, I buy it there.) It has great flavor, is lower in salt, and is much cheaper than in grocery stores.

Here are the other herbs and spices that I consider staples.

• Whole black peppercorns	• Oregano	• Paprika	• Cumin
• Coarse sea salt	• Granulated garlic	• Granulated onion	• Chili powder
• Kosher salt	• Basil	• Cayenne pepper	• Curry powder
• Thyme	• Bay leaves	• Lemon pepper	• Rosemary

Other items I keep around the kitchen:

• Matouk's hot sauce (available online)	• Sriracha (Thai hot sauce)	• Balsamic vinegar	• Cornstarch
• Tabasco® Habañero Sauce	• Kikkoman (or any quality brewed) soy sauce	• High-quality, extra-virgin olive oil	• All-purpose flour
• Pickapeppa hot sauce (the red variety)	• Hoisin sauce	• Champagne vinegar	• Concentrated beef base
	• Dark toasted sesame oil	• Red wine vinegar	• Concentrated chicken base

STARTERS, SALADS, SOUPS, AND SUCH

AT THE MINT WE DON'T SAY OR SERVE "HORS D'OEUVRES."
WE SERVE HORS D'FIELD AND STREAM.

BACON-WRAPPED DATES WITH GORGONZOLA

HAVING SPENT A LOT OF TIME IN PALM Springs, in the Coachella Valley of California—the heart of the nation's date growing region—I have driven by stand after stand selling freshly harvested dates without slowing down. That was until someone talked me into sampling this classic of tapas bars worldwide. It was love at first taste. In The Mint's version, I call for Gorgonzola but other blue cheeses work as well. Dates come in several varieties but any type should work as long as they are fresh.

SERVES 3 TO 4

- 6 THIN SLICES BACON, CUT IN HALF (TO MAKE 12 SHORT PIECES)
- 12 FRESH DATES
- 6 TABLESPOONS (2 OUNCES) CRUMBLED GORGONZOLA CHEESE

COOK THE BACON UNTIL IT IS JUST SHORT OF crisp. Set on a paper towel-lined plate to drain.

Slit the dates down the middle. Remove the pits and stuff $\frac{1}{2}$ teaspoon of Gorgonzola cheese into the cavity. Wrap the date in half a strip of bacon. You can opt to use a toothpick to keep it together if you feel it is needed.

Preheat the broiler on low and arrange the dates on a baking sheet. Broil the dates until the bacon is crisp but not burned, about 2 minutes per side—but keep a close eye on it. (You can opt to pan-sear the dates over medium heat if you so desire. Turn as necessary to ensure even cooking.) When the bacon is crisp and the cheese is melted, remove from the oven and arrange on a tray or individual appetizer plates and serve warm.

GRILLED ARTICHOKES

WHEN I WANT TO BLOW MY GUESTS AWAY WITH an appetizer without getting into an elaborate process, I whip out my old standby: grilled artichokes. They're simple, don't need a lot of prep, and people love them. There are a number of dips and sauces to serve with artichokes but my favorite is our Perfect Mayonnaise recipe (see page 242). Try it. I'll be listening for your howls of delight.

SERVES 4

4 LARGE WHOLE ARTICHOKES
4 LEMONS
1 CUP OLIVE OIL
¼ CUP LEMON PEPPER
PERFECT MAYONNAISE
  (SEE PAGE 242)

BRING A LARGE STOCKPOT FILLED WITH heavily salted water to a boil. Fill a large bowl with ice water and set aside. When the water is boiling, squeeze the juice of two of the lemons into the water, adding the rinds as well. Place the whole artichokes into the water and boil for about 20 minutes, or until the chokes are tender. You can check this by sticking a knife into the stems; they should be very tender. Cook longer if necessary. When the chokes are finished, place them in the ice water to stop the cooking.

Cut the cooled chokes in half vertically and, with a spoon or a paring knife, trim out the feathery choke with the small purple leaves, leaving the outer leaves and the heart intact.

Using your hand, flatten the chokes just a bit and place them cut-sides up on a rimmed baking sheet. Drizzle olive oil over the chokes and sprinkle a generous amount of the lemon pepper blend over them. Allow them to sit for up to 30 minutes to allow the oil and spice mix to penetrate the inner leaves. You can do this while you are preheating your grill.

Preheat a charcoal grill, gas grill, or flat griddle to very high heat and place the chokes face down. The oil and high heat should char the inside surface of the chokes. You can even burn the outside leaves a little. When you have grilled the insides of the artichokes for about 5 to 7 minutes, turn them over. Cook the outsides for another 5 to 7 minutes, remove from the heat, and serve immediately. If necessary, you can cook them in two batches, keeping the first batch warm in a low oven. Serve 1 or 2 halves per person (depending on the size of the artichokes) with the mayonnaise on the side. Slice the remaining 2 lemons into wedges, and serve alongside the artichokes.

OVEN-ROASTED GARLIC WITH CRUSTY BREAD

ROASTING HAS A MAGICAL EFFECT ON garlic. It mellows the raw garlic taste so the nutty flavor comes through in a way that is a natural for good crusty bread. We always make a bunch of roasted garlic because there are so many recipes that benefit from its unique taste, and it stores very well. When you want to serve it as an appetizer, simply throw it in the microwave for around 45 seconds and it's ready to go. Use your imagination in making use of the roasted garlic you'll have leftover. We use a lot of olive oil in the process because when the roasting is over you are left with not only the garlic itself but a goodly amount of garlic-infused olive oil to use in anything from flavoring all kinds of hot dishes to cold salad dressings. You can store garlic bulbs in the refrigerator for a least a week and the olive oil for twice as long.

SERVES 6

6 WHOLE GARLIC BULBS, UNPEELED

OLIVE OIL, AS NEEDED

CRUSTY FRENCH BREAD, AS NEEDED (ABOUT 2 MEDIUM-SIZED BAGUETTES)

PREHEAT OVEN TO 400°F.

Peel away the excess outer papery skin from the cloves of garlic, trying to keep the bulb intact. Place the garlic in an ovenproof dish and drizzle liberally with olive oil. Place the garlic in the hot oven and reduce the temperature to 325°F. Roast for 20 to 30 minutes or until it appears soft and nutty brown. Drain the oil into a separate dish. Squeeze the soft garlic from the skins, and smear it on crusty bread with the garlic-infused oil on the side.

CAJUN MUSHROOMS WITH CRAB

THIS DISH TRAVELED WITH ME FROM NEW Orleans to my first Montana restaurant, The Continental Divide, up in Ennis. It's certainly nothing fancy, just a simple mix of crab and mushrooms baked in cream. You can serve it individually in small ramekins or make it a communal dish by cooking it in a larger pan.

SERVES 8

2 BUNCHES SCALLIONS

1/4 CUP (1/2 STICK) UNSALTED BUTTER

2 POUNDS SMALL WHITE BUTTON MUSHROOMS, HALVED

1 POUND FRESH LUMP CRAB- MEAT OR 1 (16-OUNCE) CAN PASTEURIZED CRABMEAT

1/2 CUP DRY WHITE WINE

2 TABLESPOONS BASIC BLACKENING SEASONING (SEE PAGE 224), OR MORE TO TASTE

1 PINT HEAVY WHIPPING CREAM

1 TABLESPOON PAPRIKA, OR MORE TO TASTE

SEPARATE THE GREEN TOPS FROM THE white part of the scallions. Dice the whites and thinly slice the green tops and set aside separately.

Heat a large sauté pan over medium-high heat and add the butter. When the butter melts and starts to sizzle, add the diced scallion whites and mushrooms. Sauté the vegetables, continuing to stir until the mushrooms have been cooked through but not browned, about 7 or 8 minutes.

Add the crab and continue to sauté for another 3 to 4 minutes, stirring the mix occasionally. Add the wine, blackening seasoning, and cream.

Cook for another 5 minutes, stirring occasionally; the mixture should reduce and thicken. When the sauce is thick and creamy, stir in the thinly sliced scallions and turn off the heat. Spoon the mushrooms into 8 small ramekins or a medium-sized baking dish. Sprinkle a small pinch of the paprika over the top. (The mushrooms can be prepared a day ahead up to this point; cover and refrigerate until ready to bake.)

Preheat the oven to 400°F. Bake the mushrooms until they are bubbly around the edges, about 10 to 12 minutes. Serve hot.

CRAB CAKES WITH SPICY MAYO

MAYBE IT'S BECAUSE OF MY NEW ORLEANS culinary roots, or all those wonderful crab cakes from my days in Washington, D.C. at those great seafood houses that one can only find on the Eastern shore. Or maybe it was just because I was trying to use up a bunch of breadcrumbs that I had accumulated, but whatever the reason, I created my version of the classic seafood first course. As far as the spicy mayo, I took a shortcut by throwing together some mayo and spicing it up by adding some Vietnamese chili sauce with garlic, which you can find in the Asian section of your supermarket. If you are fortunate to have fresh local crab available, by all means use it. A reasonable substitute is refrigerated, pasteurized crab that normally comes in a can. To finish the crab cakes, you have two options. You can top each one with equal amounts of the mayo and serve right away, or you can run them under a hot broiler to glaze the mayo topping. We use the broiler at The Mint but either method will give you good results.

SERVES 4

CRAB CAKES

4 CUPS PLAIN BREADCRUMBS, DIVIDED

2 EGGS, BEATEN

1 TABLESPOON DIJON MUSTARD

1 TABLESPOON WORCESTERSHIRE SAUCE

1 CUP MAYONNAISE

1 POUND FRESH LUMP CRABMEAT OR 1 (16-OUNCE) CAN PASTEURIZED LUMP CRABMEAT

SEA SALT

1/4 CUP (1/2 STICK) BUTTER

SPICY MAYO

1/2 CUP MAYONNAISE

1 TEASPOON VIETNAMESE CHILI-GARLIC SAUCE

TO MAKE THE CRAB CAKES, PUT 2 CUPS OF the breadcrumbs in a shallow pie pan and set aside for coating the crab cakes. In a small bowl combine the eggs, mustard, Worcestershire sauce, and mayonnaise and set aside.

In a larger bowl add the crabmeat as well as any collected juice. Use your fingers to separate and shred the meat leaving some of the larger pieces intact. Add half of the mayonnaise mix along with 1 cup of the remaining breadcrumbs, season with salt, and toss them lightly to combine. Add enough additional mayonnaise and breadcrumbs until the mixture can be molded into 4 equal balls that will retain their shape without undue compression. Keep the mixture loose but not falling apart. Gently roll each crab cake into the breadcrumbs with just enough force to make a light crust. The balls will flatten a bit during the process.

Once the crab cakes are ready to cook, make the Spicy Mayo mixture by combining the mayonnaise and Vietnamese chili sauce.

Melt the butter in a large sauté pan over medium heat. When the butter is hot, gently place the crab cakes in the pan, being careful to keep them intact. Cook them for about 7 or so minutes and then very carefully turn them over. The outside should have a nice thick golden-brown crust. Cook the other side for around 5 minutes, until the cakes are firm.

To glaze the crab cakes with the spicy mayo topping, preheat a broiler on high. Divide the spicy mayo among the cakes and set them about 5 to 6 inches from the broiler; broil until the mayo is just golden with a crust. Alternatively, serve the cakes hot out of the pan with the spicy mayo on the side.

STEELHEAD GRAVLAX

STEELHEAD IS A GORGEOUS, ELUSIVE SEA RUN rainbow trout with mild, pink flesh. Like salmon they return to the place they were hatched to spawn. Unlike salmon, however, after steelhead spawn, they return to the sea to renew their lifecycle. Although I will not serve wild-caught trout in the restaurant, I occasionally prepare this Scandinavian classic at home in the fall, when a friend brings by a fresh-caught steelhead from the Clearwater River in Idaho, just west of the Montana state line. It doesn't happen often because just about all of us practice sustainable catch-and-release fishing.

From either fish, this is an elegant appetizer, calling for curing with a mixture of sugar, salt, and fresh dill. It is then sliced thin and served with several different garnishes and a sauce on the side. It's a beautiful presentation as well as a tasty treat.

SERVES 20

2 SIDES FRESH STEELHEAD OR SALMON (2 TO 3 POUNDS EACH), SKIN-ON

1 CUP GOOD-QUALITY COARSE SEA SALT

1 CUP PACKED LIGHT BROWN SUGAR

2 SHOTS VODKA

1 TABLESPOON FRESHLY GROUND BLACK PEPPER

4 OUNCES FRESH DILL SPRIGS

DIJON DILL MAYO SAUCE

1 CUP PERFECT MAYONNAISE (PAGE 242)

3 TABLESPOONS DIJON MUSTARD

1/4 CUP PACKED LIGHT BROWN SUGAR

CAPERS PACKED IN BRINE, FOR SERVING

FINELY DICED RED ONIONS, FOR SERVING

TO PREPARE AND CURE THE GRAVLAX:

place the fish skin-side down on a clean surface. They should be about the same size and shape. On each side, evenly distribute the salt and brown sugar and rub it into the meat. Pour a shot of vodka over each of the halves and rub it in. Take the fresh dill and distribute it evenly over one of the pieces, then carefully lay the other piece flesh-side down over the first with the dill in the middle.

Lay out sheets of foil long enough to completely enclose the fish and wrap it thoroughly in two layers. The idea is to wrap and cure the fish without leaks, which could occur as the sugar and salt leach moisture from the meat during the curing process.

Place the foil-wrapped fish on a rimmed baking tray in the refrigerator for 4 to 5 days, turning about once a day. Pour off any water that has accumulated. Keep the fish very cold.

When you are ready to serve the gravlax, make the Dijon-Dill Mayo Sauce. Unwrap the cured fish. Remove the dill, chop it finely and stir together with the mayonnaise, mustard, and brown sugar. Place the fish on a cutting board for service. The fish should be served by cutting very thin slices across the grain on the diagonal. The skin should help hold the fish together and facilitate the slicing. Arrange the slices on chilled plates and garnish with the capers, diced onions, and a dollop of the mayo sauce. Keep any remaining gravlax tightly covered in plastic wrap. It should be good for 5 to 6 days in your refrigerator.

BISON CARPACCIO

I'VE ALWAYS LOVED CARPACCIO: PAPER-THIN pieces of meat drizzled with a big, fruity olive oil, and covered with shavings of sharp Parmesan. When I started experimenting with game I found that venison, elk, and other red game meats work equally well. But my favorite is bison; the richness, texture, and deep red color of bison meat really complement this dish. There are several ways of preparing the meat. All work best if you use a fairly cylindrical piece of meat that has been semi-frozen to give you a firm cutting base. The first step is to cut paper-thin slices, so thin, in fact, that they are faintly transparent. This requires a sharp knife and a steady hand. My usual method is to slice the meat thinly, but not paper thin, and to put it between two pieces of plastic wrap. Then, using a meat hammer or a small sauté pan, I gently pound the meat, taking care to prevent holes, until it reaches the semi-transparency that I desire. Be sure to use a good-quality virgin olive oil with lots of fruit, and an equally good Parmesan cheese. A crusty, French or Italian loaf is great on the side along with a fruity Pinot Noir.

SERVES 4

4 TO 6 OUNCES BISON TENDER-LOIN, EYE OF THE ROUND, OR ANY LEAN CUT IN A ROUGHLY CYLINDRICAL SHAPE, FROZEN FOR ABOUT 30 MINUTES

$^1/_2$ TO $^3/_4$ CUP GOOD-QUALITY EXTRA-VIRGIN OLIVE OIL, OR AS NEEDED

$^1/_2$ CUP THINLY SHAVED PARMESAN CHEESE

$^1/_2$ CUP BRINE-PACKED CAPERS, DRAINED

$^1/_2$ CUP CHOPPED FRESH FLAT-LEAF PARSLEY

FRESHLY GROUND BLACK PEPPER

1 LEMON, CUT IN WEDGES

SLICE THE TENDERLOIN THINLY WITH A sharp knife, and lay the slices in a single layer between 2 pieces of plastic wrap. Using a meat hammer or a small, heavy sauté pan, gently pound the meat, taking care to do it evenly to prevent either holes or areas that are too thick, until the slices are paper thin and almost transparent.

Arrange equal portions of the meat on four salad plates, overlapping the meat and covering the bottoms of the plates. In equal amounts, and in this order, drizzle on the olive oil, then cover lightly with shaved Parmesan, capers, and parsley. Add the ground pepper, adjusting seasoning to taste, and serve at room temperature with lemon wedges.

SALMON CARPACCIO

FOR YEARS I HAVE THEORIZED THAT WILD salmon, particularly Sockeye and Coho, need to be treated almost like red meat; their strong flavor can be enhanced by sauces that sometimes one would associate with steaks. Treatments like red wine reductions, caramelized onion and mustard, wild berry compotes, things that one doesn't normally associate with seafood make good pairings with salmon. That's why the idea of Salmon Carpaccio popped into my head. It's definitely a red meat thing. In fact, I have a Bison Carpaccio (see page 28) that works equally well with beef.

Be sure to remove any skin and bones from the salmon before preparing. Also, use a very good fruity extra-virgin olive oil, as it is important to the overall taste and quality. A little salmon goes a long way so you can figure a 2-ounce portion per person will be plenty.

SERVES 8

1 POUND BONELESS, SKINLESS WILD SALMON FILLET

1 CUP GOOD-QUALITY EXTRA-VIRGIN OLIVE OIL

1 CUP GOOD-QUALITY SHAVED PARMESAN CHEESE

FRESH COARSELY-GROUND BLACK PEPPER

1 CUP CHOPPED FRESH FLAT-LEAF PARSLEY

SEA SALT

1 CUP BRINE-PACKED CAPERS, DRAINED

1 CUP FINELY DICED RED ONION

2 LEMONS, CUT INTO WEDGES

CHILL THE SALMON AND EIGHT SMALL salad plates. When both are well chilled cut the salmon fillet into 2 x 2-inch pieces of approximately similar shapes. Place each piece between two pieces of plastic wrap and, using the smooth side of a meat hammer, very carefully and gently pound the salmon to a thickness of around $\frac{1}{4}$ inch. Take the pieces of salmon and arrange them on the chilled plates, being careful not to tear the fragile flesh. Use about 5 to 6 pieces per plate (it's fine for them to overlap slightly). Cover each of the finished plates with plastic and return them to the refrigerator until ready to serve.

When ready to serve, drizzle the olive oil over the salmon, and then arrange the shaved Parmesan over the top of the salmon. Grind some fresh black pepper and sea salt over each serving, and then sprinkle the parsley over the top. Adjust seasonings to taste. On the edge of each plate arrange some capers and red onions and finally place a lemon wedge on top. Serve quickly while still cold.

TUSCAN BREAD SALAD

ONE OF THE BEST THINGS ABOUT HAVING AN independent restaurant is the fact that we can do anything we want. While The Mint is essentially a steakhouse, that doesn't mean we can't have fun with our additional offerings. Here is a summer salad inspired by panzanella in rural Tuscany using absolutely fresh tomatoes that are at their best in high summer. When we do offer this tasty little salad, it's always snapped up. Plus, it's a great way to use our day-old baguettes.

SERVES 4

1¹/₂ CUPS GOOD-QUALITY, EXTRA VIRGIN OLIVE OIL, DIVIDED

4 HEAPING CUPS DAY-OLD BREAD CUT INTO 2-INCH CUBES, WITH CRUSTS INTACT

1 TABLESPOON GRANULATED GARLIC

1 TEASPOON SEA SALT

4 CUPS CHOPPED FRESH TOMATOES (PREFERABLY EARLY GIRLS OR HEIRLOOMS)

2 CUPS DICED RED ONIONS

2 CUCUMBERS, SLICED INTO 1-INCH ROUNDS, THEN HALVED

2 CUPS COARSELY CHOPPED FRESH BASIL LEAVES

2 CUPS CRUMBLED GORGON-ZOLA OR BLUE CHEESE

PREHEAT ¹/₂ **CUP OF THE OLIVE OIL IN A SAUTÉ** pan over medium heat. When hot, add the bread, tossing to coat each piece. Continue to sauté the bread until slightly brown, then sprinkle the granulated garlic and salt over all while continuing to toss. Set aside to cool.

In a large bowl, combine the bread, tomatoes, onions, cucumbers, and basil leaves and allow the salad to rest for 5 minutes. Portion the salad into four individual serving bowls or salad plates and sprinkle the crumbled Gorgonzola equally over each.

ASIAN BEEF & SESAME SALAD

ONE OF THE SUMMER DISHES THAT MINT locals get vocal for is our Asian beef and sesame salad. Perfectly cooked rare beef and fresh and crunchy greens tied together by a tangy sesame vinaigrette makes for a great summer feast. The beef rub imparts an exotic overtone to the meat that comes together with the addition of the sesame dressing. The meat should be brought to room temperature to keep the greens from wilting. And it must not be overcooked. This recipe also works well with lamb, chicken breasts, and salmon fillets. Flank works well, or you can substitute any similar cut of beef.

SERVES 4

MARINATED BEEF

1 POUND FLANK OR TRI-TIP STEAK (SUBSTITUTE BONE-LESS CHICKEN BREASTS OR SALMON STEAKS)

$1/2$ CUP TOASTED SESAME OIL

$1/2$ CUP DARK SOY SAUCE

ASIAN RUB

$1/2$ CUP GRANULATED GARLIC

$1/2$ CUP ONION POWDER

$1/4$ CUP GROUND GINGER

$1/4$ CUP PAPRIKA

2 TEASPOONS CHINESE FIVE-SPICE POWDER

3 TEASPOONS COARSE KOSHER SALT

1 TEASPOON FRESHLY GROUND BLACK PEPPER

SALAD

1 POUND MIXED SALAD GREENS

2 CUPS SHREDDED RED CABBAGE

1 SWEET RED BELL PEPPER, FINELY SLICED

1 SWEET ONION, FINELY SLICED

1 LARGE CARROT, JULIENNED INTO 2-INCH PIECES

MINT-STYLE SESAME DRESSING (SEE PAGE 236)

$1/2$ CUP SESAME SEEDS, LIGHTLY TOASTED (OPTIONAL)

1 CUP CRUNCHY CHINESE NOODLES, TOASTED

TO PREPARE THE MEAT: COMBINE THE BEEF, sesame oil, and soy sauce in a large resealable plastic bag. Leave it to marinate for at least 1 hour and up to 3 hours before cooking. Combine the garlic, onion powder, ginger, paprika, five-spice powder, salt, and pepper for the rub and set aside.

Preheat a cast-iron skillet or sauté pan on high heat until very hot. When the pan is hot, remove the meat from the marinade and sprinkle all sides with the Asian rub. Place the steak on the hot pan and sear for about 2 minutes on each side for rare meat, or longer if you wish the meat to be more medium-rare to medium. When the meat is finished, set it aside to cool to room temperature. (If you substituted another meat, cook to the doneness you prefer, monitoring the internal temperature. For chicken, cook to 165°F; for salmon, sear only long enough to develop a crust on one or both sides.)

To assemble the salad: combine the greens, cabbage, peppers, onions, and carrots in a large bowl or in individual portions. Slice the steak across the grain in $1/2$-inch-thick strips and arrange atop the salad. Drizzle a generous amount of the sesame dressing over the salad and sprinkle the noodles and sesame seeds on top.

NOTE: The cooking process will generate a lot of smoke, so disable your smoke alarms and turn on the exhaust fan.

BUTTERMILK-FRIED QUAIL WITH STEEN'S PURE CANE SYRUP

THIS RECIPE IS STRAIGHTFORWARD AND simple, yet it has proven to be one of our most popular dishes. We get our quail farm-raised, partly boned, and ready to cook. Quail are wonderful grilled, sautéed, or roasted, but I love this recipe as an alternative to fried chicken. At The Mint we use a deep fat fryer, but at home a cast-iron skillet or even a saucepan containing 1 to 2 inches of oil works just as well. Be sure to check your oil temperature with a thermometer. Steen's Pure Cane Syrup®, produced by the historic syrup mill in Abbeville, Louisiana, is not readily available outside of the South, but substituting a good-quality honey or even molasses will work. If you want to serve this as an entrée, increase the number of quail to 6 and serve 3 halves per person.

SERVES 4

4 SEMI-BONELESS QUAIL

2 CUPS BUTTERMILK

4 CUPS ALL-PURPOSE FLOUR, SIFTED

$1/4$ CUP KOSHER SALT

VEGETABLE OIL, AS NEEDED

$1/2$ CUP STEEN'S PURE CANE SYRUP OR HONEY

REMOVE THE WINGS FROM THE QUAIL AND discard. Cut the rest of the quail in half, leaving the leg, thigh, and breast intact. Combine the quail pieces and buttermilk in a large resealable plastic bag and refrigerate the birds for at least 2 hours and up to 24 hours in the buttermilk.

Combine the flour and salt in a shallow dish. Remove each bird from the buttermilk and dredge in the flour mix.

Preheat your deep fryer or heat 2 inches of oil in a frying pan to 350°F to 360°F. Preheat the oven to 200°F. Line a rimmed baking sheet with paper towels.

Fry 2 or 3 pieces of quail at a time, being careful not to crowd the pan, and monitoring the temperature of the oil. Cook each piece for about 2 minutes per side, turning carefully so as not to disturb the flour coating. Keep the cooked quail on the lined baking sheet in the warm oven until all are cooked. Serve the quail with the Steen's syrup..

JERKED CHICKEN SKEWERS

THIS RECIPE IS DEFINITELY NOT A MONTANA dish by origin. In fact, you can find some version of jerked chicken skewers just about anywhere in the world. If you look at some of the marinades that I use for some of the Cuban recipes in this book you can see the similarities to Caribbean cooking.

I prefer to use boneless, skin-on chicken thighs for my recipe because thigh meat is juicier and tends not to dry out as quickly as chicken breasts. You can also substitute beef, pork, duck breasts, and even wild game; it's all in the marinade. These go great with Curried Coleslaw (see page 193).

SERVES 6 TO 8

1 (6-OUNCE) CAN FROZEN ORANGE JUICE CONCENTRATE, THAWED

1/2 CUP FRESHLY SQUEEZED LIME JUICE

1/2 CUP SOY SAUCE

1/2 CUP CIDER VINEGAR

1/2 CUP OLIVE OIL

2 TABLESPOONS GRANULATED GARLIC

1 TABLESPOON GROUND CINNAMON

1 TABLESPOON GROUND ALLSPICE

1 TEASPOON GROUND CLOVES

1 TEASPOON DRIED THYME

1 CUP CHOPPED SCALLIONS (WHITE AND GREEN PARTS)

1 SMALL, WHOLE HABAÑERO OR SCOTCH BON-NET PEPPER, FINELY MINCED (SUBSTITUTE 2 TABLESPOONS HABAÑERO HOT SAUCE)

HOT SAUCE, TO TASTE

8 BONELESS, SKIN-ON CHICKEN THIGHS, CUT INTO 1-INCH CUBES

3 TABLESPOONS PACKED LIGHT BROWN SUGAR

CURRIED COLESLAW (SEE PAGE 193)

IN A LARGE BOWL, WHISK TOGETHER THE orange juice, lime juice, soy sauce, vinegar, olive oil, garlic, cinnamon, allspice, cloves, thyme, scallions, habañero, 1 cup of water, and hot sauce to taste. Add the chicken thighs and toss to coat. Refrigerate the chicken in the marinade for 24 hours.

Preheat your gas or charcoal grill to medium-high heat. Prior to grilling, if using bamboo skewers, soak them in water for 30 minutes.

Skewer the pieces of chicken, setting them aside while the grill heats. Drain the marinade into a small saucepan, thin the mixture with 1 cup of water, and bring it to a boil. Reduce the heat to low while you grill the chicken. Place the chicken over the hot fire and cook, turning frequently, for 5 to 7 minutes. Stir the marinade occasionally and add the brown sugar, reducing by half to a thick consistency. The sugar in the marinade can burn quickly so keep a close watch. Serve each skewer drizzled with the reduced sauce over a bed of coleslaw.

POLENTA AND GRILLED SAUSAGE

WHETHER YOU SERVE COOKED CORNMEAL SOFT like mashed potatoes or cooked and cut into squares, polenta—like its distant relative pizza—is a great vehicle for cheese, sauces, and meat. At The Mint we serve polenta (or grits, depending on the availability of yellow corn as opposed to white) as a side for lamb, chicken, or beef. In this case, as an appetizer, we pair it with cheese, marinara sauce, and some form of sausage, baked and finished in a small round ramekin. The type of sausage you decide to use is up to you. I prefer a spicy Andouille or another form of spicy smoked sausage. The type of cheese is your choice as well; I like to use grated provolone. You can use any kind of cornmeal as long as it is coarsely ground. There are several stone-ground brands as well as other products labeled "quick polenta" and they all work well.

SERVES 6

3 LINKS SMOKED SAUSAGE, CUT INTO $\frac{1}{2}$-INCH ROUNDS

6 CUPS SOFT POLENTA WITH HERBS (SEE PAGE 217)

3 CUPS BASIC MARINARA SAUCE (SEE PAGE 243)

2 CUPS GRATED PROVOLONE CHEESE

PREHEAT THE OVEN TO 375°F.

Set a sauté pan over medium heat and cook the sausage for 3 to 5 minutes, until it is lightly browned and the fat has been partially rendered. Set aside to drain on paper towels. Spoon the soft polenta into the ramekins, so each one is about three-quarters full. Evenly distribute the sausage on top of the polenta in each ramekin.

Cover with the marinara sauce, and then sprinkle with the provolone cheese. Place the ramekins on a rimmed baking sheet and bake for about 15 to 20 minutes, or until the cheese has melted and the dish is hot through. At The Mint we finish the grits under a hot salamander. At home you can skip this step or run them under a broiler for color. Serve hot.

PEA SOUP WITH LEEKS

THIS IS THE SORT OF FOOD FARM PEOPLE eat after a long hard day in the fields. My wife Mary got this recipe from her mother, Norma Timmer, who grew up on a Dutch farm near Holland, Michigan. Like her relatives, it is about as hearty and honest as you can get. Unlike most recipes calling for ham, this recipe depends on unsmoked pig hocks, a very economical ingredient, but essential to its authenticity.

The collagen and bone in unsmoked pig hocks provide a rich, intense base. The delicate undertones bring out the flavor of the peas and other vegetables. The combination of whole and split peas adds a textural contrast that you don't find with just split peas. If you want, add a couple of diced potatoes to the vegetable mix to assure a thicker broth.

SERVES 12

- 2 UNSMOKED PIG HOCKS
- 3 BAY LEAVES
- $^{1}/_{2}$ CUP OLIVE OIL, DIVIDED
- 1 LARGE YELLOW ONION, FINELY DICED
- 5 GARLIC CLOVES, MINCED
- 2 LARGE LEEKS, THOROUGHLY RINSED, WHITES AND HALF OF THE GREENS CUT INTO $^{1}/_{2}$-INCH SLICES
- 3 STALKS CELERY, DICED
- 2 TO 3 LARGE CARROTS, GRATED (3 CUPS)
- 1 TABLESPOON DRIED THYME
- 1 TABLESPOON DRIED ROSEMARY
- 8 OUNCES WHOLE DRIED GREEN PEAS, RINSED
- 8 OUNCES DRIED GREEN SPLIT PEAS, RINSED
- 1 GALLON CHICKEN STOCK

FOR THE PIG HOCKS: PREHEAT THE OVEN TO 325°F.

In a large Dutch oven or stockpot, cover the hocks and bay leaves with a gallon of water. Bring the pot to a boil over high heat, then cover and transfer to the oven. Bake for about 1½ hours (the meat should be very tender and easy to pull from the bones); add water as needed to keep the meat covered. When hocks are done, remove them from the Dutch oven with a slotted spoon, leaving the cooking liquid behind. When the pork is cool enough to handle, pull the meat off the bones and chop into bite-sized chunks. Throw out the bones, skin, and fat. Keep the pot with the cooking liquid in the oven to keep it warm while you assemble the rest of the ingredients.

For the soup: While the hocks are cooking, add half of the olive oil to a large sauté pan over medium-high heat. Add the onions, garlic, and leeks. Cook for 5 minutes, or until translucent, then add the celery, carrots, thyme, and rosemary and cook for another 5 or so minutes, until the vegetables are tender. Add olive oil as needed to keep things from sticking.

When the vegetables are finished, add them to the Dutch oven along with all of the dried peas and the chicken stock.

Cook uncovered in the oven for 2 hours, stirring occasionally to prevent sticking. At the end of the first hour, add the reserved meat and continue to cook. You'll know when the soup is ready when the whole peas are very tender and the split peas have more or less completely broken down. If the soup is too thick, thin with a little water.

CAJUN BEEF FILÉ GUMBO

I AM ALWAYS TRYING TO COME UP WITH WAYS to use the leftover prime rib from the previous night, so, employing my experience cooking in Cajun country, I came up with a recipe for beef gumbo. Leftover beef from the grill is particularly good because the smoke adds a distinctive and delicious flavor. Be sure to make a big batch because it freezes well. Filé powder, a mixture of ground thyme and sassafras leaves, can be added just before serving to thicken the gumbo and add flavor. Be sure to make a good dark roux, but don't burn it.

SERVES 10 TO 15

1 CUP ALL-PURPOSE FLOUR

1 CUP PEANUT OR CANOLA OIL

1 CUP OLIVE OIL, VEGETABLE OIL, OR BACON GREASE, DIVIDED

3 POUNDS RAW BEEF ROAST, CUT INTO 1½ INCH CUBES, OR 3 POUNDS LEFTOVER COOKED BEEF, CUT INTO BITE-SIZED PIECES

4 GREEN BELL PEPPERS, SEEDED AND COARSELY CHOPPED

4 YELLOW ONIONS, COARSELY CHOPPED

5 BAY LEAVES

5 TABLESPOONS GROUND THYME

1 QUART BEEF STOCK (SUBSTITUTE 4 TABLESPOONS GOOD-QUALITY BEEF BASE PLUS 1 QUART WATER)

4 QUARTS WATER

1 CUP CHOPPED FRESH FLAT-LEAF PARSLEY

10 TABLESPOONS FILÉ POWDER, OR MORE TO TASTE

10 CUPS COOKED WHITE LONG-GRAIN RICE (YOU CAN SUBSTITUTE BROWN)

HOT SAUCE TO TASTE

IN A SAUTÉ PAN, MIX TOGETHER THE FLOUR and the peanut oil and cook over low heat until the flour becomes medium to dark brown (at least 20 minutes, but watch the color to make sure it doesn't burn), stirring continuously. Scrape the roux into a small bowl and set aside. (This will make more than you need, so reserve the rest for another use.)

Place a 10-quart stockpot or Dutch oven over high heat, add half of the olive oil and heat it to just below smoking point. If using raw meat, add the beef and brown on all sides. When it is finished, set aside. (If using cooked beef, skip this step and use all of the oil in the vegetables.)

Add the remaining ½ cup of olive oil and heat to just shy of smoking. When the oil is very hot, add the green peppers and onions and cook until translucent, about 3 to 5 minutes. Add the browned beef (or cooked beef, if using) to the pot and continue to cook for about 5 more minutes.

Stir in 1 cup of the roux, and when it is blended, add the bay leaf, thyme, and beef stock. Bring the stock to simmer, and then add the water gradually. Cook the gumbo for about an hour, tasting as you go; the beef should be very tender when it is done. Add the filé powder should just before serving. I usually stir 1 tablespoon into each individual bowl. Serve hot, over rice and with hot sauce to taste. Top each serving with parsley.

MEATLESS WHITE BEAN & ROSEMARY SOUP

WHILE THIS IS NOT A PURE VEGETARIAN creation because of the use of chicken stock, it is still a low-meat alternative for those who want something light and full of flavor. This is my version of a classic rustic Italian bean soup (pasta fagioli) without the pasta and tomatoes. The key to the flavor of this soup is the quality and intensity of the chicken stock and the fresh rosemary.

When I cook chicken at home, which is a lot, I almost always save the skin and bones of roasted chicken to use in a stock (see page 000). When I have accumulated enough to make a couple of gallons, I cook a batch of this soup for my long-suffering and beloved, meat-minimalist wife and soul mate. As far as the choice of beans, I prefer cannellini, or great northerns, although just about any white bean will work.

SERVES 12

- 1 POUND WHITE BEANS, COVERED IN AT LEAST 6 INCHES OF WATER AND SOAKED OVERNIGHT
- 1 GALLON CHICKEN STOCK
- 3 BAY LEAVES
- 1 TABLESPOON DRIED THYME
- 1/4 CUP FRESH ROSEMARY LEAVES, CHOPPED
- 1/2 CUP OLIVE OIL, DIVIDED
- 10 GARLIC CLOVES, SMASHED AND CHOPPED
- 2 MEDIUM YELLOW ONIONS, COARSELY CHOPPED
- 6 STALKS CELERY, CHOPPED (ABOUT 2 1/2 CUPS)
- 3 CARROTS, GRATED (ABOUT 1 1/2 CUPS)
- SEA SALT AND COARSELY GROUND FRESH BLACK PEPPER
- EXTRA-VIRGIN OLIVE OIL AND FRESHLY GRATED PARMESAN CHEESE, FOR SERVING
- 1 CUP CHOPPED FRESH FLAT-LEAF PARSLEY

TO COOK THE BEANS: DRAIN THE SOAKED beans and cover with fresh water by 2 inches in a large stockpot. Bring the pot to a boil, and then drain again. Add the chicken stock to cover the beans, and bring the pot back to a boil before reducing the heat to medium-low heat. (In my experience, this extra step of twice-boiling the beans and discarding the cooking water definitely reduces the inevitable digestive effects of eating beans.)

Add the bay leaves, thyme, and rosemary, and continue to cook the beans over medium-low heat for about 30 minutes. It is important to actually taste the beans for tenderness as you go as the cooking times will vary according to the type of bean.

While the beans cook, add half of the olive oil to a large sauté pan, and place over high heat. Add the garlic, onions and celery, and cook until translucent, about 5 minutes. Add the carrots (and more olive oil if necessary) and cook for a few minutes longer, until the carrots just start to soften. Set the vegetables aside to cool.

When the beans are mostly tender but still just a little chewy, add the reserved vegetables. The beans and the vegetables should reach their doneness at the same time without overcooking, so don't wait too long to combine them. This is a good time to check for salt and pepper.

When you are ready to serve, ladle each serving into a bowl and finish with a tablespoon or two of olive oil, Parmesan cheese, and a sprinkle of parsley over the top.

CLAM CHOWDER

WHEN PEOPLE FIRST TASTE OUR HOMEMADE clam chowder they are always surprised by how much they like it. It has in fact become one of our most requested recipes.

Why is a Montana steakhouse, located at least 1,000 miles from the nearest salt water, not nestled on some hidden tree-lined cove above Puget Sound able to serve what some have called "the best chowder ever made?" The answer is quite simply, the right blend of good ingredients. After all, any soup that combines lots of butter, bacon, and heavy cream is off to a good start. By the time you add just the right amount of clams and russet potatoes to a mix of our soon-to-be-revealed secret ingredients, this recipe alone is worth the price of this book.

In the restaurant we use a good clam base to enhance the flavor (available in some grocery stores) but you can skip this if you wish.

SERVES 12 TO 16

- 8 OUNCES SLICED THICK-CUT BACON, CHOPPED
- 3 MEDIUM YELLOW ONIONS, DICED
- 2 TABLESPOONS GROUND BLACK PEPPER
- 2 TABLESPOONS GROUND THYME
- 1 TABLESPOON GROUND TARRAGON
- 4 BAY LEAVES
- 1/2 CUP ALL-PURPOSE FLOUR
- 1/2 CUP (1 STICK) SALTED BUTTER
- 3 TABLESPOONS CLAM BASE (IF AVAILABLE)
- 2 (15 1/2-OUNCE) CANS CHOPPED SEA CLAMS, UNDRAINED
- 1 QUART WHOLE MILK
- 1 QUART HEAVY CREAM
- 3 TABLESPOONS WORCESTERSHIRE SAUCE
- 1 TABLESPOON SRIRACHA
- 3 TO 4 CELERY STALKS, DICED (ABOUT 2 CUPS)
- 3 CARROTS, DICED (ABOUT 2 CUPS)
- 1 POUND RUSSET POTATOES, UNPEELED AND DICED (ABOUT 5 CUPS)
- 1 RED OR GREEN BELL PEPPER, DICED
- KOSHER SALT TO TASTE

IN A LARGE STOCKPOT OVER MEDIUM HEAT, cook the bacon until crispy. Add the onions and cook for 5 minutes, or until translucent.

Add the butter, flour, and clam base (if using) and whisk together to form a light roux. Cook for 5 minutes over medium heat until it smells toasty, stirring constantly.

Strain the clam juice from the cans into the pot then add the milk and cream, along with the carrots, celery, pepper and potatoes. Bring to a simmer and cook over medium heat until the potatoes are just firm to the bite, around 15 minutes. Finally, add the clams.

Taste for salt and turn off the heat immediately. The chowder is ready to serve hot. (The clams are added at the end to prevent them from overcooking and becoming tough and chewy).

FISH

A FLY FISHERMAN'S DILEMMA

LIKE MOST DEDICATED FLY FISHERMEN, WE BOTH FIRMLY BELIEVE IN THE PRINCIPLE OF CATCH AND RELEASE. But, as people who also love to cook and eat fresh trout, we will, under certain circumstances, bring trout home. Of the hundreds of fish I catch over the course of a year, I may keep ten or twelve, and only those that I catch in one of the beautiful lakes and reservoirs that I can reach within minutes from my front door. I limit myself to this type of fish for several reasons. In Montana, during the late sixties, the Montana Department of Fish Wildlife and Parks decided to quit stocking our rivers and started an enlightened policy of planting hatchery-raised trout exclusively in lakes and reservoirs. Their theory was that in order for Montana rivers and streams to support a natural and healthy population of resident wild trout, they needed to refrain from introducing hatchery fish into those waters. This would limit competition for food and holding water and allow the resident trout to flourish and reproduce naturally. Because of their foresight, the program was a huge success and is the major reason that trout fishing in Montana is unmatched by any other state, except maybe Alaska.

They also found that lakes, on the other hand, can benefit from stocking programs because they have the space and food to sustain a much higher fish population than would normally be found, that planted trout in lakes would provide a greater return for recreation dollars allocated in terms of food and sport, and that their impact on wild fish would be minimal. So, for these reasons, when I do take home a trout to eat, it always comes from a lake. I find that trout are best for eating when caught right after the ice melts and the water is still very cold. The flesh is firm with good color, and the taste is at its peak.

At The Mint we serve a lot of flying fish, meaning they travel to us by commercial air.

Catch of Fish from Yellowstone River, Bozeman, Montana, 1900s

TROUT WITH TOASTED ALMONDS, BROWN BUTTER, AND LEMON (TRUITE AMANDINE)

I DON'T EAT TROUT VERY OFTEN BUT WHEN I do, I usually resort to the classic preparation still found in most Paris bistros, Truite Amandine. When I was working in New Orleans at the Louis XVI this preparation was standard fare, although we used spotted sea trout. This recipe is great for any white fish. At The Mint we use this recipe for not only trout, but also sautéed halibut, white drum, and even skate. It also works very well with snapper, redfish, smaller salmon, and a host of others.

SERVES 4

2 CUPS ALL-PURPOSE FLOUR

FINE SALT AND FRESHLY GROUND BLACK PEPPER

1 CUP (2 STICKS) SALTED BUTTER, DIVIDED

1/2 CUP VEGETABLE OIL

4 (11- TO 13-INCH) TROUT, SPLIT OPEN AND CLEANED

1/2 LEMON, PLUS MORE AS NEEDED

1 1/2 CUPS SLIVERED OR SLICED ALMONDS

1/2 CUP CHOPPED FRESH FLAT-LEAF PARSLEY

PREHEAT THE OVEN TO 250°F. POUR THE flour in a shallow dish and season generously with salt and pepper. Adjust seasonings to taste. Preheat 2 tablespoons of the butter and the oil in a large frying pan set over medium- to medium-high heat.

While the oil is heating, dredge the trout in the seasoned flour, shaking off any excess. When the oil is hot, cook the trout, turning when necessary to brown the outside and cook the fish, about 5 to 6 minutes. Keep the cooked trout in the warm oven while you make the sauce.

Pour out the oil in which the trout were cooked, and then add the rest of the butter and the juice from half a lemon (use the whole lemon if you like it tart). When the butter has melted and begun to sizzle, use a whisk to stir and scrape up all of the bits of flour remaining on the bottom of the pan from cooking the trout. Add the almonds, continually tossing them in the butter to toast evenly.

While the butter and almonds are browning, place the trout on warm plates. When the butter has foamed and the almonds are dark brown (but not burned), quickly toss on the chopped parsley, give the pan a couple of shakes, and immediately pour over the fish, distributing the almonds evenly.

CAMPFIRE TROUT

IF YOU'VE NEVER HAD A FRESH BROOK OR cutthroat trout out of a cold, clear Montana mountain lake, cooked over an open fire on the shore, then you've missed one of life's great pleasures. The whole process is simplicity itself: fresh trout, flour, butter (or bacon fat), salt and pepper, and a cast-iron frying pan. That's not to say you can't do this at home; I often do, particularly for breakfast. (Yes, I can leave home and in less than an hour return with my catch.) But usually it's something best done in the outdoors, preferably, camped beside the body of water that provided the fish.

SERVES 1

- **1 TO 2 SMALL (8- TO 11-INCH) TROUT**
- **BACON FAT OR MELTED BUTTER**
- **1 TO 2 CUPS ALL-PURPOSE FLOUR**
- **FINE SALT AND FRESHLY GROUND BLACK PEPPER**
- **BUTTERED TOAST**
- **EGGS, AS DESIRED**
- **FRESH LEMONS (OPTIONAL)**

GUT AND CLEAN THE FISH (I CUT OFF THE heads to save room in the pan). Fill a cast-iron frying pan with an inch of bacon fat or melted butter and heat over medium-high heat. The oil should sizzle angrily when you drop in a bit of flour.

Put 1 to 2 cups of flour in a paper or plastic bag along with a generous amount of salt and pepper, and shake to blend.

Place one or two fish in the bag (depending on size) and shake to completely coat the fish. Place the fish carefully in the hot oil and cook for 3 to 4 minutes, flipping until the fish has an even brown crust (do not allow it to burn). If the residual flour that is left in the pan turns black, replace it before cooking any more fish, as the burned flour will make them bitter. Serve over buttered toast and squeeze a lemon over the top, and, while you are at it, fry a couple of eggs on the side. Campfire coffee, an open fire, and a beautiful mountain lake are, of course, optional but highly recommended.

MINT-STYLE BARBEQUE SHRIMP

OUR BARBEQUE SHRIMP REALLY ISN'T BAR- bequed, it's baked. For some reason (known only to its inventor) it was so named after the place where it was first served, Pascal's Manale restaurant on Napoleon Avenue in New Orleans. Today you see variations of this recipe on menus all over the country, and there is a good reason why: it's great!

I first had it when I was cooking in New Orleans and learning the trade, so, when I came back to Montana, it just had to come with me. This dish is best with authentic American shrimp from the Gulf, particularly with the heads still on. Head-on shrimp impart much more flavor to the sauce but if you can't get them, just go with what you can get: you'll still love the results.

SERVES 4

1½ POUNDS (21- TO 25-COUNT) SHRIMP, WITH SHELLS INTACT

1 CUP (2 STICKS) UNSALTED BUTTER

1 CUP OLIVE OIL

4 BAY LEAVES

½ CUP FINELY CHOPPED GARLIC

¼ CUP DRIED ROSEMARY, CRUMBLED

¼ CUP DRIED OREGANO

¼ CUP DRIED BASIL

¼ TEASPOON CAYENNE PEPPER

1 TABLESPOON FRESH COARSELY GROUND BLACK PEPPER

2 TABLESPOONS FRESHLY SQUEEZED LEMON JUICE

2 TABLESPOONS WORCESTER-SHIRE SAUCE

FINE SALT

USING SCISSORS, CUT ALONG THE TOP OF the shell of each shrimp to devein them, leaving the shells on. This way—because they are cooked in the shell (to enhance the flavor of the sauce)—they will be easier to eat.

In a large sauté pan or saucepan melt the butter with the oil over medium heat, then add the bay leaves, garlic, rosemary, oregano, basil, cayenne, pepper, lemon juice, and Worcestershire sauce and bring to a boil. Turn the heat down and simmer for 10 minutes stirring occasionally. Turn off the heat and let the mix stand for 30 or so minutes to steep, until it reaches room temperature. Add salt, adjusting seasoning to taste.

Preheat the oven to 450°F.

Add the shrimp to the mixture in the pan, tossing well, and set the pan over medium heat. Cook the shrimp until they begin to turn slightly pink, about 4 minutes. Move the pan into the oven and cook for 10 to 15 minutes, until they look done but not overcooked. Ladle into bowls for serving, getting the bits of herbs and spices that have settled to the bottom, and serve French bread on the side for dipping. You can also serve the shrimp over linguini or thin spaghetti, tossed to coat.

PAN-ROASTED HALIBUT WITH BEURRE BLANC AND FRESH CHANTERELLES

OF ALL THE SEAFOOD DISHES WE DO AT THE Mint, this is by far the most popular. When fresh halibut and mushrooms are in season at the same time, our suppliers, Montana Fish Co. of Bozeman, can usually deliver our order within hours of the fishing boats hitting the docks in Alaska. Our chanterelles are fresh from the woods, delivered by our trusty mushroom man, Jeff Hill, who always seems to know just where the best morels and chanterelles hide. So for about two months out of the year, August and September, we are fortunate to serve fresh fish at its best. Do not use halibut steaks that are cut through the bone; use boneless fillets.

SERVES 4

- 1/4 CUP PLUS 2 TABLESPOONS (3/4 STICK) UNSALTED BUTTER, DIVIDED
- 2 HANDFULS (ABOUT 6 TO 8 OUNCES) FRESH CHANTERELLES
- 2 CUPS ALL-PURPOSE FLOUR
- FINE SALT AND FRESHLY GROUND BLACK PEPPER
- 4 FRESH (6- TO 8-OUNCE) HALIBUT FILLETS
- 1/4 CUP CANOLA OIL
- 3/4 CUP WARM BEURRE BLANC (SEE PAGE 228)
- 1 LEMON, QUARTERED
- 1/2 CUP FINELY CHOPPED FRESH FLAT-LEAF PARSLEY (OPTIONAL)

HEAT 2 TABLESPOONS OF THE BUTTER OVER medium heat and when it has melted, add the mushrooms and cook for 4 minutes tossing frequently, and then set aside.

Mix the flour with a generous amount of salt and pepper in a shallow dish. Adjust seasonings to taste. Dredge one side of the fillets (the fleshy side, not the skin side) in the seasoned flour. Add the remaining 1/4 cup of butter and the oil to the hot pan used for the mushrooms, and heat over high heat, almost to the smoking point. Add the fish, floured side down. Cook the fish for 4 to 5 minutes or until a crust has formed. Turn the fish over and cook for another 3 to 4 minutes, then remove from the heat and place on a warm plate.

Spoon 3 to 4 tablespoons of the beurre blanc either under or over the fillet and top the fish with some mushrooms. Serve immediately with a fresh lemon wedge and fresh chopped parsley for garnish and color.

PLANCHA-GRILLED SALMON WITH FRESH BASIL CHIMICHURRI

HERE IS A GREAT TWIST ON GRILLED salmon fillets. Even though the classic chimichurri sauce from Argentina is usually made from fresh oregano and parsley, I used the taste of fresh basil to enhance the flavor of plancha-grilled salmon: a reflection on how well the two flavors complement each other. The basil chimichurri may also be used in other applications, such as on grilled chicken breasts or pounded pork loin.

SERVES 4

BASIL CHIMICHURRI

1 CUP FRESH BASIL LEAVES

1 CUP FRESH FLAT-LEAF PARSLEY

1/2 CUP EXTRA-VIRGIN OLIVE OIL

6 FRESH GARLIC CLOVES

2 TABLESPOONS FRESHLY SQUEEZED LEMON JUICE

1 TABLESPOON FRESHLY CRACKED BLACK PEPPER

1 TEASPOON FINE SALT

SALMON

4 (7- TO 8-OUNCE) SALMON FILLET PORTIONS, WITH SKIN ON

OLIVE OIL, FOR SERVING

FOR THE CHIMICURRI, COMBINE INGREDIENTS in a food processor and coarsely chop by pulsing until a smooth consistency is achieved. Set aside.

For the salmon, cover the flesh side of each fillet with some of the chimicurri and allow it to sit for about 15 to 20 minutes while you preheat your plancha, cast-iron skillet, or steel griddle on the stove top or outdoor grill. When the surface is hot enough to make water sizzle, carefully place the salmon herb-side down to sear the surface and allow a crust to form, about 3 to 4 minutes (do not burn the herbs). Using a spatula, carefully turn the fillet over (keeping the crust intact) and place the fish skin-side down to finish, about 5 minutes. Monitor the cooking visually to achieve the desired degree of doneness.

Drizzle a little olive oil over the top of the fish and serve along with more chimichurri on the side to dip.

SEARED SALMON
WITH CAJUN RUB & RASPBERRY SAUCE

OVER THE YEARS, I'VE LEARNED THAT HIGH- quality, flash-frozen seafood can often be much better than so-called "fresh" fish that has been sitting on some airport loading dock. On the other hand, during the salmon and halibut season, thanks to our friends at the Montana Fish Co., we have access to the best and the freshest and, as a result, we sell lots and lots of it.

Many salmon recipes can be used with trout and occasionally I will use trout for this particular recipe, provided that the trout is large enough and—if it is a hatchery fish—that it was stocked by the state fisheries folks in one of our many lakes. I will only use one of these fish in the spring, just after the ice has melted off and they are still feeding on small shrimp and other aquatic life. Later in the season when the lake vegetation begins to come back, the fish acquire a muddy taste and, in my opinion, aren't particularly good to eat.

In this recipe the salmon is seared on a preheated cast-iron plate (plancha) or in a cast-iron skillet in a variation of the process called "blackening." In the restaurant we have a commercial exhaust system to deal with the resulting smoke. At home I usually do this on my outside gas grill.

SERVES 4

CRACKED BLACK PEPPER AND RASPBERRY SAUCE (PAGE 240)

1/4 CUP (1/2 STICK) UNSALTED BUTTER, MELTED

4 (8-OUNCE) PORTIONS BONE-LESS SOCKEYE OR COHO SALMON FILLETS WITH SKIN ON

CAJUN RUB

2 TABLESPOONS SEA SALT

2 TABLESPOONS DRIED OREGANO

2 TABLESPOONS DRIED THYME

2 TABLESPOONS PAPRIKA

2 TABLESPOONS GRANULATED GARLIC

2 TABLESPOONS FRESHLY GROUND BLACK PEPPER

1/2 TEASPOON CAYENNE PEPPER

GENTLY HEAT THE RASPBERRY SAUCE IN A saucepan over low heat; it should be slightly more liquid than the jam. Add water if needed to thin. Set aside to keep warm.

Place the melted butter in a small bowl. In a separate bowl, combine the ingredients for the Cajun rub.

Preheat a cast-iron skillet over high heat. Brush the salmon with the butter on the flesh side (not the skin side) then lightly sprinkle some of the rub on top. Do not over-season.

Carefully place the fillets rub-side down in the skillet and sear for about 1 minute, or until the surface of the fish has been lightly blackened but not burned. Carefully turn the fillet and sear skin-side down for about 2 to 3 minutes, or until the center looks cooked to your liking. (If it is a thick piece of fish, you can finish it in a 400°F preheated oven, but do not overcook or it will dry out.)

Serve with 3 or 4 tablespoons of the raspberry sauce either on top or under the fillet.

PAN-SEARED PETRALE SOLE WITH DRIED PORCINI

THIS RECIPE WAS BORN IN PATRICK'S KIT-chen in San Francisco, but we are grateful that it has turned out nicely in our kitchen here in Montana. It's quick and it's nutty and it's virtually impossible to ruin, unless you walk away from the stove.

SERVES 4

- 3/4 CUP DRIED PORCINI MUSHROOMS
- 1/2 CUP (1 STICK) UNSALTED BUTTER, MELTED
- 2 POUNDS FRESH PETRALE SOLE FILLETS, WITHOUT SKIN (DOVER SOLE OR HALIBUT IS ALSO FINE)
- FINE SALT
- 1 LEMON, QUARTERED IN WEDGES
- A HANDFUL OF CHOPPED FRESH FLAT-LEAF PARSLEY

IN A FOOD PROCESSOR OR SPICE GRINDER, grind the mushrooms into a fine powder. Brush the melted butter onto each side of the fish fillets. Place the porcini powder in a shallow dish. Dredge each piece of fish in the porcini, coating both sides. Sprinkle with salt to taste.

Fire up a cast-iron skillet over high heat; no additional oil or butter is necessary. Place the fillets in the hot skillet, without crowding the pan. Cook one side for 3 to 4 minutes, turn with a spatula, and sear the other side for 3 to 4 minutes. The fish should have a nutty-brown crust. Serve immediately with lemon wedges and parsley sprinkled on top.

BEEF

MEAT BASICS

IF HOME COOKS ENCOUNTER PROBLEMS WITH STEAKS AND CHOPS, THE USUAL REASON is that they lack the proper temperature and technique. The most important requirement in cooking red meat the Montana way, which is to say, the right way (particularly steaks and chops) is boldness; by that I mean the application of heat—lots of heat and fast. I'll illustrate.

Rick Pope, a neighbor in Bozeman, Montana, is a world-class ceramicist, fly fisherman, and a hell of a cook. He loves to recount the time a bunch of us were fly-fishing on the Big Hole River in Southwestern Montana. We'd experienced a great day of trout fishing, catching browns, rainbows, and even a few river Grayling—that rare gem-colored fish found in only a few places in the world.

The sun was sinking low over the river and little tendrils of steam were beginning to rise. As the evening chill began to settle around us, we gathered around the campfire for the essential elements of great camping—eating and drinking. We filled our tin cups with George Dickel sour mash and river water and began preparing dinner. The dinner fare included huge Montana potatoes and Walla Walla sweet onions roasted in the fire, a big bowl of tossed greens with watercress from the river, and, the requisite huge hunk of red meat.

In Rick's telling of the story, we were all beginning to weave a little from the Dickel when I told someone to open the Cabernet, check the potatoes and onions, and toss the salad. After clearing some the burning logs from the edge of the fire and banking a bunch of the glowing coals, I proceeded to fork this huge piece of moose sirloin into the fire. This incited my camp mates. (I was still in my pre-chef days and had absolutely no credibility.) This crazy dude, being me, was ruining our perfectly conceived meal by consigning this beautiful piece of meat (the whole focus of our collective culinary desires) to the flames. The scene could have been set to Wagner. The flames were shooting into the air (I had marinated the moose for a week in olive oil and herbs) and the whole thing looked like a funeral pyre. Fighting off their desperate attempts to save the meat, I pleaded for some benefit of the doubt. After all, it was my moose and if I wanted to trash it, then that was my prerogative, I argued somewhat incoherently, noting that fists were being clenched and could fly any second. Forestalling all-out mutiny I pulled the meat from the flames to the collective sigh of my would-be assailants.

After letting the meat rest for several minutes I made the first cut. Everyone held their breath as they waited to witness just how overcooked and leaden-gray the whole thing would be. Even I was nervous. But as the knife cut through the outside crust I could see red juices begin to flow—hence, the verdict that would determine my fate: perfect! To any passerby during the ensuing moments, we must have resembled a pre-historic tribe as we tore into the medium-rare roasted flesh. The only sounds were the growls and grunts of feeding animals, regressing into an ancient and forgotten past, dim eons ago before the existence of a spoken language. The orgy continued unabated until, sated at last, the meat consumed, everyone lay in penitential stupor until sleep arrived and daylight returned us to the end of the twentieth century.

I could have spared you the preceding narrative and simply advised that you should always get close enough to the fire so that the flames actually touch the meat and allow a crust to form, but where's the fun in that?

GRILLING STEAKS AND SMALL ROASTS

WE CAN'T STRESS STRONGLY ENOUGH THE NECESSITY OF MARINATING MEATS TO BE GRILLED either over an open fire or in cast iron. The tougher and thicker the cut, the longer the marinating time should be. I have found that the best way to marinate and store meats is in a resealable plastic bag. Many times when we find certain cuts like flank steak on sale we'll portion the extra cuts and marinate and freeze them in individual plastic bags until use. This makes for super-convenience, and the marinade protects the contents from freezer burn, extending the freezer shelf life.

BROTHERLY BURGERS

MY OWN CHOICE WHEN IT COMES TO BURGERS is good fresh meat ground with the right amount of fat, slightly seared on the outside, and medium on the inside with a little coarsely ground sea salt and pepper. Top with sautéed mushrooms and caramelized onions, and serve with lots of mashed potatoes (see page 208) or the Ultimate French Fries (see page 207).

MAKES 6 BURGERS

1½ POUNDS GROUND BEEF

2 TABLESPOONS GRATED WHITE ONION

2 TABLESPOONS SOUR CREAM

3 EGGS, BEATEN

1 TEASPOON THYME

FINE SALT AND FRESHLY GROUND BLACK PEPPER

BUILD A HOT FIRE OR PREHEAT A GAS GRILL or cast-iron skillet over medium-high heat. If you are using a skillet you may want to add a little olive oil.

In a bowl, mix the ground beef, onions, sour cream, eggs, and thyme together. Add salt and pepper to taste. Form the patties by hand, and cook them to your desired temperature.

There are those who love to see the sight of blood and insist upon a rare burger. In many parts of the country there are certain health department regulations that prohibit restaurants' serving a burger that has been cooked to less than a medium doneness. At The Mint, we prefer medium although we will serve rare or medium-rare upon special request.

JUST HAND ME A HAMBURGER

LET'S START OFF WITH THE OBVIOUS. A HAMBURGER IS MERELY A HAMBURGER, RIGHT?

Wrong. To me, the perfect hamburger is a piece of lean top or bottom round, chuck or sirloin, that I have just coarsely ground myself, then seared in a very hot pan, medium-rare to medium on the inside, with a crust on the outside. I then place it on a toasted sourdough roll with a Vidalia onion, a slice of a New Jersey beefsteak tomato, sea salt, coarsely ground black pepper, and a whole bunch of homemade mayonnaise.

The idea of grinding to order may sound a bit too much, but freshly ground beef is dramatically juicier and better-tasting than ground meat that has been sitting around. I buy bright red ground or chuck steak on sale and I grind very lean burgers using a very coarse grind, with just enough fat to hold them together. (I spent $30 on a little electric Sunbeam meat grinder and it works great.) I've also used elk, venison, bison, and moose with equally great and sometimes even better results. When you use wild game it is usually necessary to add a small amount of beef fat to hold the mix together. Using a little sour cream as a binder helps too. Another point to remember is the leaner the meat, the faster it cooks, so plan accordingly and reduce your cooking time.

BEEF BOURGUIGNON

I'VE ENJOYED THIS CLASSIC DISH SERVED on fine china in a Paris bistro as well as on a tin plate hot off a campfire in the backcountry of Montana. If you have the time to marinate the meat in red wine for a couple of days before cooking, you will get great results. I also believe that the flavor is even further enhanced if you cook this dish the day before you want to eat it and slowly reheat it before serving. In Montana, where we enjoy an abundance of wild game, venison or elk works perfectly for this recipe as does buffalo sirloin. To serve the bourguignon, heat some rustic French bread, toss a simple salad, and be prepared for some good eating. You have the option of serving the beef as is, or accompanied by some crusty sautéed small new potatoes, egg noodles cooked al dente, or even some Soft Polenta with Herbs (see page 217).

SERVES 6 TO 8

- 4 CUPS FRUITY RED WINE (MERLOT, BOURGOGNE)
- 2 BAY LEAVES
- 3 TABLESPOONS THYME
- 3 TABLESPOONS FRESHLY GROUND BLACK PEPPER, DIVIDED
- 4 POUNDS LEAN SIRLOIN, BRISKET, TRI-TIP, OR TRIMMED CHUCK ROAST, CUT INTO 1½-INCH CUBES
- 1 POUND BACON, CHOPPED
- 1 POUND PEARL ONIONS OR 1 LARGE VIDALIA ONION, ROUGHLY CHOPPED
- 2 LARGE CARROTS, CUT INTO ½-INCH SLICES
- ½ CUP ALL-PURPOSE FLOUR
- 1 HEAD FRESH GARLIC, PEELED AND THINLY SLICED
- 2 TABLESPOONS TOMATO PASTE
- 4 CUPS BEEF STOCK (SUBSTITUTE 2 TABLESPOONS GOOD-QUALITY BEEF BASE AND 4 CUPS WATER) PLUS MORE AS NEEDED
- 1½ POUNDS SMALL BUTTON MUSHROOMS OR LARGER MUSHROOMS, HALVED
- ½ CUP (1 STICK) UNSALTED BUTTER
- SEA SALT
- ½ CUP GRATED ORANGE ZEST (OPTIONAL)

COMBINE THE WINE, BAY LEAVES, THYME, and a tablespoon of the pepper in a large resealable plastic bag and then add the beef cubes. Marinate the beef at least overnight, or up to 2 days. Remove the marinated beef from the bag and reserve the marinade.

Preheat the oven to 400°F. Set a large Dutch oven over medium heat.

Cook the bacon until just crispy, then remove and reserve it. Pour off all but a tablespoon of the rendered fat and reserve. Add the onions and carrots and cook until slightly softened, about 5 minutes. Remove from the pan and set aside. Adding more bacon fat as needed (just to keep things from sticking), brown the beef cubes in batches to sear on all sides, about 4 to 5 minutes per batch. Add the flour and garlic to the last batch of meat and stir until slightly browned, about 2 minutes, then add the tomato paste, reserved marinade, and stock, stirring and scraping the pan to release all of the crunchy little bits of beef stuck to the bottom of the pan. Return the meat and about one-third of the sautéed vegetables to the pan.

Place the pot, uncovered, in the oven for 1 hour, stirring occasionally. Cooking it uncovered creates a nice brown crusty top, which adds great flavor.

When the meat begins to shred when pulled

apart with two forks, stir in the rest of the carrots and onions. Check liquid level, adding more stock as needed. Cook in the oven for another 35 to 45 minutes, or until the vegetables soften but haven't completely melted into the stew.

With about 15 minutes left in the cooking time, melt the butter in a skillet over high heat and sauté the mushrooms. Just before serving, add the sautéed mushrooms, cooked bacon, and the grated orange zest (if using) over the top of the stew. This will add a subtle citrus flavor.

CUBAN-STYLE BEEF FILET

WHEN I WAS EXPERIMENTING WITH THE recipe for Cuban-Style Braised Lamb (see page 116), I began to realize that oranges and beef go well together. After all, one of the classic dishes of Chinese Szechuan cuisine is orange-cooked beef, so why not try beef with mojo criollo, the great national marinade and sauce of Cuba.

MOJO CRIOLLA SAUCE

1 (12-OUNCE) CAN FROZEN ORANGE JUICE CONCENTRATE, THAWED

$1/2$ CUP FRESHLY SQUEEZED LIME JUICE

6 GARLIC CLOVES, SMASHED

1 TABLESPOON FINE SALT

1 TABLESPOON FRESHLY GROUND BLACK PEPPER

BEEF

4 (5- TO 6-OUNCE) BEEF TENDERLOIN FILETS

2 TABLESPOONS FRESHLY CRACKED BLACK PEPPERCORNS

$1/4$ CUP ($1/2$ STICK) SALTED BUTTER

TO MAKE THE MOJO CRIOLLA SAUCE, combine the orange juice concentrate with an equal amount of water and add the lime juice. Add the garlic, salt, and pepper to the mixture. Then pour the marinade over the meat in a large bowl, and marinate for 4 to 12 hours in the refrigerator.

Drain off the marinade and pat the meat dry (reserve the marinade). Put the cracked peppercorns in a dish and press one side of each filet into the peppercorns. Preheat a sauté pan on medium heat and melt the butter. When the butter is hot, it will probably start to smoke but do not allow it to burn. Add the filets pepper-side down, but be careful: the residue of the marinade may cause the hot butter to splatter. Cook about 4 minutes on one side and about 2 minutes on the opposite side. The object is to form a crust on the pepper side without overcooking the meat. It is best medium-rare.

When the meat is cooked, remove to a warm platter and cover with foil or place in a warm oven at about 200°F. Reduce the heat under the sauté pan to medium and add the remaining marinade. Reduce the mixture to the consistency of maple syrup, about 5 minutes. Serve the filets with several spoonfuls of sauce under each filet.

BEEF RIBS THREE WAYS

THERE IS A SAYING IN THE RESTAURANT BUSI- ness: "You make your money serving garbage." What this really means is that you can make money on dishes that some people would throw away, or from ingredients that are the by-product of other dishes. Beef bones are a great example. Here are three ways to do bones that I think can actually taste better than the original dishes. I like big meaty bones cut from a rib roast and separated. You can do this yourself or have your butcher do it. Basically the differ-ence lies in the type of rubs or sauce that you use. All of these recipes are for 8 leftover bones, which is the normal yield from a whole standing rib roast. You can also cook your ribs either tough or tender. A "tough" presentation comes from cooking the ribs under the broiler on the grill, as I've done here as they come off the rack. These tend to be chewier than bones that have been slow-cooked in stock for an hour or so before they are placed under a hot broiler. (You can certainly try this method: make sure the bones are completely sub-merged in liquid, and don't let it come above a gentle simmer.) I prefer tough ribs because the bones seem to retain more flavor.

I figure on 2 to 4 bones per person, depending on what else you're serving.

CHILI CURRY RIB PASTE RIBS

SERVES 2 TO 4

1/2 CUP CANOLA OR OLIVE OIL

1 TABLESPOON CURRY POWDER

1 TABLESPOON CUMIN

1 TABLESPOON CHILI POWDER

1 TEASPOON GRANULATED GARLIC

1 TEASPOON SEA SALT

1 TEASPOON FRESHLY GROUND BLACK PEPPER

8 MEATY BEEF BONES

BOOT HEEL COMEBACK BARBECUE SAUCE (PAGE 248) OR YOUR FAVORITE VARIETY (OPTIONAL)

COMBINE EVERYTHING EXCEPT the ribs in a food processor and blend to form a paste. Alternatively, use a mortar and pestle to mix. Use more or less oil for a thinner or thicker paste. Spread it all over the ribs, cover tightly, let marinate on a rimmed baking tray in the refrig-erator for at least 4 and up to 12 hours.

Preheat your broiler on high, then place the ribs in the middle of your oven and cook for 7 minutes per side, or until the ribs become well browned, turning as needed. Remove from heat and serve with sauce, if desired.

MEMPHIS-STYLE DRY RUB RIBS

1 CUP GRANULATED SUGAR
1 CUP KOSHER SALT
1/4 CUP GRANULATED GARLIC
1/2 CUP SMOKED PAPRIKA
3 TABLESPOONS CHILI POWDER
2 TABLESPOONS FRESHLY GROUND BLACK PEPPER
1 TABLESPOON LEMON PEPPER
1 TABLESPOON CURRY POWDER
1 TEASPOON DRY MUSTARD
1/2 TEASPOON CAYENNE PEPPER
8 MEATY BEEF BONES

COMBINE ALL INGREDIENTS EXCEPT THE RIBS IN A BOWL and sprinkle half of the mixture over both sides of the ribs. Cover, and refrigerate on a baking tray for 1 to 3 days. Reserve remaining rub.

Preheat the grill or broiler on low. Sprinkle the rest of the rub over the bones, and then set on the grill to lightly brown, about 10 minutes per side. Watch them closely to keep them from burning.

MANDARIN-GRILLED BEEF RIBS

1 CUP BREWED SOY SAUCE
2 TABLESPOONS TOASTED SESAME OIL
1 TABLESPOON CHINESE FIVE-SPICE POWDER
1 TABLESPOON GRANULATED GARLIC
1 TABLESPOON FINELY CHOPPED FRESH GINGER
1 TABLESPOON PACKED DARK BROWN SUGAR
1/4 CUP RICE VINEGAR
8 MEATY BEEF BONES

COMBINE SOY SAUCE, SESAME OIL, FIVE-SPICE POWDER, garlic, ginger, sugar, and vinegar in a very large resealable plastic bag (large enough to fit ribs) or in a deep roasting pan. Marinate the ribs in the refrigerator for 24 hours, turning occasionally.

Preheat your oven to 275°F. In a covered ovenproof wok or braising pan, combine the ribs and the marinade with 1 cup of water and cook them, covered, for around 2 hours until very tender.

Preheat the broiler to medium-high and broil the ribs on a rimmed baking tray, turning occasionally, until they are crispy on all sides. Brush any leftover braising liquid on the ribs to moisten them before serving.

GRILLED BEEF SATAY

I WISH I COULD SAY THAT I FIRST ENCOUN- tered satay on the streets of Bangkok. But alas, it was in a little neighborhood Thai place on Federal Boulevard, just off I-25 in Denver. Even so, it still conjures up exotic flavors even in ordinary places.

At The Mint, we cook this on a hot cast-iron plate, placing the skewers directly on the surface and then rolling them with tongs to cook evenly. You can serve this as an appetizer, or over rice with grilled skewered vegetables as a main course. The great thing about satay is that you can use all kinds of meat. Beef, game, pork, or chicken will all work well. Remember to cut the cubes about the same size for even cooking, and vary the sizes according to the kind of meat you are using: chicken and pork should be cut smaller for thorough cooking.

SERVES 6

- 2 CUPS SOY SAUCE
- 2 TABLESPOONS PACKED LIGHT BROWN SUGAR
- 2 TABLESPOONS MINCED FRESH GARLIC
- ½ CUP RICE WINE VINEGAR
- ½ CUP TOASTED SESAME OIL
- 2 TABLESPOONS FRESHLY GROUND BLACK PEPPER
- 2 TABLESPOONS PEELED AND MINCED FRESH GINGER
- ½ CUP COARSELY CHOPPED CILANTRO LEAVES
- 3 POUNDS TOP SIRLOIN OR OTHER RED GAME MEAT (VENISON IS NICE), CUT INTO 1-INCH CUBES
- 1 SMALL HEAD BUTTER LETTUCE, SEPARATED INTO LEAVES

COMBINE THE SOY SAUCE, BROWN SUGAR, garlic, vinegar, sesame oil, black pepper, ginger, and cilantro in a mixing bowl and pour over the meat in a resealable plastic bag. Marinate in the refrigerator for 24 hours.

Preheat the grill on high heat. If you are using bamboo skewers, soak them in water for 30 minutes prior to use.

Thread the meat onto the skewers, reserving the marinade.

When your grill is hot, place the meat over the hottest part of the grill and cook, turning to brown all sides, until the meat begins to show a slight char and the marinade caramelizes. It can take anywhere from 5 to 8 minutes for medium-rare doneness. When the meat is done, remove the skewers from the fire and serve them on top of the lettuce leaves. If you want a sauce to serve alongside, dilute the leftover marinade with water and bring it to a boil. Simmer it until thick, about 5 minutes. Drizzle the resulting sauce over the meat.

BEEF TENDERLOIN WITH MARSALA SAUCE

THIS IS SIMILAR TO SEVERAL RECIPES IN the book using Marsala, and also works very well with antelope. In fact, any lean, good-quality red meat will benefit from a sauce like this. It's practically instant, and the meat holds up well under the strong, sweet Marsala.

SERVES 4

4 (5- TO 6-OUNCE) BEEF TENDERLOIN FILETS

2 CUPS (4 STICKS) UNSALTED BUTTER, VERY COLD, DIVIDED

2 CUPS ALL-PURPOSE FLOUR

1 TABLESPOON FINE SALT

2 TABLESPOONS FRESHLY GROUND BLACK OR WHITE PEPPER

2 CUPS THINLY SLICED WHITE BUTTON OR CREMINI MUSHROOMS (OPTIONAL)

1/2 CUP CHICKEN OR VEAL STOCK

3/4 CUP MARSALA

FINE SALT AND FRESHLY GROUND PEPPER

CHOPPED FRESH FLAT-LEAF PARSLEY, FOR GARNISH (OPTIONAL)

SLICE EACH FILET IN HALF LENGTHWISE TO make 8 pieces. Place the filets between sheets of plastic wrap and carefully pound them with a meat mallet or small skillet until they are 3/4 inch thick.

Melt a stick of butter in a sauté pan over medium-high heat. Combine the flour, salt, and pepper in a shallow dish and dredge the filets in the seasoned flour. When the butter is very hot, place the filets directly into the pan. The important thing is to sauté the first side of the tenderloin until the blood begins to come through the light dusting of seasoned flour, about 2 minutes, then turn and cook briefly on the other side, just until a light crust forms. Remove to a warm plate. Because the meat has been pounded thin, it cooks very quickly.

Add a second stick of butter and, if you are using them, the sliced mushrooms. Cook for 1 minute, then add the stock, and Marsala, and, using a steel whisk, mix well, scraping up the residue from the pan to mix with the sauce. Cook until the mixture reduces by half, reduce the heat, and add the remaining cold butter gradually in small pieces, stirring constantly until it reaches a smooth consistency. (The butter must be cold to keep the sauce from breaking.) Add salt and a generous amount of pepper, adjusting seasonings to taste. When the sauce is ready, spoon it over the medallions, sprinkle on chopped parsley for color and serve.

NOTE: If you would rather do a Port sauce, follow the same procedure and substitute port for the Marsala.

MY FAVORITE SPICY MEATLOAF

THERE ARE TWO BASIC WAYS OF COOKING meatloaf. The first is baked in a loaf pan very much like a French terrine; the second, a freeform, hand-shaped loaf, is baked on a baking tray. The first method assures you a very moist meatloaf that has literally been cooked in its own juice. The flavor is more intense, and you end up retaining most of the fat. If your primary objective is to serve the meatloaf cold, baking it in a loaf pan is the best choice because it slices well. If you plan on serving the meatloaf as a hot entrée, then I prefer a freeform loaf fully exposed to the radiant heat of the oven. This method produces a nice crusty exterior. To achieve the best result you need to provide plenty of additional moisture to the meat mixture. I have experimented with a number of liquids including, yogurt, buttermilk, sour cream, and tomato juice, all of which are acceptable, but I prefer whole milk.

It is also important not to put too much filler in with the meat, but just enough to hold it together. I have found that stale white bread cubed, with the crust cut off, and then soaked in milk is the best filler to hold the meat together. The great thing about meatloaf is that you can use any kind of meat that can be ground—beef, assorted game, pork, veal, or even bear.

SERVES 6

- ³/₄ CUP WHOLE MILK
- 1 CUP CUBED STALE WHITE BREAD
- ³/₄ CUP OLIVE OIL
- 2 LARGE YELLOW ONIONS, CHOPPED
- 1 GREEN BELL PEPPER, CHOPPED
- 6 TABLESPOONS BASIC BLACK-ENING MIX (SEE PAGE 224)
- 1 TEASPOON CAYENNE PEPPER
- 1 TABLESPOON GROUND CUMIN
- ¹/₄ CUP GRANULATED GARLIC
- 6 TABLESPOONS WORCESTERSHIRE SAUCE
- 1 TEASPOON HOT SAUCE
- 1 CUP KETCHUP
- 3 POUNDS GROUND BEEF, GAME, OR A RED MEAT BLEND
- 3 EGGS, LIGHTLY BEATEN
- 4 BAY LEAVES

COMBINE THE WHOLE MILK AND THE BREAD in a bowl to soak.

Heat the olive oil in a sauté pan over high, and cook the onions and peppers until they are just wilted, about 3 to 5 minutes. Stir in the blackening spice, cayenne, cumin, and garlic and cook for another two minutes to blend the flavors. Place the cooked vegetables in a large bowl and allow to cool to room temperature. Stir in the soaked cubed bread, Worcestershire sauce, hot sauce, ketchup, meat, and eggs, and form into one large loaf or two smaller ones on a rimmed baking tray or in a loaf pan.

At this point, I like to cover the loaf in plastic wrap and allow it to rest for 24 hours in the refrigerator. I find that this gives the flavors time to expand and blend, very much like a classic French terrine. This stage is optional, and you still get great results by cooking the loaf right away.

Either way, when you are ready to finish the dish, preheat the oven to 375°F. Arrange the bay leaves on top of the loaf and bake for 1 hour, until the juices run clear when the loaf is poked with a fork. Serve hot or cold.

BARB'S MEATLOAF

I DON'T EVER REMEMBER ANYONE IN OUR family referring to our mother as "Mom." It was always "Barb," "BB," or numerous other nicknames. She was a wonderful woman who had a great sense of humor, took us to symphonies, was a lifelong Democrat, loved bourbon and water, and, until she finally gave it up, washed our mouths out with soap when she determined that our language spilled over the edge of decency. She wasn't the world's greatest cook and some of her creations bordered on inedible. But, when she decided to do meatloaf, she became, by far, the greatest cook in South St. Louis. Fortunately, for posterity's sake my sister, Christy O'Connor, saved her recipe. Whenever we visit her home in Kansas City, and, after I've made the rounds of my favorite eateries like Arthur Bryant's, The Smokestack, or Stroud's, our farewell supper is always Barb's meatloaf, mashed potatoes, and huge serving of nostalgia.

SERVES 6

1 CUP CUBED STALE WHITE BREAD

³/4 CUP WHOLE MILK

1 POUND GROUND BEEF

1 POUND GROUND PORK

2 LARGE YELLOW ONIONS, CHOPPED

2 TABLESPOONS GRANULATED GARLIC

1 TEASPOON FINE SALT

1 TABLESPOON FRESHLY GROUND BLACK PEPPER

1¹/2 CUPS KETCHUP, DIVIDED

2 EGGS, LIGHTLY BEATEN

4 STRIPS BACON

4 BAY LEAVES

PREHEAT THE OVEN TO 350°F.

Place the stale bread in a large measuring cup and pour the milk over it. Leave it to soak for about 10 minutes. Gently squeeze the excess milk from the bread and discard the milk.

In a large bowl, combine the meat, onions, garlic, salt, pepper, a cup of the ketchup, eggs, and the soaked bread. Form into a loaf on a rimmed baking tray. Coat the loaf with the remaining ¹/2 cup of ketchup, lay the bacon and bay leaves on top, and bake for 1 hour, or until the juices run clear when prodded with a fork.

SOUTHWESTERN MEATLOAF

I KNOW THAT THIS SOUNDS LIKE SOMETHING off the back of a Velveeta box, but take my word for it: this is a great meatloaf, juicy and full of flavor. You can use all kinds of ground meat here in various combinations, but strangely enough, beef and pork seems to work the best. It's great served hot and, even better served cold. Try it on sourdough bread with a chili mayonnaise (1 part Vietnamese chili paste to 8 parts mayo). It's the quintessential midnight snack.

SERVES 6

- ³/₄ CUP CUBED STALE WHITE BREAD
- ¹/₂ CUP WHOLE MILK
- 1 YELLOW ONION, DICED
- 4 GARLIC CLOVES, CHOPPED
- 2 TABLESPOONS OLIVE OIL
- 1¹/₂ POUNDS GROUND BEEF
- 1¹/₂ POUNDS GROUND PORK
- 3 TABLESPOONS CHILI POWDER
- 1 TEASPOON CUMIN (OPTIONAL)
- ¹/₂ CUP CHOPPED FRESH CILANTRO
- 3 TABLESPOON WORCESTERSHIRE SAUCE
- 2 TABLESPOONS FINE SALT
- 2 TABLESPOONS FRESHLY GROUND BLACK PEPPER
- 1 CUP SHREDDED CHEDDAR CHEESE
- 3 EGGS, LIGHTLY BEATEN

PREHEAT THE OVEN TO 375°F. PLACE THE stale bread in a bowl and pour the milk over it. Leave to soak for at least 10 minutes.

Set a sauté pan over medium heat and add the olive oil. Sauté the onions and garlic until translucent, about 5 minutes, and then set aside to cool to room temperature.

Combine the cooked vegetables with the ground meats, chili powder, cumin (if using), cilantro, Worcestershire sauce, salt, pepper, cheese, eggs, and soaked bread in a large bowl. After mixing well, form into a loaf on a rimmed baking sheet and bake for 60 to 90 minutes, or until the juices run clear when poked with a fork. Serve hot or cold.

Cowhands on Frank Hazelbaker's Ranch, Dillon, Montana, ca. 1935

A LITTLE LAGNIAPPE: SPICY CAJUN MEATBALLS WITH GARLIC

WHEN I WAS APPRENTICING IN NEW ORLEANS I learned to appreciate the term lagniappe (pronounced LAN-yap) which roughly translates to "something a little extra." The "extra" in this case is the garlic clove tucked away in the middle. In Cajun country, west of New Orleans, they are called "beef boulettes," savory little meatballs with a clove of garlic in the middle. When you make My Favorite Spicy Meatloaf recipe (see page 71), double it and use the extra for a batch of these great little meatballs. Served in their own gravy, they make great appetizers, or with mashed potatoes or noodles, as a main course.

SERVES 6 TO 8

1 CUP PLUS 2 TABLESPOONS OLIVE OIL, DIVIDED

3 TO 4 GARLIC HEADS, PEELED AND SEPARATED INTO CLOVES (24 CLOVES), PLUS 6 GARLIC CLOVES, CHOPPED

1¼ CUP ALL-PURPOSE FLOUR, DIVIDED

MY FAVORITE SPICY MEATLOAF (SEE PAGE 71), UP TO BAKING STAGE

3 YELLOW ONIONS, THINLY SLICED

2 TABLESPOONS DRIED THYME LEAVES

2 BAY LEAVES

1 CUP BEEF STOCK (SUBSTITUTE 1 TABLESPOON GOOD-QUALITY BEEF BASE PLUS 1 CUP WATER)

FINE SALT AND FRESHLY GROUND BLACK PEPPER

HEAT 2 TABLESPOONS OF THE OIL OVER medium heat. Sauté the whole garlic cloves in the oil for about 10 minutes until soft and slightly brown. Set aside.

Place ½ cup of the flour in a shallow dish. Start rolling the meatloaf mix into meatballs (generous golf-ball sized meatballs), and insert a cooked clove of garlic into the center of each. Roll them lightly in the flour and set aside on a rimmed baking tray.

Heat ¼ cup of the olive oil in a sauté pan over high heat. Brown the meatballs in batches on all sides, about 5 minutes per batch, and set aside. After the meatballs are browned, add ½ cup of the olive oil to the pan with the remaining ¾ cup of flour. Stir it into the oil and cook to make a dark roux for the gravy, stirring constantly for about 6 minutes. Avoid burning it. Set aside in a small bowl.

Clean out your sauté pan with a thick paper towel and then add the last ¼ cup of the olive oil. Add the onions, chopped garlic, thyme, bay leaves, and stock, and cook until the onions are soft, about 5 minutes. Add the water and stir in the roux, then add the meatballs. Cook, covered, over low heat for 45 minutes. (You may need a large covered pan to cook all of them or two standard 10-inch sauté pans.) Remove the lid and continue to cook for another 10 minutes until the gravy has reached a rich, red-brown color and desired thickness. If the gravy is too thick add some water. If it is too thin merely reduce it further over the heat. Add salt and pepper, adjusting the seasoning to taste, and serve hot.

MONSTER SIRLOIN

AS THE PROPRIETOR OF A STEAKHOUSE I FRE-
quently get asked: "What's your favorite steak?" It depends. For pan-searing a single steak, rib-eye is my favorite. But my favorite piece of meat to throw on the grill at home is a 1$\frac{3}{4}$- to 2-inch-thick center-cut sirloin, with an inch of fat around the edge.

People tend to think incorrectly of sirloin steak as one of the cheaper, inferior cuts, and a lot of the old-time Montana steakhouses still carry them on their menus. In order to keep the price down, the chefs cut them way too thin. As a result, they are often overcooked, dry, and tough. When you try to grill any steak that's less than an inch thick, you're bucking a good outcome.

On the other hand, if you are willing to pay the price to buy a good piece of meat cut the right thickness, and to use the right techniques, you are in for a true eating experience.

Just remember, fat is essential to the flavor of the cut as it melts and drips during the cooking. This allows the flame to flare up and lightly char the outside edges of the steak during the grilling process. Garnish with fresh lemons or Chimichurri Sauce (page 230).

SERVES 4

2 CUPS OLIVE OIL

3 TABLESPOONS GRANULATED GARLIC

FRESHLY SQUEEZED LEMON JUICE FROM 1 WHOLE LEMON

3 TABLESPOONS FRESHLY CRACKED BLACK PEPPER

1 TABLESPOON SEA SALT

1 (3-POUND) CENTER-CUT SIRLOIN STEAK, 1$\frac{3}{4}$-INCHES THICK

MIX THE OLIVE OIL, GARLIC, LEMON JUICE, pepper, and salt in a large lidded container. Add the steak and turn to coat both sides. Cover and marinate for 24 to 48 hours, turning occasionally.

When you are ready to prepare the steak, preheat your gas grill on the highest setting for 20 minutes. If you are using charcoal, use plenty of it and wait for the coals to give off a very hot molten glow.

Cook the meat as close to the fire as possible, allowing some of the fire to char the outside of the steak. Do not allow the meat to burn, as it will impart a bitter taste. After the crust has been formed on the presentation side, flip the meat and move it to a more indirect location on the side of your grill away from the fire, or if you are using gas, turn off one of the burners and reduce the heat on the other burners as well: cook the meat on indirect heat for desired doneness. Remember, the idea is to get the steaks close enough to the flame so that a crust will form and then to finish cooking on much less intense heat. For a rare steak, cook to 120°F; for medium-rare, 125°F to 130°F; and 135°F for medium. (You can also finish the meat in a 400°F oven rather than on the grill if you choose.)

Remove steak and place on a carving board, cover with foil and allow the meat to rest for 10 minutes before slicing. Remember, it is the chef's prerogative to cut a small slice for tasting and temperature prior to serving.

To serve, take a good carving knife and cut 1-inch slices diagonally across the grain. Serve the meat on a warm platter in its own juices.

BACKYARD-BLACKENED NEW YORK STEAKS

WHEN I WAS APPRENTICING IN NEW ORLEANS, a soon-to-be-famous chef, Paul Prudhomme, was developing a new style of cooking he called blackening. He started searing redfish or red drum on a cast-iron skillet and the crusty, spicy fish grew so popular that the species became threatened with extinction.

Upon further research, I learned that the concept of blackening originated in Argentina, where cooks use cast-iron plates called planchas over wood fires to cook a variety of beef recipes. I used this technique of cooking and searing on cast iron for years at my old restaurant, the Continental Divide in Ennis. We find it to be just as popular on steaks we serve at The Mint. We use Chef Prudhomme's basic principles but with less salt and cayenne, and we season on one side only. This prevents the spices from overwhelming while still pushing the blackened texture. This works just as well on chicken breasts, pork chops, salmon, and most firm white fish such as halibut. Keep these cuts less than 1 inch thick or you will have to finish them in the oven.

Home cooks face some limitations when blackening. Most home exhaust systems simply cannot cope with the amount of smoke generated. You can do this in the kitchen if you have a great ventilation system, but I would recommend using your outdoor gas grill to deal with the problem of smoke. The key to success is high heat, so be sure that your grill is beyond the smoking stage. The idea is to char and mellow the flavors of the seasoning mix and use them to form a crust that will seal in the moisture of the cut you are preparing, without burning it.

SERVES 4

6 TABLESPOONS MELTED BUTTER

4 TEASPOONS BASIC BLACKENING SPICE MIXTURE (PAGE 224)

4 (13- TO 16-OUNCE) NEW YORK STEAKS, ABOUT 1½ INCHES THICK

1 LEMON, CUT INTO WEDGES

PREHEAT YOUR OVEN TO 400°F. PREHEAT A large cast-iron skillet on the stovetop to the point where small pieces of butter will burst into flames when dropped on the surface. Alternatively, preheat an outdoor grill on high heat.

Brush the meat with butter on both sides and sprinkle the spice mixture on the side you wish to blacken. Carefully place the seasoned sides down on the hot skillet. If you don't see lots of smoke and even a brief flare-up you probably haven't preheated it enough.

Cook the seasoned side for 3 to 5 minutes without moving the steaks, long enough to form a good crust, then turn and cook the other sides for another 3 to 5 minutes. At this point, the meat should be rare to medium-rare: 120°F for rare, and for medium-rare, 125°F to 130°F. If you wish to cook the meat longer, finish cooking the steaks in the oven for 5 to 15 minutes, depending on your preferred degree of doneness. Remember, you can always put an under-cooked steak back in the oven. Once it is overcooked, then you're cooked.

Serve hot with lemon wedges on the side.

PLANCHA-GRILLED FLANK STEAK, ARGENTINE-STYLE

I DOUBT THAT THERE ARE TWO PLACES IN the world as far removed yet so geographically similar as Montana and Argentina. Great mountain ranges and vast tracts of grasslands provide the perfect habitat for raising great beef and lots of it. As a matter of fact, the terrain is so similar that if a director for a Western movie were to select a location for a shoot either place would serve equally well. Some of my friends who are fishing guides work in Montana in the summer and Argentina in the winter, and they tell me that the rivers are similar enough that the trout take many of the same flies. Another similarity is that both places are home to dedicated beef eaters who take their food seriously and love to devour great chunks of grilled meat at every opportunity. Regardless of where you live, this is basic meat culture at its absolute best!

Once again that workhorse of Argentine cooking, the plancha—or cast-iron skillet—is my cooking tool of choice. (Although a hot charcoal fire will serve admirably as well.) My favorite cut is flank steak, but beef tri-tips trimmed of excess fat work just as well. This recipe also lends itself to various types of game including elk, moose, and deer. The meat should be of a uniform thickness, no more than $1\frac{1}{2}$ inches, and should be cooked over a very hot fire or on a preheated cast-iron skillet no more than medium-rare, and then sliced thinly with a very sharp knife across the grain.

SERVES 6

4 POUNDS FLANK STEAK, TRI-TIP, OR SIMILAR CUTS OF BEEF OR OTHER BIG GAME ANIMALS, WELL-TRIMMED OF FAT

$1\frac{1}{2}$ CUPS OLIVE OIL

2 TABLESPOONS GRANULATED GARLIC

FRESHLY SQUEEZED LEMON JUICE FROM 1 LEMON

2 TABLESPOONS FRESHLY CRACKED BLACK PEPPER

1 TABLESPOON SEA SALT

CHIMICHURRI SAUCE (SEE PAGE 230) OR GARLIC MUSTARD SAUCE (SEE PAGE 241), FOR SERVING

COMBINE THE MEAT WITH THE OLIVE OIL, garlic, lemon juice, pepper, and sea salt in a resealable bag, and marinate in the refrigerator for 24 hours.

If you are using charcoal, prepare a very hot fire and allow the coals to glow bright orange. A grill basket directly over the flames will produce great results. For a gas grill, preheat on high for 15 minutes with a cast-iron skillet directly over the burners. Alternatively, preheat a cast-iron skillet over high heat on the stovetop.

Drain the marinade from the meat. Place the meat close enough to the flames to produce a light char, but do not allow the meat to burn and turn bitter. Cook for about 3 to 4 minutes per side, allowing the heat to form a crust on the outside of the steaks. Do not overcook. If you are not sure of the internal temperature, don't hesitate to slice off a little and see for yourself. You should always err on the side of rare, as the temperature will continue to rise once you take it off the heat.

To serve, cut $\frac{1}{2}$-inch-thick slices at an angle across the grain and serve with chimichurri or garlic mustard sauce.

IRON-SEARED NEW YORK STEAK, MINT-STYLE

MOST RESTAURANT KITCHENS USE GAS grills as char broilers. In my opinion, these appliances do not generate enough heat and, because of their design, don't allow the meat to be cooked close enough to the heat source. To compensate, we place our meat directly on superheated steel plates to sear and seal the outside of the steaks. A cast-iron skillet also works very well. Then we finish the meat to the desired temperature in a hot oven. This will work with any meat up to 3 inches thick. Essentially we are blackening the meat without using blackening spices. The oil and seasoning from the marinade will also generate some flame, adding texture and flavor during the searing process. If you do this at home, make sure your kitchen has a great ventilating system, because where there's fire, there's smoke.

When I make this at home, I usually place the plancha or cast-iron skillet directly over the burners on my backyard gas grill. Simply remove the grate and the burner covers and place the cooking surface directly on top of the burners. The best way to determine the degree of doneness is to use a quick-read meat thermometer. An extra treat would be to serve the meat with Chimichurri Sauce on the side (see page 230).

SERVES 4

- 4 (8-OUNCE) NEW YORK STEAKS, 1³/₄-INCH THICK
- 2 CUPS OLIVE OIL
- 3 TABLESPOONS GRANULATED GARLIC
- 3 TABLESPOONS FRESHLY CRACKED BLACK PEPPER
- FRESHLY SQUEEZED LEMON JUICE FROM 1 LEMON
- CHIMICHURRI SAUCE (SEE PAGE 230) OR DIJON BUTTER (SEE PAGE 234), FOR SERVING (OPTIONAL)

MARINATE THE STEAKS IN THE OLIVE OIL, garlic, pepper and lemon juice in a 2-gallon plastic resealable bag or non-reactive container for at least 24 hours in the refrigerator.

Preheat your oven to 400°F. Preheat a cast-iron skillet, grill, or sauté pan for 15 to 20 minutes at highest heat. If using an outdoor grill, you can remove the grate and burner covers and place an old cast-iron skillet directly on the burners for better heat conduction. Test it by dropping a small piece of butter on the hot surface. If it bursts into flames, the grill is ready.

When ready, sear the steaks for 5 minutes on the top (the presentation side) without moving and 2 to 3 minutes on the bottom, or until a good crust has formed and the meat is charred, but not burned. Remove from the grill and place the meat in the preheated oven to cook to desired doneness: about 5 minutes for rare, 120°F; 9 to 10 minutes for medium-rare 125°F to 130°F; and 8 to 12 minutes for medium, 135°F. (Allow at least 5 minutes of resting time.) Anyone who wants their steak cooked more than that should save their money and eat a pair of old Nikes.

Serve on heated plates with several tablespoons of chimichurri on the side or Dijon compound butter to melt over the top if you like.

PAN-SEARED DELMONICO STEAK

WHEN I LIVED IN WASHINGTON, D.C., YEARS ago one of my favorites dining spots was a great little restaurant on M Street in Georgetown called "Le Steak." The menu consisted of only two or three items, all steak, and all very good. My favorite was a simple pan-seared Delmonico with red wine sauce served with perfectly cut and cooked pomme frites. I liked the combination so much that I came up with my own take on their classic and simple preparation. We serve our fries at The Mint in the French style, fresh cut and twice cooked.

A Delmonico steak is another name for a boneless rib-eye. You can also use a small New York cut as either one works great. The key to this recipe is a lot of butter and high heat.

SERVES 4

STEAK
3 TABLESPOONS CLARIFIED BUTTER (SEE PAGE 236)

4 (10-OUNCE) BONELESS RIB-EYE STEAKS CUT 1½ INCHES THICK, AT ROOM TEMPERATURE

RED WINE PAN SAUCE
3 TABLESPOONS CLARIFIED BUTTER (SEE PAGE 236)

2 TABLESPOONS FINELY CHOPPED SHALLOTS

1 TEASPOON FRESHLY CRACKED BLACK PEPPER

½ CUP RED WINE

DASH OF WORCESTERSHIRE SAUCE

½ CUP (1 STICK) SALTED BUTTER, CUT INTO SMALL PIECES AND KEPT COLD

FINE SALT AND FRESH CRACKED BLACK PEPPER

3 TABLESPOONS CHOPPED FRESH FLAT-LEAF PARSLEY

ULTIMATE FRENCH FRIES (SEE PAGE 207), FOR SERVING

SET A 12-INCH SAUTÉ PAN ON MEDIUM-HIGH heat, and add enough of the clarified butter to just coat the bottom. Just before the butter begins to smoke, add the steaks and cook without moving until a crust has formed, about 4 to 5 minutes, then turn and cook the other side for 3 to 4 minutes. Because they are relatively thin cuts they should be cooked to rare or medium-rare.

When finished, place in a 200°F oven to keep warm, and cook remaining steaks in batches, if necessary, adding more clarified butter as needed.

To make the red wine sauce, add clarified butter to the sauté pan, then the shallots and black pepper. Cook the shallots for a minute or two, until softened. Deglaze the pan with the red wine, add a dash of Worcestershire sauce, and reduce the contents by half, about 10 minutes. Remove the pan from the heat. Have a whisk and the cold cut butter at hand. Begin to whisk the butter into the sauce one piece at a time. Keep adding and whisking until all the cold butter has been incorporated and the sauce is creamy. Add salt and pepper to taste. Stir in the parsley, spoon the sauce over the steaks, and serve with the hot French fries on the side.

PAN-FRIED TENDERLOIN STEAKS WITH ROSEMARY

I INSIST ON CREATING A CRUST ON ANY STEAK I cook to add flavor and contain the juices. Normally this can be done over a hot fire, on a gas grill when you allow the flames to touch and sear the meat, or on a hot cast-iron sear plate sitting on a gas grill. Any of these techniques will work well. But what if you live in a place with long winters and you have to cook inside? Obviously smoke becomes an issue, particularly if, like me, you are stuck with a downdraft exhaust system.

So how do I cook a steak with the desired crust in the winter, with no smoke? Simple—I fry it like a piece of bacon. After all, doesn't bacon get crispy if you fry it long enough? In this recipe I use 7- to 8-ounce tenderloins, and flatten them to a thickness of 1³/₄ inches thick. You can use rib-eyes or New Yorks, even top sirloin, just keep the thickness about the same.

SERVES 4

FINE SALT AND FRESHLY GROUND BLACK PEPPER

4 (8-OUNCE) TENDERLOIN, RIB-EYE, NEW YORK, OR TOP SIRLOIN STEAKS, CUT AND PRESSED TO 1³/₄-INCH THICK

1 CUP OLIVE OIL

3 FRESH ROSEMARY BRANCHES

QUARTERED LEMONS, FOR SERVING (OPTIONAL)

GENEROUSLY SALT AND PEPPER THE steaks, adjusting the seasoning to taste. Allow the steaks to reach room temperature. Set a 10-inch to 12-inch sauté pan or a cast-iron skillet over medium-high heat and add the oil to about half an inch in depth. Add the rosemary branches to the oil as it heats to just below the point of smoking. If the rosemary begins to burn, remove it from the pan.

Add the steaks and cook the presentation side (the tops) for about 8 minutes to allow a crust to form. Flip and cook for another 6 to 7 minutes. Check for temperature either by meat thermometer, or by feel: you'll want 125°F for medium-rare.

Remove from pan, and cover with foil for 10 minutes. Serve with fresh lemon wedges.

PAN-ROASTED CÔTES DU BOEUF, LOUIS XVI-STYLE

BACK IN THE PREHISTORIC 1980S, WHEN I was working for Daniel Bonnot at the Louis XVI restaurant in New Orleans, we used to do a wonderful French bistro classic, *Côtes du Boeuf aux Herbes* which literally means "a beef chop with herbs." It was a 2-inch-thick bone-in rib-eye that had been marinated in herbs and olive oil, cooked like a steak in a 1200°F oven, and carved tableside. This dish was sold for $30 for two. That would translate into $60 to $70 in today's money.

At The Mint we offer essentially the same thing: a rib-eye for two that usually runs over two pounds of lip-smacking certified Angus beef. In this case, it is boneless. Before it goes on the fire, we bring it to room temperature and flavor it with sea salt and coarsely ground pepper. Since none of us is likely to have an oven in our kitchen that can reach even 1000°F, I developed a technique using a cast-iron skillet and a 500°F oven that gives you the same results. Make sure your ventilation system is up and running. Outside, cook it on a cast-iron skillet positioned right over the burners on your gas grill. Serve with Potatoes au Gratin (see page 212), fresh grilled asparagus, and a big red wine.

SERVES 6

- 1 (32- TO 38-OUNCE) BONELESS RIB-EYE, 3 INCHES THICK
- 1 CUP OLIVE OIL
- 3 TABLESPOONS FRESHLY CRACKED BLACK PEPPER
- 1/4 CUP GRANULATED GARLIC
- 1/4 CUP FRESH ROSEMARY LEAVES
- 2 TABLESPOONS KOSHER SALT

PLACE MEAT, OLIVE OIL, PEPPER, GARLIC, and rosemary in resealeable plastic bag and marinate in the refrigerator for 48 hours.

Just before cooking, preheat your oven to 400°F. Preheat a cast-iron skillet for 10 minutes over high heat on the stovetop or directly over the burners on a gas grill.

Drain the marinade from the meat and sprinkle the salt on both sides of the meat. Next, before you place the steak in the hot skillet, sprinkle a tablespoon of the marinade on the steak. Slide it with a spatula onto the hot skillet. It's definitely going to pop and splatter. Cook on high for 7 minutes without moving until a crust forms, then turn the meat over and sear the other side for 2 minutes. When both sides are browned, put the skillet in the oven and turn the oven off.

Let the meat sit in the cooling oven for 7 to 10 minutes. Use your meat thermometer to determine the internal temperature. For rare to medium-rare, remove the meat when the temperature reads 120°F. Cover and allow the meat to rest for 20 minutes before carving. By the time you are ready to serve the meat, its internal temperature should be in the 125°F range and the results should be a perfectly cooked medium-rare.

If you are using a gas grill, follow the same instructions including finishing in the oven. I do not recommend rib-eyes being cooked less than medium rare as cooking a rib-eye rare can produce a tough and stringy result.

SLOW-COOKED BEEF BRISKET

OVER THE YEARS I HAVE TRIED ALL KINDS of cookers, pits, and kettles: they were messy, cumbersome, and they all required constant monitoring. The fire was either too hot or not hot enough, and the minute you walked away, the whole thing would explode into a raging inferno. It wasn't until I started working for Sunbeam Corporation's Outdoor Products Division as their chef that I finally got real and bought a gas grill. Once I started using it, I discovered why propane and natural gas grills have come into their own, especially for slow-cooked barbeque.

Whether you cook brisket on a gas grill or even in an oven, for best results and great flavor use a good rub, and then cook the brisket long and slow. I always do a whole brisket because the leftovers freeze well.

SERVES 8

1 (6- TO 10-POUND) BEEF BRISKET, PARTIALLY TRIMMED, WITH A 1-INCH FAT CAP REMAINING

2 CUPS PAPRIKA

2 CUPS PACKED LIGHT BROWN SUGAR

1 CUP FINE SALT

1/2 CUP MILD CHILI POWDER

1 CUP GRANULATED GARLIC

1/2 CUP ONION POWDER

1/2 CUP CURRY POWDER

1/2 CUP FRESHLY GROUND BLACK PEPPER

1 CUP CIDER VINEGAR

WITH A SMALL SHARP KNIFE, SCORE THE FAT cap on the brisket with inch-long slashes, not cutting all the way through to the meat. In a bowl, combine the paprika, sugar, salt, chili powder, garlic, onion powder, curry, and pepper. Generously sprinkle the rub over the brisket, and wrap in it plenty of plastic wrap. Store it in a roasting pan or large bowl for 2 to 3 days in the refrigerator.

When you are ready to cook, remove the brisket from the refrigerator and bring it to room temperature. Remove the plastic wrap and place the beef on a rack over a drip pan with about an inch of water (at least 4 cups) mixed with the cider vinegar. Preheat a gas grill on low: turn on one burner to its lowest setting and place the meat as far away from the heat as you can.

Add some water-soaked wood chips to a small foil packet (poke a few holes in the packet to allow smoke to escape) and tuck it over the active burner. You want the chips to smoke but not burn.

Try to keep the grill temperature at or below 200°F during the smoking and cooking process. Keep a supply of soaked chips handy to replenish during the first 3 to 4 hours of cooking. Baste the meat periodically and add more water if necessary to maintain an inch of liquid. Cook long and slow for at least 5 to 6 hours, or until the internal temperature reaches 185°F and the meat is very tender: you should be able to pull it apart with a fork.

Alternatively, preheat the oven to 200°F. Place the beef on a rack over a drip pan with about an inch of water (at least 4 cups) mixed with the cider vinegar. Cook the brisket for about 5 hours, or until it is fork-tender. Add more water if necessary to maintain that level of liquid.

When the brisket is ready to serve, if you want to, you can utilize the basting liquid by mixing it with your favorite barbeque sauce to accompany the meat or even use the liquid to flavor a batch of beans. Slice thinly across the grain to serve.

BRAISED BARBEQUE BEEF BRISKET

MY BUDDY ALLEN PIERCE, WHO HAILS FROM an old Texas family, gave me this recipe that he insists goes all the way back to the trail drives of the nineteenth century. I have a hard time believing that a typical chuck wagon cook had even heard of Worcestershire sauce (although it does predate much of Texas history), much less had a bottle under the seat of his wagon. The cast-iron Dutch oven, however, as hard working and reliable as a high plains herding dog, was indispensible to any self-respecting trail cook.

Traditional or not, this is a great way to do "faux" barbeque beef when you don't want to make the effort of slow-cooking it on the grill. Think of it as kind of a cowboy-style "sloppy Joe." You can even use a crockpot, but if you do, be sure to brown the meat really well before you start the slow cooking process, otherwise you will end up with a gray, featureless mess.

I like to double the amounts and freeze some in resealable bags to break out on cold Montana Sundays watching football with friends. Serve with pinto beans and coleslaw, with rustic bread on the side.

SERVES 4

1 (3-POUND) POINT-CUT BRISKET

2 CUPS BEEF STOCK (SUBSTITUTE 1 TABLESPOON GOOD-QUALITY BEEF BASE PLUS 2 CUPS WATER)

2 CUPS KETCHUP

$1/2$ CUP PACKED LIGHT BROWN SUGAR

1 (12-OUNCE) BOTTLE OR CAN OF BEER (I LIKE A HEAVY PORTER OR STOUT)

1 TABLESPOON WORCESTERSHIRE SAUCE

3 TABLESPOONS LIQUID SMOKE, OR MORE TO TASTE

1 TABLESPOON VINEGAR-BASED HOT SAUCE

$1/2$ CUP OLIVE OIL

PLACE THE MEAT IN A LARGE RESEALABLE plastic bag or non-reactive bowl. Mix together the beef stock, ketchup, sugar, beer, Worcestershire, liquid smoke, and hot sauce, and pour over the meat. Marinate in the refrigerator for 2 to 3 days.

To cook, place a large Dutch oven on the stovetop, add olive oil, and heat over high heat.

Drain the meat from the marinade, reserving the marinade. Brown all sides of the meat, about 10 minutes per side, until it is nice and brown. It will pop and splatter so watch out. When the meat has a crust on all sides, add the marinade, bring to a simmer, reduce the heat to low, and cook covered for around 4 hours, or until the meat can be pulled apart with a fork.

Remove the meat from the sauce and reduce the sauce until it has thickened to the consistency of thin ketchup.

BEEF FILETS WITH BRANDY AND BLACK PEPPERCORNS

THIS DISH BORROWS FROM CLASSIC FRENCH bistro cooking at its best—simple and straightforward—as I learned it cooking in New Orleans. It went out of style long ago and you never see it on menus (except occasionally mine), but to me it is a luscious link to the history of the earlier twentieth century before the onset of "nouvelle cuisine."

The filets are sautéed in a very hot pan, and the browned bits left behind are then utilized to make one of the great dishes in any cuisine. This dish is a perennial classic and when we run this as a special at The Mint, it quickly sells out.

Serve with crusty roasted potatoes or wild rice with a Cabernet, Zinfandel, Merlot, or other hearty red wine. If this sinful recipe gives you guilt pangs—even I get them on rare occasions—then do as I do: substitute venison or elk tenderloins.

SERVES 4

- 4 (5- TO 6-OUNCE) BEEF TENDERLOIN FILETS, $1^3/_4$ TO 2 INCHES THICK
- 3 TABLESPOONS FRESHLY CRACKED BLACK PEPPER
- $^1/_4$ CUP ($^1/_2$ STICK) UNSALTED BUTTER
- $^3/_4$ CUP BEEF STOCK (SUBSTITUTE 1 TEASPOON GOOD-QUALITY BEEF BASE PLUS $^3/_4$ CUP WATER)
- $^1/_4$ CUP BRANDY
- $^3/_4$ CUP WHIPPING CREAM
- $^1/_4$ CUP FINELY CHOPPED FRESH FLAT-LEAF PARSLEY
- FINE SALT

PREHEAT A HEAVY CAST-IRON SAUTÉ PAN over high heat. Press one side of each filet into the cracked pepper to lightly coat. Have all the other ingredients ready to add in the final stages of cooking as it will go very fast. Add the butter to the pan and allow it to get very hot and begin to smoke. Add the filets, pepper-side down and cook for about 5 minutes. Make sure to allow the hot butter and pepper to form a dark crust on the filets. Gently turn the meat, taking care not to knock off the pepper, and cook for 3 to 5 minutes on the other side for rare, about 120°F, and just under a minute longer on each side for medium-rare, 125°F to 130°F. Do not overcook!

When the meat is finished, remove to a warm plate or low oven and cover with foil. Immediately add the beef stock and the brandy to the pan. There will be flames but they should die down quickly as the alcohol burns off. After the flames have subsided, turn the heat down to medium and add the cream. Reduce the liquid to about half of its original volume, all the time stirring and scraping the bits of residue off the bottom of the pan. If you want to avoid the flames, add the brandy after the other liquids; you may still get flames but not as many. When the sauce has reduced to the desired thickness, add salt if needed along with the chopped parsley. Adjust seasoning to taste. If the sauce becomes too thick you can thin it with more cream. Stir well, and pour equal amounts of the sauce on warmed plates. Place the cooked filets over the sauce and serve immediately.

BEEF SHORT RIBS WITH ORANGE, FENNEL, & KALAMATA OLIVES

THE COMBINATION OF BONE AND THE skin that encases the short rib produces a rich and heady sauce, redolent of beefy flavors; frankly, as long as you cook them to a literal "falling off the bone" stage, it's almost impossible to produce a bad dish. My brother, Tony, a great cook in his own right, showed me this interesting way of cooking short ribs which I have used at The Mint with good results. Serve with black beans and rice (see page 188), oven-roasted red potatoes, or Soft Polenta with Herbs (see page 217).

SERVES 4

6 TABLESPOONS OLIVE OIL, DIVIDED, PLUS MORE AS NEEDED

2 CUPS RED WINE, DIVIDED

3 MEDIUM YELLOW ONIONS SLICED, DIVIDED

$1/2$ CUP FROZEN ORANGE JUICE CONCENTRATE, THAWED

1 TABLESPOON GRANULATED GARLIC

1 TABLESPOON FENNEL SEEDS

1 TABLESPOON DRIED OREGANO

3 BAY LEAVES

1 TABLESPOON FRESHLY GROUND BLACK PEPPER, PLUS MORE AS NEEDED

6 WHOLE BEEF SHORT RIBS WITH LOTS OF MEAT, CUT BY YOUR BUTCHER INTO 3 INCH PIECES

2 TABLESPOONS ALL-PURPOSE FLOUR

1 TABLESPOON TOMATO PASTE

2 QUARTS BEEF STOCK (SUBSTITUTE $1/2$ CUP GOOD-QUALITY BEEF BASE AND 2 QUARTS WATER

2 CUPS PITTED KALAMATA OLIVES, SLICED IN HALF

1 (15-OUNCE) CAN DICED TOMATOES, DRAINED

SALT TO TASTE

COMBINE 2 TABLESPOONS OF THE OLIVE OIL, 1 cup of wine, 1 sliced onion, the orange juice concentrate, garlic, fennel seeds, oregano, bay leaves and pepper in a 2-gallon resealable plastic bag, add the meat, shaking well, and refrigerate for 24 hours.

Preheat the oven to 325°F.

Remove the ribs from the marinade, and reserve the marinade. Place a large ovenproof Dutch oven or pot on the stovetop over medium-high heat. Add the remaining 4 tablespoons of olive oil and when the oil is hot, brown the short

ribs on all sides, turning occasionally. Set the ribs aside. In the same pot, sauté the remaining 2 sliced onions until translucent. Turn the heat down to medium-low, stir in the flour, and cook for 3 minutes to create a light roux. Throw in the tomato paste followed by the remaining 1 cup of red wine, scraping up any browned bits from the bottom of the pan. Add the reserved marinade and continue to cook for 30 seconds. Next add the beef stock, stirring until well combined.

Add the meat to the pot and bring to a boil: the liquid should just cover the meat. Place the pot in the oven and cook covered for 1 hour. Remove the cover and check the ribs for doneness: they should be tender without falling off the bone. Uncover the pot and cook in the oven for another 45 minutes. When the meat easily pulls away from the bone, add the kalamata olives and the diced tomatoes. Place the pot on the stovetop, remove the ribs to a bowl, and raise the heat to a simmer to reduce the sauce. Monitor carefully; do not let the sauce burn or scorch while reducing. If the sauce is too thick, add some water to thin. Taste for salt, return the ribs to the sauce, reheat, and serve in large bowls.

SALISBURY STEAK

SALISBURY STEAK IS ONE THOSE ROADHOUSE things that used to be a staple in the old-time Montana "supper clubs." Whether from a sense of nostalgia, or because I used to like them so much as a kid, I occasionally serve this roadhouse classic as a "comfort food" special, and the response is great.

When we can get them, we use organic, grass-fed beef from locally raised steers from a ranch located on the shores of Ennis Lake in the upper Madison Valley. These grass-fed cows are perfect for this kind of dish. They offer great flavor with very little fat.

Serve with mashed potatoes or mounds of fresh-cooked French fries. This may not be as healthy as the good doctor would like, but in Montana, we have a common saying: "What the hell?"

SERVES 4

2 MEDIUM YELLOW ONIONS, FINELY DICED

1 TEASPOON GRANULATED GARLIC

2 TABLESPOONS WORCESTERSHIRE SAUCE

1 TABLESPOON SEA SALT

1 TABLESPOON FRESHLY GROUND BLACK PEPPER

2 POUNDS GROUND SIRLOIN

2 TABLESPOONS OLIVE OIL

GRAVY

1/4 CUP (1/2 STICK) UNSALTED BUTTER OR 1/4 CUP OLIVE OIL

1 THINLY SLICED YELLOW ONION

1 CUP THINLY SLICED BUTTON MUSHROOMS

1 TEASPOON FRESHLY GROUND BLACK PEPPER

2 TABLESPOONS ALL-PURPOSE FLOUR

2 CUPS BEEF STOCK (SUBSTITUTE 2 TEASPOONS GOOD-QUALITY BEEF BASE PLUS 2 CUPS WATER)

FINE SALT

BLEND THE ONION, GARLIC, WORCESTER- shire, salt, and pepper into the meat, then, form four 8-ounce patties.

Heat a 12-inch sauté pan over medium-high heat and add olive oil. Pan-fry the patties until brown on the outside, about 2 minutes per side.

Set the meat aside. It's best to undercook the meat here because it will cook some more when you reheat the patties in the gravy.

In the same pan, heat the butter over medium-high heat, and sauté the onions, mushrooms, and pepper, until the onions are golden, about 5 minutes. Gradually stir in the flour. Cook for another 3 minutes as the mix forms a light roux.

Add the stock, mixing well until the sauce thickens. Reduce the heat to a simmer and add the patties. Finish cooking the patties in the gravy, about 10 minutes, turning once or twice to absorb the flavors. Taste for salt, and serve hot.

CHOOSING RED MEAT

THE GREATEST CHEF IS ONLY AS GOOD AS THE RAW MATERIALS HE OR SHE HAS TO WORK WITH.
With good meat you can sometimes get bad results, but with bad meat you always get bad results. You don't have to be a meat expert to recognize what is good and what to avoid, if you take advantage of the resources at your disposal.

When choosing meat, employ four tests: age, color, cut, and aroma. Some of the things to avoid when buying red meat are: a purplish or brownish-red color; fat that is gray or yellow; too much marbling; not enough marbling; meat that gives off too much juice; a coarse and granular structure; and coloring variation, two different tones of dark red and light.

On the question of quality, a federal grading system imposes uniform standards on meat. Fat content, color, flavor, and tenderness are graded by the following marks that are placed directly on the cuts of meat. They are Prime, Choice, Good, Commercial, and Utility.

PRIME AND CHOICE meats should have a fine, compact grain and be a bright red. The meat should be elastic to the touch. Marbling, that is, the interlacing of fat, should be apparent and uniform. This should be a good indication of tenderness. Marbling gives meat internal moisture and flavor, particularly when grilled, seared, or cooked over high heat.

GOOD, COMMERCIAL, AND UTILITY are lesser grades and their appearance shows. These grades will have a coarser texture, and there will be a lot less marbling or none at all. The surface of the meat will appear rougher, and the feel may be softer and more pliable. These grades are generally much cheaper and are usually slow-cooked, braised, or stewed. They can still have a lot of flavor, and, as we demonstrate, can be every bit as good as prime or choice, when properly rubbed or marinated. For example, a cheap cut of chuck or some cuts of game that would normally require long roasting or braising can give great results on the grill by being tenderized first by lengthy marinating and secondly by the way they are carved for the table.

These characteristics can tell you a lot about quality and age, as well as the type of food the animal ate. An old bull will be dark red without much marbling, if any. You can cook it a hundred ways and it still will be tough and tasteless. Grass-fed beef should be bright red and without fat, which can be a bonus if you are avoiding the higher cholesterol content of lesser cuts. Milk-fed veal calves should have a fine-grained texture that is almost white. If the flesh is red, the calf was probably grass or grain-fed and allowed to grow too old.

OLD-FASHIONED SWISS STEAK AND GRAVY

WHEN I WAS GROWING UP, THIS DISH WAS A family staple. Then, for reasons never explained, it was no longer in style. I discovered this classic again in the seventies when I moved to Montana, where it has always been a mainstay of ranch kitchens and small town cafés. From the Western Café in Bozeman, to the M&M in Butte, it is basically the same: juicy floured slabs of crusty beef, simmered long and slow in its own gravy, and served with mounds of mashed potatoes. The idea of this recipe is to braise or slow-cook the beef to fork tenderness and smother it with onions and gravy.

SERVES 4

STEAK

2 POUNDS BONELESS ROUND STEAK, CUT INTO FOUR 1-INCH-THICK SLICES

1 CUP ALL-PURPOSE FLOUR

1 TEASPOON FINE SALT

1 TEASPOON FRESHLY GROUND BLACK PEPPER

1 TEASPOON GRANULATED GARLIC

1 TEASPOON PAPRIKA

$^{1}/_{4}$ CUP ($^{1}/_{2}$ STICK) SALTED BUTTER

3 TABLESPOONS OLIVE OIL

GRAVY

1 MEDIUM YELLOW ONION, THINLY SLICED

5 GARLIC CLOVES, FINELY DICED

2 CUPS BEEF STOCK (SUBSTITUTE 2 TEASPOONS GOOD-QUALITY BEEF BASE PLUS 2 CUPS WATER)

With the coarse end of a meat hammer or the bottom of a small pan, pound the meat to a thickness of $^{1}/_{2}$ to $^{3}/_{4}$ inch. It's easier and less messy if you put the meat between two pieces of waxed paper or plastic wrap.

Stir together the flour, salt, pepper, garlic, and paprika, and place it in a shallow dish. Dredge and thoroughly coat the meat in the seasoned flour and let it rest for about 30 minutes.

Heat the butter and oil in a large sauté pan over medium heat, and cook the steak to a golden brown on both sides, about 3 to 4 minutes per side. Remove the meat from the pan and set aside while you prepare the gravy.

Add the onions and garlic to the pan and cook until translucent, about 3 minutes, and then add the beef stock. Be sure and scrape all the brown bits from the cooking, making sure the gravy is well blended.

Reduce the heat to low, and place the meat back in the pan, overlapping slightly if necessary. Cover tightly and cook for another hour or until the meat is fork-tender and the gravy has thickened. If the gravy becomes too thick, simply add more stock or water.

CHICKEN-FRIED STEAK

IN THE DAYS BEFORE MASS CHICKEN PROD-uction facilities, chickens were considered a luxury, while beef was plentiful and cheap. Some enterprising cook decided that cheap cuts of beef could be pounded, cooked like fried chicken, and sold at a higher price than plain old pot roast. Chicken-fried steak became the rage in Depression-era cuisine and it quickly spread from Texas to the rest of the country.

I realize most people don't have a restaurant-style deep fryer so I wrote this recipe to demonstrate the way I do it at home: on the top of the stove in a cast-iron skillet. Any good fried chicken recipe works. You merely use a seasoned, pounded, piece of beef in place of chicken, and start cooking. Of course, the gravy is a must with this dish. In fact, it's the gravy that raises this dish from the ordinary to the sublime. Mashed potatoes on the side would be a sound addition.

SERVES 4

STEAK

1 (2-POUND) TOP ROUND STEAK, CUT INTO 8-OUNCE SLICES

1 CUP ALL-PURPOSE FLOUR

1 TABLESPOON PAPRIKA

1 TEASPOON GRANULATED GARLIC

FINE SALT AND FRESHLY GROUND BLACK PEPPER

2 CUPS WHOLE MILK

1 EGG, LIGHTLY BEATEN

LARD, CANOLA, PEANUT, OR OLIVE OIL, AS NEEDED FOR FRYING

COUNTRY GRAVY

2 TABLESPOONS ALL-PURPOSE FLOUR

1 CUP HALF-AND-HALF

1/2 TEASPOON ONION POWDER

1/2 TEASPOON GRANULATED GARLIC

1 CUP BEEF OR CHICKEN STOCK (SUBSTITUTE 1 TEASPOON GOOD-QUALITY BEEF OR CHICKEN BASE PLUS 1 CUP WATER)

1 TABLESPOON FRESH COARSELY GROUND BLACK PEPPER

COVER THE TOP OF EACH PIECE OF MEAT with plastic wrap or waxed paper, then, with a coarse side of a meat hammer, or the bottom of a small pan, pound the hell out of the meat until it is about 1/2-inch thick. Remember, you have to tenderize the meat through pounding rather than long, slow cooking like Swiss steak, so put your shoulder into it. As I'm tenderizing the meat, I continually run my hand over each piece to check for a uniform thickness. Season with salt and pepper on both sides, adjusting seasoning to taste. Set aside.

Stir together the flour, paprika, garlic, salt, and pepper to taste in a large shallow dish. In another dish, stir together the milk and egg.

Add the oil to a depth of 1 inch in a large cast-iron skillet and preheat over medium-high heat to 350°F. You can also check the oil temperature by carefully flicking a tiny drop of water into the oil. If it fizzles and spatters immediately, the oil is ready.

While the oil is heating, prepare the meat by coating both sides of each piece with the seasoned flour, then the milk mixture, then back into the seasoned flour.

Place the steaks in batches in the hot oil without crowding the pan, and brown well on both sides. Remove them to a paper towel-lined plate. Pour off most of the oil from the pan, keeping about a quarter of an inch. Reduce the heat to medium, and reheat the remaining oil. When the oil is hot, put the meat back into the pan and pan-fry for about 5 minutes per side to cook through. You want to achieve a brown crunchy texture. Remove the steaks and set aside in a low oven while you make the gravy in the skillet.

Pour off most, but not all, of the fat (leaving a tablespoon or two), being careful to retain the crunchy bits of flour that have accumulated during the cooking process. Over medium heat, add the flour to the pan residue and brown slightly. Then add half-and-half, onion powder, garlic, stock, and pepper, and stir briskly while scraping the bottom of the pan. Remember, there is already salt from the seasoned flour and stock, so don't over-salt the gravy. When the gravy has reached the desired thickness remove from the heat.

Put the steaks on plates and serve the gravy either over or under the meat, with prodigious amounts of mashed potatoes covered in even more gravy.

BUTTE MINERS BEEF AND POTATO PIE

ANOTHER LEGACY OF THE WELSH MINERS who migrated to Butte in the heyday of copper and silver mining was a hearty dish that was, in essence, an Americanized version of shepherd's pie. Made with beef instead of lamb, it was a variation of the pasties that they carried in their lunch buckets for their noonday meal deep in the darkness of the many mines that dotted what was then known as "the richest hill on Earth."

By adding kalamata olives, tomatoes, and a number of herbs and spices, including smoked paprika and cumin, I was able to take this rather bland and uncomplicated dish to another level in taste and texture. It has since become a Sunday night favorite at the restaurant and a leftover bonus at my house.

PIE FILLING

1/2 CUP OLIVE OIL

1 YELLOW ONION, DICED

1 RED OR GREEN BELL PEPPER, CHOPPED

3/4 CUP GRATED CARROTS (ABOUT 2 CARROTS)

2 POUNDS LEAN GROUND BEEF, ELK, OR BISON

2 TABLESPOONS DRIED ROSEMARY

2 TABLESPOONS DRIED OREGANO

1 TABLESPOON SMOKED PAPRIKA

2 TEASPOONS GROUND CUMIN

1 TEASPOON DRY MUSTARD POWDER

1 TABLESPOON GRANULATED GARLIC

1 1/2 CUPS RED WINE

1 (14-OUNCE) CAN DICED TOMATOES, DRAINED

2 CUPS PITTED KALAMATA OLIVES, CUT IN HALF

FINE SALT AND CRUSHED RED PEPPER FLAKES

PIE TOPPING

4 LARGE IDAHO POTATOES, PEELED

1 CUP WHOLE MILK

1/4 CUP OLIVE OIL

6 EGG YOLKS

FINE SALT AND FRESHLY GROUND BLACK PEPPER

OVER MEDIUM-HIGH HEAT, PREHEAT A VERY large cast-iron skillet with the olive oil for several minutes until hot, then add the onions, pepper, and carrots. Cook until the vegetables begin to soften but not brown, about 5 minutes. Add the meat, breaking up the large chunks with the side of the spoon until the meat is browned and begins to blend with the vegetables. Add the rosemary, oregano, paprika, cumin, mustard, and garlic. Continue cooking the mixture for another 5 minutes, all the while stirring and chopping with your spoon, and then add the wine, tomatoes, and olives.

Reduce the heat and simmer until the liquids have been somewhat reduced but there is still enough to keep the mixture moist. Taste, and add salt and red pepper flakes, adjusting the seasoning to taste. Remove from the heat while you prepare the topping.

Cut the potatoes into 1 1/2-inch pieces and place in a medium saucepan. Cover with cold water, and bring to a boil. Cook until the potatoes are fork-tender, about 10 minutes, then drain.

While the potatoes are cooking, warm the milk in a small saucepan. Blend the hot milk and olive oil with the potatoes and mash. Blend in the egg yolks until they have all been incorporated into the mix. Add salt and pepper, adjusting the seasoning to taste and set aside.

Preheat your oven to 400°F.

Take the mashed potatoes and spread them evenly over the top of the meat in the skillet. Use a spatula to smooth the surface. Bake, for 30 to 45 minutes, or until the top begins to brown and becomes slightly crisp, but not burned. Serve in wedges, like a pie.

BUTTE PASTIES

WHEN I MOVED TO MONTANA I KEPT HEARING about a local treat called pasties that had achieved cult status in Butte. Until then, I always thought that pasties were something strippers wore to circumvent local decency ordinances. Pronounced "PAST-eaze" rather than "PASTE-eaze," these are hand-sized baked meat pies that miners took into the mines for lunch. A large part of the early population of Butte was comprised of miners and their families who had emigrated from Cornwall and Wales to work the "pits," as the mines were called locally. The miners' wives, each of whom had their own inherited family recipes, usually prepared Cornish pasties. As the mines of Butte flourished, so did restaurants and shops specializing in these tasty little pockets of meat and potatoes. Today, only one shop remains in Butte, appropriately named The Pasty Shop. While the shop seems to be part culinary museum and part restaurant, pasties still endure in many Butte home menus. Every once in a while I make up a batch to take along for a shore lunch when we float the Madison River fly-fishing for trout. My co-author and I share the opinion that the combination of cold beer and pasties enjoyed under a big cottonwood tree, followed by a nap, makes for one of the better experiences of Montana fly-fishing.

Most of the time I cheat and buy off-the-shelf pie dough (two pie crusts in a package) at the grocery store. It will do in a pinch and it works fine for both fried and baked pies. If you want to be authentic, use this recipe.

MAKES 6 PASTIES

PASTRY DOUGH
5 CUPS ALL-PURPOSE FLOUR

1 TEASPOON FINE SALT

1 TABLESPOON GRANULATED SUGAR

1/2 TEASPOON BAKING POWDER

1 1/2 CUPS (3 STICKS) COLD UNSALTED BUTTER OR COLD VEGETABLE SHORTENING, CUT INTO SMALL PIECES

2 EGG YOLKS

FILLING
1/2 CUP OLIVE OIL

1 1/2 POUNDS LEAN BEEF OR GAME, COARSELY GROUND OR FINELY DICED

4 STALKS CELERY, FINELY DICED

1 MEDIUM YELLOW ONION, FINELY DICED

3 GARLIC CLOVES, DICED

1 TABLESPOON DRIED THYME

1 TABLESPOON FRESHLY GROUND BLACK PEPPER

3 LARGE WHITE POTATOES, PEELED, BOILED UNTIL TENDER, AND FINELY DICED

2 TABLESPOON ALL-PURPOSE FLOUR

2 TABLESPOONS GOOD-QUALITY BEEF BASE

SEA SALT

1 EGG, LIGHTLY BEATEN

TO PREPARE THE DOUGH, SIFT THE FLOUR, salt, sugar, and baking powder together into a mixing bowl. Cut in the butter and blend with a pastry cutter or two knives until it looks like a coarse meal. In a separate bowl, beat together the egg yolks and 1/2 cup of water.

Gradually add the mixture to the dry ingredients until it is fully incorporated. Form into a disc, wrap in waxed paper or plastic wrap, and refrigerate for about 1 hour.

Divide the dough into 6 equal portions. Roll the dough out into a circle on a lightly floured surface, each about 8 or 9 inches in diameter.

(continued)

Think of the filling as finely diced beef stew or corned beef hash with a little gravy, which is exactly what it is. Heat a large sauté pan over medium-high heat and add the oil. Add meat, and sauté for about 5 minutes, until it just begins to brown. Add the celery, onions, garlic, thyme, and pepper, and cook until the vegetables are wilted, about 10 minutes. Stir together ½ cup of water with the flour to make a slurry. Scrape it into the pan, then add the potatoes and beef base, and cook until it thickens to coat the back of a spoon. Cool the filling to room temperature before using in the pastries.

Preheat the oven to 350°F. Place 4 heaping tablespoons of the filling in the center of each pastry, then paint the inside edge of the 9-inch circle of dough with the beaten egg. Fold the pastries into half circles and crimp the edges closed using a fork. Cut a couple of small vents for steam.

Bake the pies on a rimmed baking sheet for 30 minutes, or until the pastries are golden-brown. Serve hot or at room temperature. These pies freeze perfectly for months; wrap them well.

PRAISING RANCHERS

MORE THAN 70 PERCENT OF MONTANA'S 147,046 SQUARE MILES ARE CONSIDERED GRAZING LAND. Forty million acres are privately owned. The U.S. government's Bureau of Land Management oversees the rest. The sheer vastness of the land accommodates a lot of living things. Among the greatest beneficiaries, besides antelope, bison, elk, deer, and beef cattle are sheep. More than 20 breeds graze the rolling foothills of the west summer pastures to the central sweet grass valleys for winter protection to the short grass plains bounding the great Missouri River and Yellowstone Basin and the Big Horn River.

Having lived and worked in Montana for a quarter-century, I've gotten to know a lot of ranchers as neighbors, purveyors, and restaurant customers. To me, ranchers personify the traditional values of hard work, trustworthiness, pride, resiliency, and independence. Ranchers helped inspire this cookbook.

Today, the reality of ranching is what it has always been: bitter cold nights of spring calving when the only times a rancher's hands are warm are when they're inside a mother cow helping with a birth. Mending fences and the other chores occupy endless to-do lists that also include dealing with bankers, bureaucrats, broken-down equipment, and packs of coyotes, in no certain order. Sweat pours forth in many forms, none more prodigious than when it comes from worrying about the weather and the price of beef. It takes a tough-minded person to hold onto and work a piece of land that others know could be developed into more profitable use. I'm grateful to those ranchers who shun the sub-dividers and developers who wave easy money in their faces. Stubborn, independent, yes, but those are the qualities that defined the American experience for what it was, in Montana.

NACHITOCHES MEAT PIES

A THOUSAND MILES SOUTH OF BUTTE IS A little town on the Cane River in western Louisiana where they have been eating meat pies since the late 1700s. Nachitoches is a charming little town of antebellum houses nestled along a beautiful bayou laced with Spanish moss. At Lasyone's you can buy a classic meat pie just like the ones sold by the street vendors and shops almost 200 years ago. The only difference is now they fry them in canola oil rather than lard. The concept is similar to the Butte pies but the Nachitoches pies are fried instead of baked, and the filling is much spicier. Wrap them well and these fully cooked pies will freeze for months.

MAKES 12 PIES

- 1 RECIPE PASTRY DOUGH FOR SAVORY PIES (SEE PAGE 99)
- 2 TABLESPOONS OLIVE OIL
- 1½ POUNDS LEAN GROUND BEEF OR GAME
- 1 MEDIUM YELLOW ONION, CHOPPED
- 1 STALK CELERY, CHOPPED
- 1 MEDIUM GREEN BELL PEPPER, CHOPPED
- 3 TABLESPOONS CHOPPED GARLIC
- 1 TABLESPOON BLACKENING SPICE MIX (SEE PAGE 224)
- ¼ TEASPOON CAYENNE PEPPER
- ½ TEASPOON FRESHLY GROUND BLACK PEPPER
- 1 TABLESPOON ALL-PURPOSE FLOUR
- 1 TABLESPOON GOOD-QUALITY BEEF BASE
- CANOLA OR VEGETABLE OIL, AS NEEDED FOR FRYING
- 1 EGG, LIGHTLY BEATEN

DIVIDE THE PASTRY DOUGH INTO 12 PORtions. Roll out each one on a lightly floured surface into a circle about 5 inches in diameter. Cover and set aside.

In a large skillet, heat the oil over high heat and add all of the meat, onions, celery, peppers, garlic, blackening spice mix, cayenne, and black pepper. Sauté for about 10 minutes, until the vegetables are soft and translucent, then add the flour and stir well. Cook for another 5 minutes, and then stir in the beef base and 1 cup of water. Cook until the mixture is thickened and the liquid has been almost totally absorbed. The filling should not be runny; you will be frying the pies in hot oil and you want to avoid spattering. Cool the mixture to room temperature before filling the pies.

Heat at least 4 inches of canola oil in a deep pot or electric fryer to 350°F.

Place about 2 to 3 tablespoons of the filling in the center of each pastry circle. Paint the edges with the beaten egg, then fold over and seal the edges by crimping the edges shut with a fork.

Fry the pies in batches until golden-brown on both sides, turning once in the oil, about 5 minutes. Drain on a paper towel-lined plate and serve warm with plenty of hot sauce and cold beer.

VACA FRITA

VACA FRITA, WHICH MEANS "FRIED COW" IN Spanish, would seem to be the last thing you would find on the menu of a steak and potatoes place in Montana. It's classic Cuban, and the first time I had it was in Little Havana in Miami. Although it's a long way from Calle Ocho to Main Street, Montana, when the word gets out that we're featuring this tribute to Latin cuisine as a special on our menu, our customers flock to The Mint eager to gobble up this dish.

Be sure to shred the beef as finely as you can, fry it extra crispy, and top with sautéed onions. Serve with black beans and rice (see page 188) on the side. At The Mint we use our thin cut, deep-fried onion rings to give this dish our own special treatment, but the traditional way is with the onions sautéed in the pan.

SERVES 6

- 1 WHITE ONION HALVED, PLUS 2 WHITE ONIONS, VERY THINLY SLICED, DIVIDED
- 6 FRESH WHOLE GARLIC CLOVES PLUS 4 CLOVES, MINCED, DIVIDED
- 4 BAY LEAVES
- 1 QUART BEEF STOCK (SUBSTITUTE 4 TEASPOONS GOOD-QUALITY BEEF BASE PLUS 1 QUART WATER)
- 2-POUND FLANK STEAK OR TRI-TIP, TRIMMED OF FAT
- 4 TABLESPOONS FRESHLY SQUEEZED LIME JUICE
- 1 CUP FROZEN ORANGE JUICE CONCENTRATE, THAWED
- 1 TEASPOON SEA SALT
- 1 TABLESPOON RED PEPPER FLAKES, DIVIDED
- 1/2 CUP OLIVE OIL, DIVIDED

COMBINE THE HALVED WHITE ONION, 6 whole cloves of garlic, the bay leaves, and stock in a large pot over high heat. When it reaches a boil, add the meat, reduce the heat, and simmer for about 90 minutes, testing with a fork to be sure the beef is very tender. Set the meat aside to cool and save the resulting stock for another use.

When the meat has cooled, shred the beef by pulling it apart into small pieces with a fork or your fingers. When the meat has been shredded put it into a large container with the lime juice, orange juice concentrate, 2 cups of water, salt, and 1 teaspoon of red pepper flakes for at least 3 hours or overnight.

Remove the meat from the marinade and press into a colander to release as much of the moisture as you can.

Heat half of the olive oil over high heat in a large sauté pan and carefully add the meat in small batches (the hot oil will splatter). Cook the beef until crisp, about 10 minutes, turning once. When finished, remove the meat to a serving platter and cover with foil to keep warm.

Add the rest of the oil to the pan. When it is hot, add the remaining 2 sliced onions and 4 cloves of minced garlic and fry until slightly caramelized. Top the meat with the sautéed onions and garlic and serve. If you want more spice, add the remaining 2 teaspoons of red pepper flakes.

CAMPFIRE COFFEE CHILI

I CREATED THIS RECIPE FOR MY FRIEND BOB LEE, the founder and former owner of Hunting World Inc., a worldwide retailer of luggage, outdoor clothing, and hunting and fishing accessories. Bob is great sportsman and conservationist, and worked with the Chinese government to preserve and study rare sheep in the remote mountains of northern China.

Bob's ranch, Windy Water, overlooks Ennis Lake and the Bear Trap Wilderness area of the upper Madison River in Southwest Montana. Every year around Thanksgiving, I know where to find him, stalking the backcountry for a late-season big game hunt. I also know that he'll have a big pot of campfire chili simmering on the back of the stove during the length of his stay.

To the typical "bowl of red" Texas chili eater, Bob's ingredients may seem bizarre; actually they remind me of Cincinnati-style chili, which Texans swear isn't chili at all. It is a concoction with a slightly sweet and complex flavor that works well with elk, bison, moose, or deer. If you use beef, very lean cuts—like a top round trimmed of fat—will give you a reasonable facsimile of wild game. The addition of coffee creates a slightly smoky undertone that really makes this an interesting variation. Make a big batch because the chili only gets better with age. If you have the opportunity to cook this recipe in an iron pot over an open fire you will have definitely reached the pinnacle of true comfort food. If no open fire is available, it still tastes great off the top of your kitchen stove. Serve with cornbread or tortillas and a good stout microbrew or a big Zinfandel. Optional toppings include chopped jalapeños, diced chiles, chopped raw onions, grated Monterey Jack cheese, sour cream, and any combinations thereof.

SERVES 8 GENEROUSLY

½ CUP OLIVE OIL, DIVIDED

3 POUNDS WILD GAME MEAT (ELK, MOOSE, OR VENISON, TRIMMED OF ALL FAT, OR VERY LEAN BEEF), CUT INTO ½-INCH CUBES

6 MEDIUM YELLOW ONIONS, COARSELY CHOPPED

2 QUARTS STRONG BREWED COFFEE

2 CUPS MILD NEW MEXICAN CHILI PASTE (SEE NOTE) OR 1 CUP GROUND ANCHO CHILI POWDER

½ CUP GRANULATED GARLIC

¼ CUP DRIED OREGANO

3 TABLESPOONS GROUND CUMIN

1½ CUPS MOLASSES

¼ CUP UNSWEETENED COCOA POWDER

1½ CUPS TOMATO PASTE

5 TABLESPOONS GOOD-QUALITY BEEF BASE

5 (14-OUNCE) CANS BLACK BEANS, DRAINED

3 TABLESPOONS MASA HARINA (CORN TORTILLA FLOUR) (OPTIONAL)

FINE SALT AND CAYENNE PEPPER

HEAT A VERY LARGE STOCKPOT OVER HIGH heat, and add 2 tablespoons of the olive oil. Add the meat in batches, searing it on all sides. Remove the browned meat to a bowl, allow the heat to recover, and add more oil as needed.

When all the meat has been browned and set aside, add the onions and cook for 5 minutes, stirring occasionally, until they become transparent.

Add the coffee and stir well, getting the browned bits of meat off the bottom of the pot. When it begins to boil, add 1 quart of water and the chili paste, garlic, oregano, cumin, molasses, cocoa powder, tomato paste, and beef base. When the liquid begins to boil again, add the reserved meat, bring back to a boil, and then reduce the heat to a simmer.

Cook the chili for about 1½ hours, or until the meat is fork-tender. Add black beans and cook for another 30 minutes. (If you need more liquid, add up to a quart of water as it cooks.) If you like a thicker chili, stir ½ cup of cold water into the masa harina to make a thin paste, then stir it into the chili; cook for another 10 minutes. Adjust the flavor and heat with salt and cayenne pepper.

Serve in warm bowls.

NOTE: You can use regular mild chili powder, but the flavor is much better if you make your own purée out of the dried mild New Mexican chiles commonly found in any large supermarket. I recommend using 10 to 12 large or 18 to 22 medium chiles. Break open the chiles to get rid of the seeds and stems, put the chiles in a saucepan, add enough water to cover, and boil for 20 minutes. Run the whole mixture through a food processor until the chiles are converted to a smooth paste. Commercial chili powder contains additional seasonings, so look at the listed ingredients and modify the recipe accordingly so as not to overdo it. As in all my chilis, I add the salt and cayenne pepper at the end to my taste.

CHUCK-WAGON CHILI

IN PERHAPS AN OBLIQUE REFERENCE TO THEIR own mongrel selves, many trail-drive chuck-wagon cooks would refer to their chili concoctions uniformly as "Son of a Bitch Stew." They threw in whatever they could scrounge—jack rabbits, rattlesnakes, maybe even armadillos. They made it so spicy-hot that nobody knew what they were eating. And it was a "manly" point of honor not to question the cook.

I like to think of myself as a chuck-wagon cook in a past life because I always revert to simple comfort food and one-pot dinners. Unfortunately, this kind of food is not necessarily what the people who eat in my restaurant are looking for, so I inevitably end up cooking it at home. That doesn't bother me because some of the greatest recipes come from home kitchens.

It would be an understatement to say that among chili lovers the subject of what constitutes the classic and true "bowl of red" can create a lot more controversy than politics or religion. My favorite is a simple combination of the best ingredients I can put together: New Mexican chili pods that have been rehydrated and made into a paste, cumin made from toasted and hand-ground seeds, fresh garlic, good Mexican oregano, and the best lean game or beef that I can find. I love all forms of chili, but when I want what I believe to be the best and truest form of chili, the version that one would have experienced in the early days of the West, this is the way I do it. This is as close to the original "Son of a Bitch Stew" as you can get.

If you are a hot freak like me, and you want to add some heat to this dish, you have a couple of options. You can use cayenne pepper, or even better, you can add a tablespoon of chopped chipotle peppers. Chipotles are jalapeños that have been smoked, and they usually come canned in an adobo sauce. I like to serve the chili with various garnishes including, but not limited to, pinto beans, chopped onions, shredded Cheddar or Monterey Jack, chopped jalapeños, and even various shapes of pasta. It freezes well and, like all comfort foods, improves with age.

1 CUP OLIVE OIL, DIVIDED

5 POUNDS LEAN GAME OR BEEF, CUT INTO 1/2-INCH PIECES, OR VERY COARSELY GROUND

3 LARGE YELLOW ONIONS, CHOPPED

10 GARLIC CLOVES, CHOPPED

1 1/2 CUPS RED CHILI PASTE, OR 10 TABLESPOONS ANCHO CHILI POWDER (SEE NOTE, PAGE 106)

1/4 CUP GROUND TOASTED CUMIN (SEE NOTE)

3 TABLESPOONS DRIED OREGANO

5 TABLESPOONS GOOD-QUALITY BEEF BASE

1 TABLESPOON CHOPPED, CANNED CHIPOTLE PEPPERS IN ADOBO SAUCE (OPTIONAL)

3/4 CUP MASA HARINA (CORN TORTILLA FLOUR)

HEAT A VERY LARGE DUTCH OVEN OR STOCK-pot over high heat, and add 2 tablespoons of the olive oil. Add the meat in batches, searing it on all sides. Remove the browned meat to a bowl, allow the heat to recover, and add more oil as needed for each batch.

Add more oil to coat the pan, and cook the onions and garlic until transparent, about 3 minutes. Return the meat to the pot and add 1 quart of water along with the chili paste, cumin, oregano, beef base, and chipotle peppers. Mix well, bring to a boil, then reduce the heat and simmer for 1 to 1 1/2 hours, or until the meat is fork-tender.

Stir the masa into 1 cup of cold water to make a paste. Gradually add the paste to the chili, allowing time for it to cook and thicken. If you want the chili thicker, add more of the masa paste.

NOTE: To toast the cumin, put 1/2 cup of seeds in a hot, dry sauté pan and cook, constantly tossing until they have been toasted and browned, 1 to 3 minutes. Immediately remove them from the hot pan. Use a mortar and pestle to grind the seeds.

MINT-STYLE PRIME RIB

British upper classes became involved in Montana cattle ranches. It didn't matter if they were owners, investors, or actual ranchers; there was a constant stream of Brits who boarded trains and came to Big Sky Country. As a result, at any given time there was always enough of them around to put together two sides of a gentlemen's cricket match.

I can also picture that after a match, some wayward Englishman, starving for a taste of home, obtained a slab of beef rib, rubbed it with salt and pepper, threw it in the oven until it was "properly" done, and served it to his stoic countrymen. Whatever their legacy, the Brits inspired Montanans to develop their own devotion to prime rib, often doffing their ranch work clothes for fine white shirts or blouses and shiny boots, heading for their local supper clubs to enjoy their favorite dining-out dish.

At The Mint we try to keep it simple (we use boneless at the restaurant, but at home I favor the bone-in). Take the roast, rub it with a mix of kosher salt and very coarsely ground pepper, and allow the roast to reach room temperature (out of reach of the dogs).

When you're estimating quantities, a good rule of thumb is to figure 1 pound per person if the roast is bone-in, and about a 1$\frac{1}{2}$-inch to 2-inch slice per person if boneless. Like a lot of dishes, I usually cook more than I need because the leftovers are always great. We like to have people over for New Year's Eve for Prime rib. Some of them inevitably spend the night because of too much wine, too much bad weather, or a combination of both. Then it became a ritual to do Leftover Roast Beef Hash and eggs on New Year's Day from the leftovers (see page 110).

SERVES 6 TO 8

$\frac{1}{2}$ CUP KOSHER SALT

$\frac{1}{2}$ CUP FRESHLY CRACKED BLACK PEPPER

$\frac{1}{2}$ CUP GRANULATED GARLIC

1 (5- TO 6-POUND) FOUR-BONED RIB ROAST

HORSERADISH SAUCE

1 CUP SOUR CREAM

1 CUP MAYONNAISE

$\frac{1}{2}$ CUP GOOD-QUALITY HORSERADISH

COMBINE THE SALT, PEPPER, AND GARLIC IN a small bowl. Rub the seasoning mix on the outside of the roast. Allow it to come to room temperature, usually a couple of hours.

Preheat the oven to 225°F.

Set the prime rib in a large roasting pan. Cook the prime rib for about 2 hours, then begin monitoring the internal temperature with a meat thermometer. (I don't set a time because each roast is different; not only the weight, but also the altitude can be a factor.) After 2 hours, insert a meat thermometer. Be certain you're reading from the center of the roast, not touching the bone. When the internal temperature reaches 110°F, turn the heat to 475°F for 30 minutes or so to brown the outside. For a medium-rare prime rib, check the meat again, looking for an internal temp of 120°F. (For a rare doneness, 115°F; for medium doneness, 130°F.) Remove the meat from the oven and cover it loosely in foil—or, as my father-in-law does, wrap in newspaper—to allow the meat to "rest" for about 30 minutes. This allows the internal temperature to rise by about 10 degrees and the juices to flow evenly within the meat, just enough time to do a Yorkshire Pudding (see below).

Stir together the sour cream, mayonnaise, and horseradish and serve alongside the prime rib.

YORKSHIRE PUDDING

LET'S FACE IT: IF YOU'RE GOING TO EAT A prime rib dripping with fat and flavor, what's another 10,000 calories? This savory pudding makes use of all the delicious pan drippings from the prime rib (see previous page).

SERVES 4

1 CUP BLEACHED ALL-PURPOSE FLOUR
1 TEASPOON FINE SALT
3 EGGS
1¼ CUPS WHOLE MILK
1 (14-OUNCE) CAN GOOD-QUALITY BEEF BROTH

IN A MIXING BOWL, COMBINE THE FLOUR, salt, eggs, milk, beef broth, and a tablespoon of water and set aside.

Pour off all but 1 to 1½ cups of the fat from the hot roasting pan; reserve the excess fat for cooking Leftover Roast Beef Hash (see opposite)! Be careful to leave the browned residue from the cooking undisturbed in the pan to flavor the pudding. With a flat spoon or whisk, scrape up the browned bits on the bottom of the roasting pan and stir them around in the pan juices. Put the roasting pan back in the oven and turn it to 450°F. When the oven reaches 450°F, remove the pan from the oven and pour the batter evenly into the hot pan. Bake the pudding for around 30 minutes or until the mixture puffs up and is dark golden. Remove from the oven and serve directly from the pan.

LEFTOVER ROAST BEEF HASH

IT NEVER FAILS, AT THE RESTAURANT, WHEN we've prepped a large amount of what we think that night's customers will order, they will inevitably order whatever it is we are low on. Do a lot of roast chicken and they will order beef. Do a lot of beef, and everyone orders the seared tuna. On the other hand, leftover prime rib can be a good thing because I can use it to make one of my favorite dishes: Roast Beef Hash.

Be sure and save some of the beef fat from the prime rib, as it is the most flavorful (though not the healthiest) way to cook a great batch of hash. Serve it hot with a couple of fried eggs over the top. If you really want to go all-out, do some homemade biscuits with lots of Steen's Pure Cane Syrup or, another option, serve them with a paste made by blending equal parts butter and honey. A cold, spicy, Bloody Mary on the side isn't the worst of ideas but of course the booze is optional.

SERVES 6 TO 8

3 LARGE RUSSET POTATOES, DICED INTO 1/2-INCH PIECES

1/2 CUP (1 STICK) UNSALTED BUTTER, OLIVE OIL, OR BEEF FAT

1 LARGE YELLOW ONION, FINELY DICED

1 TABLESPOON DRIED THYME

1/2 TEASPOON MUSTARD POWDER (OPTIONAL)

1 TEASPOON GRANULATED GARLIC

4 CUPS COLD ROAST BEEF LEFTOVERS DICED INTO 1/2-INCH PIECES

1/2 CUP HEAVY CREAM (OPTIONAL)

FINE SALT AND FRESHLY GROUND BLACK PEPPER

12 TO 16 EGGS, COOKED TO YOUR LIKING

1 CUP CHOPPED FRESH FLAT-LEAF PARSLEY

PLACE THE POTATOES IN A SAUCEPAN AND cover with cold water. Bring to a boil and cook the potatoes until slightly fork-tender, about 10 minutes, then drain well and set aside in the hot pan (the drier the potatoes the better, so toss them occasionally while they're still hot to help the water evaporate).

In a very large pan or skillet, preheat the oil on medium-high heat. When the oil is hot, add the onions and cook until translucent, about 5 minutes. Then add the potatoes, thyme, mustard powder, and garlic. Allow the bottom to brown and develop a good crust before turning with a spatula.

Mix in the beef and continue to cook until the mixture is crisp. When the hash just begins to crisp up, add a little of the cream (if using) to bind and moisten the mix. The addition of cream can result in a crispier texture as it cooks away. Press the mixture into the bottom of the pan. When the hash is sufficiently browned, remove with a spatula to hot plates and serve with poached or fried eggs on top. Sprinkle with parsley.

LAMB AND PORK

ALTHOUGH THEY ARE NOT CONSIDERED AS IMPORTANT TO MONTANA'S HISTORY AND today's economy as beef is, lamb, and to a lesser degree, pork, have been and continue to be important to our diets. Prior to the 1950s, lamb was a large enough part of Montana's economy that our growers supplied Americans with a large percentage of the lamb that was consumed domestically.

Throughout the Mountain West, Basque herders—refugees from oppression, discrimination, and civil wars in Spain—tended huge flocks, numbering as many as 2,000 heads, protecting them from coyotes, wolves, and grizzlies, moving them across the sweeping grasslands and into valleys for protection from winter winds. Accompanied only by their inestimable shepherd dogs, their wagons, and cast-iron stoves, they posted themselves for months on end, watching over their woolly wards and moving them to new pastures when the grass got eaten low. You could see them occasionally, on the streets of Butte or Miles City or other towns and hamlets that dotted the grazing grasslands. You knew they had delivered their flocks and come to collect their pay. Many run ranches themselves now. Some continue to work as they have for generations, solitary and out of sight for most of the year. But when they deliver the goods, well, there's nothing that compares to grass-fed local lamb. We get ours from Sweet Grass Natural Lamb down in Big Timber and I know Patrick, my friend and fellow author, gets his from farmers in Sonoma County, where he hangs out on his own farm. Not long ago he called to report that he walked into his local butcher shop, ordered small lamb loins and was told by the proud purveyor: "Congratulations, you've just bought what's left of the grand prize winner at the Sonoma County Fair!"

I know that most of the country has had little choice but to buy lamb imported from New Zealand, but more and more local lamb is appearing in markets across the country. So, as in all things, we advocate asking for "local first." Once you try it, you'll realize, with the first bite, what've you've been missing. At The Mint, we're only half exaggerating when we say we like our lamb to be raised within bleating earshot.

Carl Jarrett watching the flock, Harvat Ranch, Livingston, Montana, June 1940

Edwin Harvat in corral, Harvat Ranch, Livingston, Montana, January 1937

CUBAN-STYLE BRAISED LAMB

LIKE MOST CHEFS I OFTEN SEEM TO BE GOING off on ethnic tangents. Normally the Cuban thing hits me sometime in the month of February when Montana is under an Arctic chill and spring seems eons away. One of my favorite Cuban recipes is called Fricassee de Pollo, a sour orange-flavored chicken dish. When I substituted the lamb for chicken, the results were great; so give it a try. Have some friends over, put on some salsa, and crank up the volume; it will make you think of warm sunny places and drinks with lots of rum and fruit in them! Con mucho gusto! Even my wife Mary, who eats like a bird, asked for seconds. Black beans and rice (see page 188) make mighty nice compadres.

SERVES 6 TO 8

1 (12-OUNCE) CAN FROZEN ORANGE JUICE CONCENTRATE, THAWED

1/2 CUP LIME JUICE

1 TABLESPOON FINE SALT

1 TABLESPOON FRESHLY GROUND BLACK PEPPER

5 GARLIC CLOVES, MINCED

1 (3- TO 4-POUND) BONELESS LAMB SHOULDER OR LEG, CUT INTO 2-INCH CUBES (SUBSTITUTE CHICKEN OR PORK)

3/4 CUP OLIVE OIL, DIVIDED

3 MEDIUM YELLOW ONIONS, DICED

2 GREEN BELL PEPPERS, DICED

1 (6-OUNCE) CAN TOMATO PASTE

1 CUP PITTED GREEN OLIVES

1 CUP RAISINS

1/2 CUP CAPERS IN BRINE, DRAINED

1 POUND RUSSET POTATOES (I PREFER UNPEELED), CUT INTO 1-INCH CUBES

COMBINE THE ORANGE JUICE CONCENTRATE, an equal amount of water, the lime juice, salt, pepper, and garlic to make a marinade. Place the marinade in a large lidded container (or in a resealable plastic bag), add the lamb, and marinate in the refrigerator for at least 4 hours, but preferably overnight.

Remove the lamb from the marinade and drain, reserving the meat and marinade separately. Preheat half the olive oil over medium-high heat in a large, nonstick sauté pan and carefully add the lamb one piece at a time. Don't crowd the pan; you want to sear the meat to a nice brown color. Be careful as the sugar in the orange juice can burn and the result would be bitter. Add more oil if necessary and continue cooking in batches until all of the lamb has been browned. Set the lamb aside and add the onions and green peppers to the pan. Sauté until soft, about 5 to 8 minutes. Remove the onions and peppers from the pan and set aside.

Preheat the oven to 325°F.

Add the reserved marinade to the sauté pan and bring to a boil, scraping up any brown bits. Then transfer the liquid to a large roasting pan and set it over two burners on the stove top over medium-high heat. Stir in the sautéed vegetables, lamb, tomato paste, olives, raisins, capers, and potatoes and bring to a boil. Be sure there is enough of liquid to just cover the meat, adding water as needed.

Place in the oven and cook, uncovered, for about an hour, testing the meat and potatoes for tenderness. Cook until you are satisfied with the texture, adding a splash of water as needed to thin out the sauce. Be sure to dish up plenty of the sauce with each serving. This dish can be done a day or two ahead of time, as it only gets better with age.

BRAISED LAMB SHANKS WITH WHITE BEANS

LAMB AND WHITE BEANS OFFER A PLEASANT marriage of rustic flavors and textures that is perfect for cold weather fare, meaning we serve it regularly for about six months at our restaurant in Montana. We happily oblige our customers who've spent a day skiing at nearby Big Sky with lamb shanks, crusty sourdough bread, and a hearty Zinfandel. A good rule of thumb is one shank per person, although two is not out of the question if you are really hungry, as most of our customers always seem to be.

Whether I do lamb or veal shanks, I always use a roasting pan from beginning to end. Cooking everything in one pan seems to produce flavors that are more pronounced and intense. Serve with great bread; try my Toasted Garlic Bread with Parmesan-Cheese Crust (see page 186).

SERVES 4

- 1 POUND DRIED WHITE BEANS (NAVY OR GREAT NORTHERN)
- 1 CUP OLIVE OIL, DIVIDED
- 4 TO 6 LAMB SHANKS (ABOUT 3 POUNDS TOTAL)
- 3 MEDIUM YELLOW ONIONS, SLICED
- 15 GARLIC CLOVES, PEELED
- 2 TABLESPOONS LEMON ZEST
- 1 CUP ALL-PURPOSE FLOUR
- 3 TABLESPOONS DRIED ROSEMARY
- 3 BAY LEAVES
- 2 CUPS WHITE WINE
- 2 CUPS CHOPPED FRESH FLAT-LEAF PARSLEY, DIVIDED
- 2 (24-OUNCE) CANS GOOD-QUALITY WHOLE TOMATOES, DRAINED, WITH JUICES RESERVED
- 4 LEMON WEDGES, FOR GARNISH

SOAK THE WHITE BEANS OVERNIGHT IN water, covering by a few inches.

Drain the beans and add fresh water, covering by a few inches. Bring the beans to a boil, then reduce to a simmer for about 1 to 1½ hours, or until the beans are tender but still slightly chewy. Drain and set aside.

Preheat the oven to 350°F.

Set a roasting pan over two burners, both turned to medium-high heat. Add half the olive oil to the pan and heat until almost smoking. Add the lamb shanks (carefully to avoid splattering) and brown thoroughly. Remove and set aside. Add the rest of the oil, onions, garlic cloves, and lemon zest, and sauté until golden, about 6 minutes. Gradually sprinkle in the flour, allowing it to form a roux-like consistency and stir until it turns light brown, about 3 minutes. Add the rosemary, bay leaves, wine, 2 cups of water, 1 cup of the fresh parsley, and the juice from the tomatoes. (Reserve the tomatoes.) Put the shanks back in the pan. They should be more or less submerged.

Cook uncovered in the oven for 1 hour or until the lamb is beginning to get tender. Take out the shanks, stir in the beans and reserved tomatoes, and put the shanks back in; cook for another 30 minutes. When the beans and lamb are very tender, dish into warm bowls, garnish with the remaining fresh parsley and a lemon wedge, and serve. Don't forget some great bread.

GRILLED FRENCH COUNTRY-STYLE MARINATED LEG OF LAMB

THE FRENCH STYLE OF COOKING SOMETIMES has a reputation for lots of elaborate preparations, including complex sauces and reductions. This recipe is exactly the opposite. It is the essence of simplicity and really captures French country cooking at its best. Sometimes I think grilling is the best method, because the essence of smoke adds a little more depth to the flavor, but the leg of lamb can also be roasted, and it is magnificent.

Don't forget to use your meat thermometer to cook it just the way you like it.

SERVES 6

- 3 TABLESPOONS FRESH ROSEMARY
- 3 TABLESPOONS FRESH THYME
- 3 TABLESPOONS FRESH OREGANO
- 1/2 CUP OLIVE OIL
- 2 TABLESPOONS SEA SALT
- 1 LARGE SHALLOT, DICED
- 1 (4- TO 6-POUND) BONELESS LEG OF LAMB
- 2 CUPS DRY WHITE WINE (IF COOKING IN THE OVEN)

IN A FOOD PROCESSOR, COMBINE THE rosemary, thyme, oregano, olive oil, salt, and shallot and process to make a paste.

Trim off any excess fat from the lamb and score all over with a sharp knife, making cuts half an inch deep. Rub the leg with the paste and place in a large lidded container or resealable plastic bag. Pour the wine over the lamb and marinate it for a day, refrigerated, turning occasionally.

To grill the lamb on a gas grill, turn one burner to a medium to low setting and put a small foil packet of pre-soaked wood chips directly over the flames underneath the grate. (Poke holes in the packet to allow smoke to escape.) You want the fire hot enough to make the wood smoke but not so hot as to burn the meat. Set the lamb directly over the fire to brown it on all sides, turning occasionally. When there's a crust all around, move it away from the heat to finish cooking indirectly, at least another 45 minutes. The meat is done when the internal temperature reaches 120°F for rare, 130°F for medium-rare, and 140°F for medium. The leg of lamb should rest at least 10 minutes before carving; that said, it will continue to cook slightly during the resting period so don't let it rest too long.

Alternatively, you can cook the lamb in the oven. Preheat the oven to 375°F. Cook the lamb in a roasting pan for approximately 10 minutes per pound, using a meat thermometer to monitor the temperature. Allow the meat to rest for 10 minutes before serving. One advantage to roasting is the availability of pan drippings for a sauce. While the lamb rests, deglaze the pan with the wine, bring to a boil, and reduce by half. Add a little water if it reduces too much. Serve this resulting sauce with the lamb after carving.

GRILLED HERB-MARINATED LAMB CHOPS

VERY OFTEN THE SIMPLEST WAY CAN BE THE best when it comes to cooking. Of course it doesn't hurt to have access to great Montana-grown lamb from the people at Sweet Grass Natural Lamb just down the road from us at Big Timber, or from the folks at Willow Springs Ranch, whose operation is literally in our backyard in Belgrade. Charcoal-grilled is my first choice, but you can also sear these chops on the skillet like we do at The Mint. Either way, if you keep it simple you can't go wrong: cooked slightly charred, with a good bottle of Pinot Noir. Serve hot, with our Rosemary Shallot Sauce for Lamb (see page 247). Two other favorite choices are the Béarnaise (see page 227), or Choron (see page 227), a béarnaise with tomato flavor.

SERVES 4

- 1 CUP OLIVE OIL
- 5 CLOVES FRESH GARLIC, MINCED
- 1 TABLESPOON FRESHLY CRACKED BLACK PEPPER
- 2 TABLESPOONS CHOPPED FRESH ROSEMARY
- 1 TEASPOON SEA SALT
- 6 TO 8 SMALL LOIN CHOPS

STIR TOGETHER THE OIL, GARLIC, PEPPER, rosemary, and salt to form a marinade. Combine the chops and the marinade in a resealable plastic bag. Marinate the chops for 24 to 48 hours in the refrigerator.

Build a very hot fire in a charcoal grill, or preheat a gas grill on high heat. Alternatively, preheat a cast-iron skillet over high heat until it is smoking. Place the chops directly over the heat and allow the flames to come into contact with the meat to deeply brown and sear, but not burn, the meat. If cooking indoors, place the chops on the hot skillet and sear without moving. Cook for approximately 3 to 4 minutes per side to achieve a medium-rare interior.

ICELANDIC SHEEP AT WILLOW SPRING RANCH MONTANA, LLC IN BELGRADE, MONTANA.

Katy and Richard Harjes left a big-city life to establish an organic sheep ranch in the foothills of the Bridger Mountains. They taught themselves—and relied on the kindness of neighbors—as they worked through their early years of ranching: feeding and care of their new flock, lambing, and incorporating the use of livestock guardian dogs to protect against predators. They now ship their certified organic, grass-fed lamb to customers and restaurants across the country. Their lamb is served with pride at The Mint, and in other fine establishments.

JERKED LEG OF LAMB

Every once in a while, particularly in winter, I've got to get away. I usually go where it's warm and, if I'm lucky, my brother Nick leaves his Kentucky horse farm to join me. We share a passion for fishing and food and discovering new dishes.

This is a great recipe that I picked up a few years back on a Caribbean bonefish fishing trip. It comes from a funky little restaurant called the Harbor Rest located near Deadman's Cay on the windward side of Long Island, one of the outer islands in the Bahamian chain. After a long day of casting into the wind on bonefish flats, we ordered a couple of cold Kaliks (the national beer of the Bahamas) and proceeded to dive into this wonderful mutton dish, plucked hot and juicy right off the coals.

I suggest a boneless leg of lamb, butterflied open, flattened and marinated. If you can find coconut rum, by all means use it in the marinade, and drink it at your own peril, or you can use Mount Gay or any other dark heavy rum. Red or black beans and rice (see page 188) is the perfect accompaniment.

SERVES 6

- ½ CUP COCONUT OR DARK RUM
- ¼ CUP OLIVE OIL
- 3 BAY LEAVES
- ¼ CUP FRESHLY SQUEEZED LIME JUICE
- 1 LARGE YELLOW ONION, FINELY CHOPPED
- 6 GARLIC CLOVES, MINCED
- 3 SHALLOTS, FINELY DICED
- 1 JALAPEÑO, FINELY DICED
- 1 TABLESPOON THYME
- 1 TEASPOON ALLSPICE
- ½ TEASPOON GROUND CLOVES
- 1 TABLESPOON SEA SALT
- 1 (4- TO 6-POUND) BONELESS LEG OF LAMB

COMBINE THE RUM, OLIVE OIL, BAY LEAVES, lime juice, onion, garlic, shallots, jalapeno, thyme, allspice, cloves, and salt in a saucepan and set over medium-high heat. Cook, stirring frequently, until the mixture comes to a boil. Remove from the heat and allow it to cool to room temperature.

Cut small slits all over the fat side of the lamb. Place it in a resealable plastic bag with the cooled marinade. Marinate in the refrigerator for at least 24 hours.

Preheat your gas or charcoal grill at a high heat. Cook the lamb fat-side down for 5 minutes. Turn and cook the other side, browning the outside, for another 5 minutes. Move the lamb off the direct heat to another part of the grill and finish cooking until the internal temperature at the thickest part reads 130°F on a meat thermometer; check after 45 minutes. Remove from the grill, cover, and allow it to rest for 10 to 15 minutes. Slice across the grain and serve.

KENTUCKY BARBECUE LEG OF LAMB

When I visit my brother Nick in Kentucky bluegrass country, I always try to first stop in Owensboro, Kentucky, just over the Indiana state line. In an opinion I share with others, Owensboro is the national capital of barbecue lamb, or mutton, as the locals refer to it. Mutton is generally defined as the meat from an adult sheep and, although widely consumed around the world, in this country we prefer lamb because it's milder. Still, a number of legendary mutton barbecue places with fitting names such as The Moonlight, Shady Rest, The Old Hickory Pit, and George's give Owensboro its chops, so to speak. Each has its own style of sauce, and the recipes vary slightly. But with help from smokers, the strong mutton flavor can be easily offset. The secret to getting a good smoky flavor is to soak some wood chips in water for a couple of hours before you use them.

SERVES 6 TO 10

- 1 (4- TO 6-POUND) BONELESS LEG OF LAMB
- 2 CUPS CHICKEN STOCK (SUBSTITUTE 2 TABLESPOONS GOOD-QUALITY CHICKEN BASE PLUS 2 CUPS WATER)
- 1/4 CUP MOLASSES
- 2 TABLESPOONS PACKED DARK BROWN SUGAR
- 1/2 CUP CIDER VINEGAR
- 1/2 CUP STRONG BREWED COFFEE
- 1/2 CUP KETCHUP
- 2 TABLESPOONS WORCESTER-SHIRE SAUCE
- 1 TABLESPOON CHILI POWDER
- 1 TABLESPOON GRANULATED GARLIC
- 1 TABLESPOON ONION POWDER
- 1 TEASPOON CUMIN
- 1 TEASPOON RED PEPPER FLAKES

PLACE THE LAMB IN A 2-GALLON PLASTIC resealable plastic bag (consider double bagging). Stir together the stock, molasses, sugar, vinegar, coffee, ketchup, Worcestershire, chili powder, garlic, onion powder, cumin, and red pepper flakes. Pour about two-thirds of it over the lamb in the plastic bag and marinate in the refrigerator for 2 days. Reserve the rest of the marinade, tightly covered.

Soak about 1 cup of wood chips in water for an hour. Preheat a gas grill with all of the burners on a high setting.

Place the wet wood chips in a foil packet with holes punched in it directly over one of your gas burners. Place the lamb at the opposite end of the grill from the chips and cook on high for 5 minutes on each side. Turn off all of the burners except the one under the chips, and reduce it to low heat. Continue to cook the lamb on the indirect heat for approximately 4 hours.

During the last hour baste the lamb frequently with some but not all of the reserved marinade. If it looks like the meat is cooking too fast and burning, move it up to the warming rack in the lid of your grill. If you don't have a rack put a couple of pieces of foil under the lamb and let it continue to cook from the top. The finished lamb should have an internal temperature of around 160°F.

Cook the remaining marinade in a saucepan over low heat, reducing to about half of its volume. Slice and serve using the reduced marinade as a sauce.

MILANESE-STYLE LAMB CHOPS

THERE IS A GREAT ALTERNATIVE TO THE traditional way of grilling or broiling lamb chops. In Milan, I discovered this dish that involves sautéing lamb rib chops with breadcrumbs and Parmesan cheese and finishing the dish with brown butter and capers. Every time we did this as a special at the Continental Divide it sold out. We've enjoyed the same success at The Mint. Once you try it you'll know why. Remember to cook the chops quickly because they have been pounded and are thin, and also to turn the chops very carefully to preserve the wonderful crust. This recipe also works very well with venison or veal chops. Serve with a simple lemon butter pasta or risotto.

BREADED CHOPS

12 BONE-IN LAMB CHOPS (FROM THE LOIN OR RIB)

2 CUPS PLAIN BREADCRUMBS

2 CUPS PARMESAN CHEESE

2 TABLESPOONS WHITE PEPPER

2 EGGS, LIGHTLY BEATEN

2 CUPS MILK

OLIVE OIL, AS NEEDED FOR COOKING

2 TABLESPOONS UNSALTED BUTTER

CAPER BUTTER SAUCE

1/4 CUP CAPERS

1 CUP (2 STICKS) UNSALTED BUTTER

3 TABLESPOONS FRESHLY SQUEEZED LEMON JUICE

1/2 CUP CHOPPED FRESH FLAT-LEAF PARSLEY

FINE SALT AND FRESHLY GROUND BLACK PEPPER

1 LEMON CUT IN WEDGES, FOR SERVING

COVER EACH RIB CHOP WITH PLASTIC WRAP or waxed paper and, with a meat hammer or bottom of a small frying pan, very carefully pound them down to about 1/2 inch in thickness, taking care not to splinter the bone.

Mix the breadcrumbs, Parmesan, and pepper and set aside in a shallow dish for dredging. In a mixing bowl combine the eggs and milk. Dip the chop in the egg wash and dredge it in the breadcrumb mix, then dip it back into the wash and dredge it in the breadcrumb mix a second time. Carefully set the chop aside for a few minutes to allow the coating to set up.

In a sauté pan, pour olive oil to a depth of 1/2 inch, add the butter, and heat over medium-high. When the mixture is hot and melted but not burning, carefully lay the chops in the hot oil and cook until the crust until golden brown, about 3 minutes, being careful not to dislodge the delicate crust that has formed. Turn and cook briefly on the other side, no more than 2 minutes but long enough to form a crust. Do not overcook or burn the breading mixture. Place the cooked chops on a warm platter while you make the sauce.

To make the sauce, turn the heat under the pan to high and add the capers, butter, and lemon juice. Cook over high heat, and, with a steel whisk or spatula, scrape up the pan residue that has accumulated to help season the sauce. When the butter has begun to foam and turn brown, add the chopped parsley, adjusting the salt and pepper to taste. Spoon it over the chops, garnish with lemon wedges, and serve.

PLANCHA-GRILLED LAMB CHOPS WITH APPLE JELLY REDUCTION SAUCE

THIS SIMPLE WAY OF DOING LAMB CHOPS is my favorite. They're cooked on a gas grill with a plancha, (cast-iron or stainless steel plate), and excellent served with a full-bodied Pinot Noir.

SERVES 4

GRILLED CHOPS

¾ CUP OLIVE OIL

5 GARLIC CLOVES, CHOPPED

2 TABLESPOONS CHOPPED FRESH ROSEMARY

1 TABLESPOON FRESHLY CRACKED BLACK PEPPER

1 TEASPOON SEA SALT

8 LAMB CHOPS

APPLE JELLY SAUCE

1 CUP CHICKEN OR LAMB DEMI-GLACE

2 TABLESPOONS CHOPPED FRESH ROSEMARY

½ CUP APPLE JELLY

1 TEASPOON FRESHLY CRACKED BLACK PEPPER

1 TEASPOON BALSAMIC VINEGAR

STIR TOGETHER THE OLIVE OIL, GARLIC, rosemary, pepper, and salt in a crude paste and spread on top of each chop. Allow the chops to sit herb-side up in the refrigerator, covered, for 2 to 12 hours.

If you are using a gas grill, place a cast-iron skillet directly on top of the burners and preheat for at least 15 minutes on the highest setting. Gently place the chops, herb-side down, so that the garlic and rosemary coating come into contact with the hot surface. The mixture should char but not burn, as that would make the garlic bitter. After 4 to 5 minutes, gently turn the chops and cook for another 4 or 5 minutes until medium-rare. Set on a warm platter to rest and make the sauce.

Mix together the demi-glace, rosemary, apple jelly, pepper, and vinegar in a small pan and cook over medium heat, reducing the mixture by half, about 6 minutes. Spoon about a tablespoon of sauce directly over each plate, and serve one chop per plate.

RACK OF LAMB WITH DIJON HERB CRUST

ONE OF THE FIRST THINGS I LEARNED UNDER Chef Daniel Bonnot at the Louis XVI restaurant in New Orleans was how to do his classic rendition of Rack of Lamb en Croute. In this case the crust wasn't the usual puff pastry but a savory blend of breadcrumbs, herbs, and Dijon mustard. That was a long time ago, but this dish has an ageless quality that few dishes can boast.

Some chefs like to "French" the lamb racks prior to cooking, which involves trimming all of the fat around the loin and cutting the fat and connective tissue off the rib bones themselves all the way to the eye. I'm lazy and I like to cook the racks the way they come, with the fat and meat that cling naturally to the bones. It gives me something to gnaw on. Trimming may improve the appearance but I'll take the fat.

SERVES 2

ROASTED LAMB

1 WHOLE RACK OF LAMB (7 TO 8 BONES)

3 TABLESPOONS OLIVE OIL

2 TABLESPOONS CRUMBLED DRIED ROSEMARY

1 TABLESPOON SEA SALT

BREADCRUMB TOPPING

1/4 CUP OLIVE OIL

1/2 CUP DIJON MUSTARD

2 CUPS PLAIN BREADCRUMBS

2 TABLESPOONS CRUMBLED ROSEMARY

1 TABLESPOON THYME

1 TABLESPOON SEA SALT

1 TABLESPOON FRESHLY GROUND BLACK PEPPER

PREHEAT THE OVEN TO 500°F.

Rub the rack with the olive oil, rosemary, and salt and bring to room temperature before cooking. Roast the lamb in a roasting pan for 10 minutes, turning frequently to just sear the top and bottom. Remove from the heat and allow the meat to cool. This can be done a day ahead; wrap the rack of lamb well and refrigerate until ready to proceed.

For the breadcrumb topping, stir the olive oil and mustard together. In a shallow dish, stir together the breadcrumbs, rosemary, thyme, salt, and pepper. Brush the mustard mixture onto the lamb, then roll the rack in the breadcrumb mixture, patting all over to ensure a complete coating on all sides.

Preheat the oven to 400°F.

Place the lamb, bone-side down, in a roasting pan and cook in the oven for approximately 15 minutes, until the crust has browned and the internal temperature has reached 125°F. Be sure to place the thermometer in the thickest part of the lamb, away from the bones. Allow the lamb to rest, covered, for 5 to 10 minutes before cutting into individual chops and serving.

SOUTHWESTERN-STYLE ROAST LEG OF LAMB

I PREFER A BONELESS LEG HERE BECAUSE the marinade has a better chance of penetrating the meat. Either way, marinate it, throw it in the oven, and carve it. The marinade is then reduced and used for a great sauce. Incidentally this recipe works very well for a pork roast of the same size; just remember to cook it longer, until a thermometer shows 140°F in the thickest part of the roast. The only question here is what to serve with it. A couple of great sides would be Chili and Garlic Mashed Potatoes (see page 208) or Corn Macque Choux (see page 199.)

SERVES 6

4 GARLIC CLOVES, COARSELY CHOPPED

2 TABLESPOONS DRIED OREGANO

3 TABLESPOONS CHILI POWDER

2 TABLESPOONS GROUND CUMIN

1/2 CUP CIDER VINEGAR

1/2 CUP ORANGE JUICE

1/2 CUP OLIVE OIL

1/4 CUP PACKED DARK BROWN SUGAR

1 TABLESPOON FRESHLY CRACKED BLACK PEPPER

1 TEASPOON FINE SALT

1 BONELESS LEG OF LAMB (ABOUT 5 POUNDS), TRIMMED OF FAT

COMBINE THE GARLIC, OREGANO, CHILI powder, cumin, vinegar, orange juice, oil, sugar, pepper, and salt and whisk together until the sugar and salt dissolve. Put the leg of lamb in a large, heavy-duty plastic resealable bag, pour the marinade over it, and marinate in the refrigerator for at least 24 hours or for as long as 3 days. Remove the roast from the fridge 2 hours before cooking to bring to room temperature.

Preheat the oven to 450°F.

Remove the roast from the bag, reserving the marinade, and set it in a roasting pan fitted with a large rack. Cook the first 10 minutes at 450°F to sear the meat then turn the oven down to 350° to finish. Roast the lamb for another 1 hour and 15 minutes, or until the internal temperature reads 130°F to 140°F for medium-rare to medium doneness. For medium to medium-well the internal temperature should be around 155°F, but in Montana, well-cooked lamb is a sacrilege.

Remove the roast from the oven and place it on a cutting board, preferably with recessed edges to catch the drippings and cover loosely with aluminum foil. This will allow the juices, which flowed to the center during cooking, to redistribute to all portions of the roast. Allow it to rest for 15 minutes before carving.

If you like, put heatproof dinner plates and a platter in the still-warm oven to warm while the meat rests and you prepare the sauce.

Drain off all but about 2 tablespoons of fat from the roasting pan. Pour in the reserved marinade and set the roasting pan over two burners over medium-high heat. Bring to a boil, stirring the sauce constantly to keep it from burning, and scrape the toasty bits of meat from the bottom of the pan. Allow the sauce to reduce and thicken to barely coat the back of a spoon. If you need more liquid, thin with a small amount of water.

Place the leg of lamb on a cutting board. Cut 1/4-inch angled slices. Transfer the slices to a platter and serve with the pan sauce.

IRISH STEW

BACK IN THE DAY, BUTTE WAS THE RICHEST CITY PER capita in the United States, and the overriding reason was mining. People from all over the world came to work in the mines, and although most ethnic groups frequented their own saloons, Irishmen, on the other hand, patronized them all. Friends of mine, whose families passed along stories of the early days, swear that in nearly every tavern, regardless of ethnic ownership, Irish stew was offered for free, in hopes that the customers would drink as heartily as they ate.

I'm dedicating my spicy Irish stew to my great-aunt Margaret Mullen, a fiery woman whose lasting legacy was not her cooking—I have no memory of her cooking anything except boiling water for tea—but her love of eating. For some reason known only to her, she really had a thing for Irish stew. It never ceased to amaze me how she could sit all 90 pounds of herself at the table and devour what seemed to be half her weight in stew.

I have added a few more herbs, and certainly a lot more pepper than Aunt Margaret would have liked, to put a little more zing in this old dish, which reflects her personality more than her palate. Serve it with crusty bread and a slightly chilled Beaujolais or maybe a Guinness.

SERVES 6 TO 8

- 1/2 CUP OLIVE OIL, DIVIDED
- 3 POUNDS BONED LEG OF LAMB, OR SHOULDER, CUT INTO 1-INCH CUBES
- 2 TABLESPOONS ALL-PURPOSE FLOUR
- 1 CUP DRY WHITE WINE
- 2 GARLIC CLOVES, CHOPPED
- 3 CUPS CHICKEN STOCK (SUBSTITUTE 3 TEASPOONS GOOD-QUALITY CHICKEN BASE PLUS 3 CUPS WATER)
- 2 BAY LEAVES
- 1 TABLESPOON DRIED ROSEMARY
- 1 TABLESPOON DRIED THYME
- 1 TEASPOON DRIED MARJORAM

- 2 LARGE CARROTS, SLICED INTO THIN DISCS
- 2 MEDIUM YELLOW ONIONS, FINELY DICED
- 3 POUNDS RUSSET POTATOES, PEELED AND CUT INTO 1-INCH CUBES
- 1/2 HEAD GREEN CABBAGE, COARSELY SHREDDED (OPTIONAL)
- 2 TABLESPOONS SEA SALT
- 2 TABLESPOONS FRESHLY GROUND BLACK PEPPER
- 1 POUND GREEN PEAS (FROZEN WORKS FINE)

PUT HALF THE OLIVE OIL IN A SAUTÉ PAN AND lightly cook the lamb to a delicate shade of light brown, in batches if necessary, adding oil as needed. Return all the meat to the pan, sprinkle the flour over the meat, and stir it in to form a light roux. Pour in the white wine, deglazing the pan and scraping all of the bits and pieces that have accumulated off the bottom. Add the chopped garlic and set the pan aside, off the heat.

Preheat oven to 350°F.

Pour the contents of the pan into a 4- to 6-quart baking dish. Add all of the stock, bay leaves, rosemary, thyme, and marjoram, and then braise in the oven uncovered for 45 minutes or until the meat is slightly tender.

While the meat is braising, pour some of the remaining olive oil into a sauté pan over medium-high heat and cook the carrots and onions for 5 to 10 minutes, stirring frequently.

Add the sautéed carrots and onions, potatoes, and cabbage (if using) to the baking dish, stir, and braise for another 45 to 60 minutes, until the meat is very tender and the vegetables are soft. Add salt and pepper to taste. Just before serving, stir in the peas and allow them to heat up.

IRON-SEARED PORK LOIN WITH FRESH HERBS

I'M A FAN OF FRANCIS MALLMAN, THE PRE-eminent Argentine chef, whose book *Seven Fires* is one of my favorites. He details using wood for the kind of cooking that Argentines are famous for, and his recipes are simple and wonderful. I'm proud to say that a lot of my cooking resembles his. Searing meats over hot cast iron has been a mainstay of my restaurants and I am gratified to find out that there was some method to my madness. Mallman prefers fresh chopped rosemary for his herb rub, which is great, but just about any fresh herb will work.

What follows is a relatively cheap and satisfying dish that can be accompanied by just about anything. I like roasted potatoes and vegetables also cooked on the same hot cast iron as the meat.

The importance of a hot grill cannot be understated, so leave yourself plenty of time to preheat your grill. One good way to determine proper heat is to drop a tiny amount of olive oil onto the grill. If it sizzles vigorously, the grill is ready.

To serve, I like to drizzle a tablespoon of honey or sweet soy sauce on top and allow the heat of the pork to melt it.

SERVES 4

4 (6-OUNCE) BONELESS PORK LOIN CHOPS, ABOUT $^3/_4$-INCH THICK

KOSHER SALT

1 CUP CHOPPED FRESH HERBS OF YOUR CHOICE (ROSEMARY, THYME, OR OREGANO, ALONE OR IN ANY COMBINATION)

$^1/_2$ CUP CHOPPED GARLIC

FRESHLY GROUND BLACK PEPPER OR RED PEPPER FLAKES

1 CUP OLIVE OIL

6 TO 8 TABLESPOONS HONEY OR SWEET SOY SAUCE

BRINE THE CHOPS WITH $^3/_4$ CUP OF SALT dissolved in a gallon of water for 2 to 3 hours in the refrigerator.

Drain the pork. Place the chops between two sheets of plastic wrap or parchment paper and pound the chops to $^1/_2$-inch thick. Pat them dry with paper towels.

Stir together the herbs, garlic, and salt and pepper to taste. Pat it all over one side of the chops.

Lay the chops on a rimmed baking sheet, and allow them to rest in the refrigerator from 1 to 6 hours.

Prior to cooking, allow the pork to reach room temperature. Preheat the grill on high heat, at least 20 minutes.

Using a spatula, carefully place the chops herb-side down on the hot grill and allow several minutes for a crust to form without burning. When turning, be sure to get the spatula under the crust without dislodging it and gently turn the chops over. Cook the other side until the pork reaches 160°F inside, about 4 minutes, and then place the chops in a warm oven until ready to eat. Before serving, drizzle the pork with the honey or soy sauce.

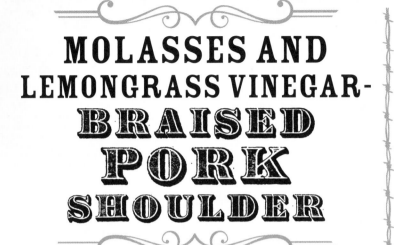

MOLASSES AND LEMONGRASS VINEGAR-BRAISED PORK SHOULDER

THIS IS A VARIATION OF THE SLOW-COOKED Pork Shoulder with Pomegranate Molasses Rub (see page 133). I wanted to do something with a product developed by my Argentine friend Virginia Wax, a wonderful amateur chef in her own right who has created a new lemongrass vinegar: its delicate overtone adds a whole new depth to any dish. She sells this product under the name of Auntie Si, a name bestowed upon her years ago by my stepdaughter Addison McHenry. You can buy this product online at www.auntiesi.com.

I recommend a cast-iron Dutch oven. It lends itself to the long, slow cooking necessary to perfect this recipe, but any covered pot will do. If the pork has been injected with a brining solution by the producer, skip the brining step here.

SERVES 6 TO 8

- ³/₄ CUP KOSHER SALT, PLUS MORE AS NEEDED
- 1 (5- TO 6-POUND) BONE-IN PORK SHOULDER
- ¹/₄ CUP OLIVE OIL
- ³/₄ CUP MOLASSES OR STEEN'S PURE CANE SYRUP
- ¹/₄ CUP FRESHLY CRACKED BLACK PEPPER
- 2 LARGE YELLOW ONIONS, SLICED
- 15 WHOLE GARLIC CLOVES
- 1 CUP CHICKEN STOCK (SUBSTITUTE 1 TABLESPOON GOOD-QUALITY CHICKEN BASE PLUS 1 CUP WATER)
- ¹/₂ CUP AUNTIE SI'S LEMON-GRASS VINEGAR (SUBSTITUTE SEASONED RICE VINEGAR)
- 4 BAY LEAVES
- 2 LARGE GARNET YAMS, PEELED AND CUT INTO ¹/₂-INCH CUBES

DISSOLVE ³/₄ CUP OF SALT IN 2 GALLONS OF water, and brine the roast in the refrigerator for 24 hours prior to cooking.

Preheat the oven to 250°F.

Heat the olive oil in a large Dutch oven or a heavy covered roasting pan over high heat. Brown the fat side of the roast and remove from the pan. Brush the roast with the molasses and sprinkle with salt and a generous amount of the cracked pepper, adjusting seasoning to taste.

Add the onions and garlic to the hot pan and cook until slightly caramelized. Then add the stock, lemongrass vinegar, and bay leaves and return the meat to the pot. Put the covered pot in the oven and cook undisturbed for 3 hours, then check for tenderness. If the meat is just shy of fork-tender, cook for another 30 minutes then check again. At this point, add the yams and cook for another 45 minutes until the meat is close to falling off the bone.

If you want to reduce the sauce, remove the pork and yams from the pot and reduce to desired consistency. Return meat and yams to the pot, and serve hot.

SLOW-COOKED PORK SHOULDER WITH POMEGRANATE MOLASSES RUB

THIS DISH BY MY CO-AUTHOR PATRICK could easily fit into a comfort food section of our book, except that we intend for all sections to be comfortable. Or if we had a "cheap eats" section, it would certainly belong, because this cut, sometimes called the butt, is indeed economical. When cooked slow and easy for succulence, with an influence of both sweetness and tartness from the molasses, it delivers a deeply satisfying payoff. Depending on the size (don't underestimate because this is such a comfort dish that guests consume second and third portions by picking away with their fingers) it's a wonderful leftover, either alone or for pulled-pork sandwiches. Serve on a big platter surrounded with steamed or roasted winter squash or yams drizzled with peanut oil and sprinkled with chopped cilantro or parsley. Applesauce is also welcome.

SERVES 6

FINE SALT AND FRESHLY GROUND BLACK PEPPER

1/4 CUP VEGETABLE OR CANOLA OIL

1 (5-POUND) PORK BUTT (BOSTON BUTT) OR BONELESS SHOULDER

2 TABLESPOONS WORCESTERSHIRE SAUCE (OPTIONAL)

1/2 CUP POMEGRANATE MOLASSES

1/2 CUP (1 STICK) UNSALTED BUTTER

1/2 CUP CIDER VINEGAR

1/2 CUP VEGETABLE STOCK

PREHEAT OVEN TO 225°F.

Sprinkle salt and pepper all over the meat. In a 4-quart Dutch oven, heat the oil over high heat and brown the pork on all sides. Meanwhile, combine the molasses and butter in a small saucepan and heat until just melted together. Turn the meat fat-side up in the pan and brush lightly with Worcestershire (if using). Paint the top of the meat thickly with the buttered molasses. Pour the vinegar and stock around (but not over) the meat in the Dutch oven. The liquid is there to provide steam and a subtle infusion of tartness.

Cover the Dutch oven and place in the oven. Leave it to cook. Don't check on it for at least 4 hours (I prefer to cook for 5). The meat should be falling-apart tender.

Remove from the oven and set the meat on a big platter. You should be able to carve the meat with a fork or even a serving spoon.

PORK CHOPS WITH HONEY, CHIPOTLES, AND LIME

PORK PLAYS A GREAT HOST TO JUST ABOUT any accompaniment. Here is a little southwestern twist for something different from your regular summer barbecue. Chipotles are jalapeño peppers that have been smoked; they are available packed in cans with adobo sauce in most large grocery stores.

We like to do our pork chops about 1³/₄-inches thick. The long marinating time helps maintain a higher moisture level, which means a juicier chop.

SERVES 4

MARINADE
¹/₂ CUP OLIVE OIL

2 TABLESPOONS GRANULATED GARLIC

1 TABLESPOON KOSHER SALT

1 TABLESPOON FRESHLY GROUND BLACK PEPPER

THE JUICE OF 1 LIME

4 (6-OUNCE) BONELESS PORK CHOPS, 1³/₄ INCHES THICK

CHIPOTLE SAUCE
2 TABLESPOONS OLIVE OIL

1 YELLOW ONION, FINELY DICED

³/₄ CUP HONEY

¹/₄ CUP BROWN MUSTARD

1 TABLESPOON MINCED CANNED CHIPOTLE PEPPERS

1 TABLESPOON GROUND CUMIN

1 TABLESPOON PAPRIKA

¹/₂ TEASPOON GRANULATED GARLIC

¹/₂ TEASPOON ALLSPICE

GARNISH
2 FRESH LIMES, CUT INTO QUARTERS

COMBINE THE OLIVE OIL, GARLIC, SALT pepper, lime juice, and ¹/₄ cup of water in a bowl and whisk thoroughly. Place the chops and the pepper marinade in a resealable plastic bag for at least 4 hours in the refrigerator. Drain the chops, reserving the marinade, and pat dry.

For the chipotle sauce, heat the olive oil in a saucepan over medium heat and sauté the onions until translucent, about 5 minutes. Add the reserved marinade and ¹/₂ cup of water, bring to a boil, then add the honey, mustard, chipotles, cumin, paprika, garlic, and allspice. Reduce the heat to medium and simmer for 10 minutes or until the sauce has reduced by half and begins to thicken.

Preheat a cast-iron skillet on high heat, until a drop of water sizzles vigorously on its surface. Place the marinated pork chops, presentation-side down on the hot surface to sear and brown. This usually takes around 5 to 7 minutes. Be sure that this side has a good, dark, slightly crusty appearance before turning. Flip the chops and reduce the heat to medium and sear for 2 to 3 minutes. Spoon some of the chipotle sauce over each chop. (If the sauce has gotten too thick, add a little water to thin.) Place a large lid over the chops to finish the cooking (or if you don't have one, make a dome out of foil): this will create a steaming effect that should help to retain moisture while you finish the cooking, usually around another 10 minutes. At this point, the meat should be medium or slightly pink in the middle and 140 to 145°F: a perfectly cooked juicy chop ready to serve. While the chops are finishing, slowly reheat the additional sauce so that it will be hot when the meat is done.

Serve the chops on a warm plate topped with the sauce, and garnished with the lime.

PORK SCHNITZELS WITH PANKO AND BROWN SAGE BUTTER

AMONG PORK'S GREAT VIRTUES IS ITS versatility. Most sauces that work with chicken and veal will work with pork. This preparation tastes a good deal like wiener schnitzel but uses pork instead of veal, thus making it a whole lot cheaper.

I use Japanese-style breadcrumbs (panko) in this recipe rather than the traditional breadcrumbs because I like the extra crispy texture, but you can use either one. Some chefs use a well-trimmed pork sirloin instead of the boneless loin. Either cut lends itself to slicing across the grain, but for our purposes I like the loin.

SERVES 6

- 2 POUNDS BONELESS PORK LOIN
- FINE SALT AND FRESHLY GROUND BLACK PEPPER
- 2 EGGS, LIGHTLY BEATEN
- 2 CUPS WHOLE MILK
- 1 CUP ALL-PURPOSE FLOUR
- 2 CUPS PANKO (JAPANESE BREADCRUMBS)
- 1/4 CUP OLIVE OIL
- 1 CUP (2 STICKS) UNSALTED BUTTER, DIVIDED
- 12 TO 15 FRESH SAGE LEAVES
- 5 TABLESPOONS FRESHLY SQUEEZED LEMON JUICE
- 1/2 CUP CHOPPED FRESH FLAT-LEAF PARSLEY
- 6 LEMON WEDGES (FOR GARNISH)

CUT THE PORK LOIN INTO 1-INCH PIECES across the grain, and then, placing each piece between two pieces of plastic wrap, carefully pound the pieces to an even thickness of 1/4 inch with a meat mallet or a small sauté pan. Run your hand over the meat to ensure an even thickness without holes. Season with salt and pepper.

Set up three pie pans or shallow bowls; in one, stir together the beaten eggs and milk; in another place the flour; in the third, place the panko. Have a baking sheet nearby to hold the breaded cutlets before cooking.

Dip each cutlet, one at a time, into the egg mixture, then into the flour, coating both sides, then back into the egg for a second time, and finally into the panko. Make sure that both sides are well coated. As you complete each piece, place it on the baking sheet until all the pork is breaded.

When all of the cutlets are ready, add the olive oil and 1 stick of the butter to a large sauté pan and turn the heat to medium-high. You will know when the pan is ready when a small drop of water dropped in the pan sizzles.

Carefully place the cutlets in the hot oil mixture and cook both sides until lightly browned. Do not crowd the pan, and watch carefully to be sure the meat isn't browning too quickly. Cook just long enough to let one side become golden-brown, then turn to finish the other side. Remove finished cutlets to a baking tray in a warm oven.

Pour off any excess oil and turn the heat to high. Quickly add the remaining stick of butter, sage leaves, and lemon juice. Stir until the butter begins to foam and turn brown, and the sage leaves are crispy. Add the parsley and stir briefly, then remove from the heat. Remove the cutlets from the oven, pour the sizzling sauce over the meat, and serve with the lemon wedges.

RIBS!

WHEN I THINK OF AMERICA'S TEMPLES OF BAR-becue, I picture huge brick pits, stained dark with years of smoke and sauce, of hickory fires smoldering under slabs of slow-cooking pork. I see juicy, mahogany-colored morsels of crunchy ribs nestled among mounds of tart coleslaw and creamy potato salad. I can smell the aroma from at least a block away. It's also not hard to imagine, that with a little time and planning, you can reproduce the great taste of Memphis or Kansas City pit barbecue in your own backyard. The two essentials to great ribs are smoke and long, slow cooking.

There are two kinds of ribs: baby backs, which are lean, or spareribs, which I prefer. Spareribs must contain at least eleven ribs and may include some portions of the sternum and diaphragm. They usually contain some gristle and fat, but they are far juicier, and thus have a lot more flavor than the baby backs. On the other hand, baby backs are more tender and easier to work with (Patrick prefers them) so either type has its advantages.

No matter what type of ribs you prefer, the secret to great flavor is a great rub! The right mix of salt, sugar, and spices will create a built-in flavor that complements the smokiness from the grill. Rubs also add color and help create a bronze and crusty exterior to your ribs.

My favorite way to serve ribs is to the way they do it all over the South. First, get a couple of pieces of cheap white bread, cover the bread with sauce and lay the ribs on top, then cover everything with sauce. The bread soaks up the sauce and makes for messy but great eating. Serve with Curried Coleslaw (see page 193). Potato salad also makes a great sidekick (see page 213).

SERVES 6

2 RACKS ST. LOUIS SPARERIBS, CUT INTO THIRDS, OR 3 BABY BACK RIB RACKS, CUT INTO HALVES

3 CUPS PACKED DARK BROWN SUGAR, DIVIDED

2 CUPS SMOKED PAPRIKA

1 CUP KOSHER SALT

1/2 CUP CHILI POWDER

1/2 CUP CURRY POWDER

1/2 CUP ONION POWDER

1/2 CUP LEMON PEPPER

1/4 CUP GRANULATED GARLIC

2 CUPS APPLE CIDER OR APPLE JUICE

BARBECUE SAUCE OF YOUR CHOICE (SEE PAGE 248), FOR SERVING

MIX TOGETHER 2 CUPS OF THE SUGAR, paprika, salt, chili powder, curry powder, onion powder, lemon pepper, and garlic. Generously sprinkle the rub over both sides of the ribs and refrigerate them in large 2-gallon resealable plastic bags for 3 or 4 days. Less time is acceptable, but the longer the better. Any excess rub will keep for months in a tightly-sealed jar.

Preheat the grill on low heat. (A gas grill is ideal here because you can use the lowest settings and ensure a steady, even heat source. For a charcoal barbecue, place the ribs on a warming rack farthest from the heat source, and build the fire on the opposite side of the grill.)

Place a packet of moistened wood chips directly over the flames, and when they start to smoke, put the ribs on the grill. Alternatively, use a smoke box accessory or an old 6-inch frying pan over one of the burners, fill with pre-soaked wood chips (usually hickory), and set the heat just high enough to cause them to smoke. Add more chips as needed.

Make a basting liquid by stirring together the apple cider, remaining sugar, and 2 cups of water. Place it in a drip pan under the ribs on the indirect side. *(continued)*

Smoke-cook the ribs on indirect heat, covered, for at least 3 hours over heat that is no higher than 250°F. Baste the ribs with a brush every hour. The thin sauce will moisten and add color to the ribs without burning them. (Save your regular barbecue sauce until later).

If you feel the need, turn them every hour or so, but I recommend leaving them alone for the first 2 hours. The ribs should be burnished and tender; you should be able to wiggle an individual rib, almost pulling it apart from the rest of the rack.

Remove the ribs from the grill, slather them with a generous coating of barbecue sauce, and allow them to cool down slightly. Then wrap them thoroughly in plastic wrap. That's right: wrap them in plastic (I was skeptical the first time I followed these directions) and put them on a sheet pan in a 200°F oven for 60 to 90 minutes. This is absolutely the best method for finishing and holding the ribs until they are ready to be served. The plastic will hold in the moisture and intensify the interaction between the meat and the sauce and will produce a great product as opposed to a total meltdown.

You can tell when the ribs are done by tearing away one of the little ribs on the small end and eating it. If the meat pulls away easily and it tastes good, the ribs are ready to eat. The texture should be moist and tender. You can cook the ribs up to this point and refrigerate them until ready to serve, tightly wrapped in the plastic and foil.

Just before I am ready to serve the ribs I remove the plastic, put them back on the grill over a medium fire for a few minutes, and slather them with more sauce in order to build up a little "bark." That is a process of building up layers of sauce on the meat. Watch closely because the sugar in the barbecue sauce will burn if left unattended.

Cut the ribs into serving portions. I usually cut the ribs into 3 or 4-bone portions depending on whether I'm cutting from the small end or the large end. Baby backs are usually served in half-slab portions.

BISON

BISON MAN

WHEN YOU HEAR THE NAME TED TURNER, THE LABEL "RUTHLESS BILLIONAIRE" PROBABLY pops into your head. But he is more than a label. He's also famous for his ecological contributions and activism to control world population growth, his involvement in the Goodwill Games, and any of a dozen other notable and often controversial causes. Yet beyond these weighty endeavors, the one that lights his eyes is his protection of buffalo, correctly referred to as the American bison. Not only is he the state's largest private landowner, he and his ranch hands tend to the world's largest bison herd, numbering well more than 30,000 animals.

You've probably already guessed that I admire Ted. On a personal level, he is friendly, amusing, and down to earth. He has been a great customer in both my restaurants, and a good neighbor. He purchased four big ranches that would have certainly been subdivided, developed, and sold off in 20-acre tracts. Instead he kept them intact, put a lot of money into stream and range improvements, and stocked them with a whole bunch of bison. In fact his love of the breed got him into the business of buying large ranches to protect livestock in both North and South America.

A few years ago, Ted and I were sitting on the deck at his Snowcrest Ranch on the Ruby River, in southwestern Montana, drinking wine and watching the sun go down. Having just consumed grilled bison tenderloin from one of the herd grazing on the river bottom below us, Ted filled me in on how it all started.

"When I was a kid, I was fascinated with bison, and their place in American history," he said. (Ted is very careful to refer to his shaggy wards quite correctly as "bison" and not "buffalo".) "I devoured every book I could find about them and their eventual extermination; and so, when I had a few bucks, I bought three and kept them on my dad's farm in South Carolina. Later, I bought a place near Tallahassee, increased my herd to 100, and began to think that maybe someday I would like to get a few more."

With typical Turner determination he did just that. Starting in Montana, then New Mexico and Nebraska, he has expanded his bison empire over 1.5 million acres. Recently his purchases of ranches in Brazil and Argentina have made him the largest private landowner in the world. I asked him about his plans to enlarge his herds—how many is enough: fifty thousand, a hundred thousand? He gazed at his wine glass, took a long pull, savored it, and replied: "I never talk about what I'm going to do, just about what I've done."

Bison in Montana are raised on ranches throughout the state and their numbers are growing rapidly. So common is bison that sirloins and ground products have taken their places alongside beef in grocery meat cases—including your neighborhood Safeway or Whole Foods. Bison contains little or no marbling because of its low fat content, which accounts for its attraction among weight watchers. We find it just plain delicious.

BISON PEANUT SATÉ

FIRST-TIME CUSTOMERS ALWAYS SEEM bewildered by my preparing an iconic American animal in the manner of Bangkok street food. I can't say I blame them. But in fact this recipe is a great way to use just about any kind of red meat. You get the best results from cooking this dish over a hot open fire, or on preheated cast iron, but you can get good results by using a preheated broiler. Be sure and marinate the meat for at least four hours, and if you are using bamboo rather than metal skewers, soak them for an hour before use. Another serving option is to toss some cooked noodles with the peanut sauce and place the meat over the top for a main course.

SERVES 4

BISON SATE
2 TO 3 POUNDS BISON TENDERLOIN

1 CUP SOY SAUCE

$^{1}/_{2}$ CUP RICE VINEGAR

2 TABLESPOONS SESAME OIL

$^{1}/_{2}$ TEASPOON HOT CHILI PASTE OR SRIRACHA SAUCE

2 GARLIC CLOVES, CRUSHED

2 TABLESPOONS FRESHLY SQUEEZED LIME JUICE

2 TABLESPOONS PACKED DARK BROWN SUGAR

PEANUT SAUCE
1 CUP NATURAL CRUNCHY PEANUT BUTTER

$^{1}/_{2}$ CUP SOY SAUCE

2 TABLESPOONS SESAME OIL

2 TABLESPOONS PACKED DARK BROWN SUGAR

2 TABLESPOONS FRESHLY SQUEEZED LIME JUICE

$^{1}/_{2}$ CUP FRESH CILANTRO LEAVES

2 GARLIC CLOVES

2 WHOLE SCALLIONS, TRIMMED AND CHOPPED (WHITE AND GREEN PARTS)

WHOLE LETTUCE LEAVES, FOR SERVING

CUT THE TENDERLOIN INTO 1-INCH CUBES. Mix together the soy sauce, vinegar, sesame oil, chili paste, garlic, lime juice, and sugar, and marinate the bison in this mixture in the refrigerator for at least 4 hours, up to 12 hours. While the meat is marinating, prepare the peanut sauce.

In a food processor, blend together the peanut butter, soy sauce, sesame oil, brown sugar, lime juice, cilantro, garlic, and scallions until smooth. Set aside at room temperature.

Preheat a grill or a cast-iron skillet on high heat. Alternatively, preheat a broiler on high. Place 5 to 6 pieces of the meat on each skewer and cook, rotating occasionally, for 5 minutes (or longer if you want the meat more well-done). Place on a serving plate over a layer of lettuce leaves and drizzle the sauce over the top of the skewers.

SICILIAN-STYLE BISON

I CAME UP WITH THIS RECIPE YEARS AGO FOR my now late friend A.J. McLane, who used it in an article for *Esquire* magazine. He also used it in his monumental game cookbook *A Taste of the Wild* published in 1991. I called it "Buffalo in the Style of Tuscany." In retrospect, "Sicilian-style" would have been a more appropriate description because of the use of tomatoes, anchovies, and capers. No matter what you call it, this is a great recipe for bison, elk, moose, or even beef tenderloin either prepared whole, or cut into medallions.

SERVES 4

- 1/2 CUP OLIVE OIL, DIVIDED
- 1 TEASPOON FINELY CHOPPED FRESH THYME
- 1 TEASPOON FINELY CHOPPED FRESH ROSEMARY
- 1 TABLESPOON FRESHLY CRACKED BLACK PEPPER, PLUS MORE AS NEEDED FOR SERVING
- 2 GARLIC CLOVES, FINELY CHOPPED
- 1 1/2 POUNDS BISON TENDER- LOIN, CUT INTO 1 1/2-INCH MEDALLIONS
- 1 TABLESPOON ANCHOVY PASTE OR 3 ANCHOVY FILLETS
- 3 TABLESPOONS CAPERS
- 1/4 CUP PURÉED SUNDRIED TOMATOES OR 2 TABLE- SPOONS TOMATO PASTE
- 1/2 CUP BEEF DEMI-GLACE OR 1 CUP BEEF STOCK
- 1 CUP MARSALA WINE
- 1 HANDFUL CHOPPED FRESH FLAT-LEAF PARSLEY

COMBINE ALL BUT 3 TABLESPOONS OF THE olive oil, the thyme, rosemary, black pepper, and garlic in a resealable plastic bag. Marinate the bison in this mixture at room temperature for about 3 hours.

To cook on the stove top, heat a cast-iron skillet almost to the smoking point. Add the meat to the pan, not disturbing any pieces of garlic and herbs sticking to the meat, and quickly sear both sides until rare or medium-rare, about 2 to 3 minutes per side. Or you can grill the meat by preheating a very hot charcoal fire and cooking the bison directly over the heat, allowing the flames to envelope and sear the meat. Either way, keep the meat warm in a very low oven while making the sauce.

Add the remaining 3 tablespoons of olive oil, anchovy paste, and capers to the hot skillet. Stir and cook briefly, until the anchovy paste just starts to dissolve, then add the tomato purée, beef demi-glace, and Marsala, and reduce until sufficiently thickened to the consistency of ketchup.

Arrange the medallions with the sauce on warm plates, then grind a little pepper over the tops and toss on some fresh parsley for extra color.

BISON TENDERLOIN
WITH COMPOUND BUTTER

THIS HAS ALWAYS BEEN ONE OF OUR TOP sellers. But because it is delicate, it should not be cooked more than medium-rare. Because it is expensive, about $20 a pound, there's no room for error. My kitchen guys are the greatest and they usually get it right on the mark.

SERVES 4

4 (8-OUNCE) BISON TENDER-
LOIN FILETS (EACH ABOUT
2 1/2 INCHES THICK)

1/4 CUP OLIVE OIL OR MELTED
BUTTER

SEA SALT AND FRESHLY
GROUND BLACK PEPPER

MAÎTRE D'HÔTEL BUTTER
(SEE PAGE 234)

PREHEAT YOUR CHARCOAL FIRE OR GAS grill to a very high temperature. When the fire is ready, brush the filets with oil then season the meat all over with salt and pepper, adjusting the seasoning to taste.

Place the meat over the hottest part of the grill and cook for about 5 to 7 minutes per side. Test for temperature by poking the meat with your finger: really soft means rare meat, slightly firmer means it's medium-rare. Don't ever cook bison steaks of any kind beyond medium-rare. They have very little internal fat and they will dry out quickly. If you test one with a meat thermometer it should be between 120°F and 125°F.

As soon as you remove the steaks from the heat cut a 1/4-inch-thick slice from the roll of compound butter and allow it to melt over the meat. Serve immediately.

DUTCH-OVEN BISON STEW

TODAY, IT'S NOT LIKE IT WAS IN THE MID- nineteenth century, when the bison population ran in the millions before it was nearly wiped out. That said, between Yellowstone National Park in the south, Ted Turner's ranch holdings in the middle, and the National Bison Refuge at Moise in the northwest, together with smaller bison ranching operations in between, Montana has become a virtual bison factory. I think it's great (although many cattlemen would take serious issue with that statement). Bison meat is very high in protein, low in fat, and damn good eating, and this simple recipe is one of the best.

You don't have to cook this dish in a Dutch oven over an open fire for it to be outstanding, and furthermore, you don't have to serve it steaming hot on tin plates, in a hunting camp, pitched by the side of a rushing mountain stream, but it helps.

SERVES 6 TO 8

1/2 CUP OLIVE OIL

4 POUNDS BISON CHUCK OR ROUND ROAST, CUT INTO 1 1/2-INCH CUBES

2 LARGE YELLOW ONIONS, COARSELY DICED

1/3 CUP ALL-PURPOSE FLOUR

2 CUPS BEEF STOCK (SUBSTITUTE 2 TABLESPOONS GOOD-QUALITY BEEF BASE PLUS 2 CUPS WATER)

1 CUP DARK BEER OR PORTER

2 TO 3 MEDIUM CARROTS, CUT INTO 1-INCH PIECES

3 TABLESPOONS THYME

3 BAY LEAVES

1 (6-OUNCE) CAN TOMATO PASTE

3 TABLESPOONS GRANULATED GARLIC

1 TEASPOON ALLSPICE

4 RUSSET POTATOES, PEELED AND CUT INTO 1 1/2-INCH PIECES

FINE SALT AND FRESHLY GROUND BLACK PEPPER

1/2 CUP CHOPPED FRESH FLAT-LEAF PARSLEY (OPTIONAL)

IN A HOT DUTCH OVEN, HEAVY POT, OR braising pan, heat the oil over high heat. Sear the bison on all sides and set aside. Add the onions and sauté for 5 minutes. When they turn translucent, add the flour. Stir in well and when the flour has browned a bit, add the seared meat. Pour in the beef stock and beer, stirring well to dislodge the cooked meat, flour, and onions from the bottom of the pot. Bring to a simmer and add the carrots, thyme, bay leaves, tomato paste, garlic, and allspice. Cook uncovered over low heat for 3 hours, gently stirring occasionally from the bottom, adding more liquid if necessary. When the meat is fork-tender but not falling apart, add the potatoes and cook until they are tender, about 20 minutes. Add salt and pepper, adjusting seasoning to taste. The gravy should be fairly thick. If it is too thick, thin with water or beef stock.

Serve in warm bowls with a bit of fresh chopped parsley for color and plenty of crusty bread and butter.

GRILLED BISON HANGER STEAK

LIKE ITS BEEF COUNTERPART, BISON HANGER steak is a less expensive cut and although it is slightly tougher than the more familiar cuts, it has a great deal more flavor. We marinate the meat for 24 hours, partially flatten it, and quickly sear it over a cast-iron plate at very high heat. It is comparable to flank or tri-tip steak in that after cooking it must be thinly sliced across the grain before serving. A cast-iron pan is ideal for this as its smooth surface will sear without overcooking, plus it allows the herb and spice mixture to adhere to the surface of the steak when it is served.

SERVES 4

1 CUP OLIVE OIL

1 TABLESPOON CHOPPED FRESH ROSEMARY LEAVES

2 TABLESPOONS FRESHLY SQUEEZED LEMON JUICE

1 TABLESPOON CHOPPED GARLIC CLOVES

1 TEASPOON SEA SALT

1 TEASPOON FRESHLY CRACKED BLACK PEPPER

2 POUNDS BISON HANGER STEAK, FLATTENED TO 1-INCH THICKNESS

HERBED TOPPING

1 CUP OLIVE OIL

$^1/_2$ CUP WHOLE FRESH ROSEMARY LEAVES

$^1/_2$ CUP CHOPPED GARLIC CLOVES

3 TEASPOONS FRESHLY GRATED LEMON ZEST

1 TEASPOON COARSELY GROUND SEA SALT

COMBINE THE OLIVE OIL, ROSEMARY, LEMON juice, garlic, salt, and pepper in a 1-gallon resealable plastic bag. Add the bison and allow it to marinate in the refrigerator for 12 to 24 hours.

When you are ready to cook the meat, lay a plancha or cast-iron sear pan directly over the burners on your gas grill and preheat on high.

While the grill is heating up, mix the topping by combining the olive oil, rosemary, garlic, lemon zest, and salt in a shallow dish. When you are ready to begin cooking, press the meat very firmly into the mixture with your palms so that it adheres to the top side of the meat.

When the cooking surface is hot and almost smoking, carefully lay the meat herb-side down on the hot surface, allowing the heat to form a crust. Cook for 3 to 4 minutes, then, using a spatula, very carefully turn the meat, keeping the crust intact. Cook for 2 minutes or so on the bottom side. The meat should be medium-rare; do not overcook. Remove the meat from the fire and put it on a cutting board. Slice the steak into $^3/_4$-inch slices and divide it evenly among warm plates. Serve.

WILD GAME

IN MONTANA, WE LIKE TO SAY, "IF IT'S BEEN LYING IN THE ROAD FOR AT LEAST FOUR DAYS, it's well-aged." Seriously, when we talk of game we are usually referring to big game: elk, venison, moose, and antelope. For our purposes, we're going to include game birds as well. These animals (unless they have been farm-raised) have usually been shot, field-dressed, cut, and frozen. Like Patrick, my fellow author, I used to hunt four-legged game but don't anymore. I'd like to think I've reached an age that governs me from killing anything. In truth, I'm too lazy. Besides, I'm surrounded by friends willing to get up on sub-zero mornings, trudge up mountains through two feet of snow, track an animal, shoot it, clean it, haul it down the mountain, cut it up, wrap it and deliver it to my kitchen door.

I suppose if it weren't for generous friends, I might be driven back into the woods to satisfy my craving for a perfectly seared venison backstrap. But as the old saying goes, I keep my friends close so that I can stay close to home.

Game should be hung at a temperature just above freezing for one to two weeks. I always seam my meat (the European-style of boning and cutting meat into pieces that are defined by the muscle and sinew). If you take yours to be cut commercially, instruct them to bone everything out first. There is nothing that can destroy the flavor of wild game as quickly as bone dust from a meat saw. I also take great pains to remove all fat and hair, as they can also impart a rancid taste to the meat.

With the meat prepared this way you cook it literally any way you want to. I usually cut the pieces into a size and thickness suitable for marinating and grilling, which is my preferred method of cooking. Trim pieces and cuts too tough or small for grilling are best ground or used for stews and chili.

Hunting Camp, Gallatin Canyon, Montana, ca. 1915

After a Day's Hunt, Karst's Ranch, Gallatin Canyon, Montana, ca. 1915

WILD DUCK AND SAUSAGE GUMBO

WHEN IT COMES TO WING SHOOTING, I DEFER to Patrick, my fellow author, who continues to hunt pheasant and upland birds. In fact, it's no secret among my friends and former hunting companions that I was, and undoubtedly still am, one of the worst wing shooters ever to pick up a shotgun. Those ducks that were fortunate enough to fly within the range of my sights had at least a 90 percent chance of survival: pretty good odds from the duck's point of view. Tie in poor shooting with cold, wet weather, and the inevitable happened: I gave all of my duck-hunting paraphernalia away years ago and now depend on the largess of my hunting friends to supply me with the occasional duck dinner.

I enjoy wild duck cooked just about any way, but this is one of my favorite recipes. The usual practice in Montana, unlike other parts of the country, is to remove the breast and discard the rest of the duck. But for those willing to go the extra mile and eviscerate and pluck the duck, leaving the whole bird intact, there is an opportunity to enjoy many more interesting preparations than merely a skinless duck breast. You can easily halve the yield for fewer birds, if you have less generous friends.

SERVES 8 TO 10

- 4 WHOLE DUCKS, PLUCKED, SKIN-ON (ABOUT 10 POUNDS TOTAL)
- 5 BAY LEAVES
- 1/4 CUP DRIED THYME
- 10 TO 12 FRESH GARLIC CLOVES, THINLY SLICED, TO TASTE
- 1/2 TEASPOON CAYENNE PEPPER, OR MORE TO TASTE
- 1 CUP BACON GREASE (RENDERED FROM ABOUT 6 SLICES OF COOKED BACON)
- 1 CUP ALL-PURPOSE FLOUR
- 1/2 CUP CANOLA OIL
- 3 LARGE YELLOW ONIONS, DICED
- 3 GREEN BELL PEPPERS, DICED
- 4 STALKS CELERY, DICED (ABOUT 3 CUPS)
- 2 CUPS DICED SMOKED HAM
- 1 POUND ANDOUILLE OR POLISH SMOKED SAUSAGE, CUT INTO 1-INCH ROUNDS
- 3 TABLESPOONS FILE POWDER (OPTIONAL)
- KOSHER SALT
- 6 TO 8 CUPS LONG-GRAIN WHITE RICE, COOKED ACCORDING TO PACKAGE DIRECTIONS

SET TWO VERY LARGE STOCKPOTS OF WATER to boil over high heat; they should be large enough to hold all of the whole duck carcasses.

Begin by removing the duck breasts with a boning knife, slicing vertically along the breastbone and through the ribs. Then remove the legs and thighs from the duck. Place the legs and thighs, remaining carcasses, the bay leaves, thyme, garlic, and cayenne in the uncovered stock pots and turn the heat down to medium to just a simmer. After 45 minutes remove the legs and thighs from the water and set them aside to cool briefly. Pull the meat off the bones, setting it aside, and return the skin and bones to the pot. Continue to simmer the duck carcasses uncovered for another 2 hours to create a duck stock; the liquid will reduce by about half. Strain the stock through a fine sieve, discarding the solids, and keep it warm in one large pot. You want to end up with about 2 1/2 gallons of strained and reduced duck stock. (*continued*)

While the stock is simmering, dice the reserved duck breasts into 1-inch chunks.

Heat the bacon grease in a large sauté pan over medium heat. Whisk in the flour and cook to make a dark roux, whisking constantly for about 10 minutes until it obtains a frosting-like consistency and is coffee-colored. Remove it from the pan and set aside.

Heat a second large sauté pan over medium-high heat and add the canola oil. When it is shimmering, add the onions, peppers, and celery and cook until the vegetables are translucent, about 5 minutes. Add the vegetables and the dark roux to the pot of stock, stirring in carefully to avoid any spilling. The roux should melt into the stock and begin to thicken it.

Add the reserved duck thigh and leg meat, the chopped breast meat, ham, and sausage to the stock and simmer covered for 1 hour, or until the gumbo is thick and the duck meat is tender. Just before serving, stir in the file powder (if using).

Taste for seasoning, adding salt and cayenne if needed, and serve over rice.

PRAIRIE CHICKEN AND GREEN CHILE STEW

THIS IS THE KIND OF DISH THE CHUCK- wagon cook would throw together on special occasions or when there was more than the usual overnight stay. Maybe the trail boss decided to rest the herd for a particularly tough stretch ahead, or maybe they were waiting for a flooded river to fall. In any event, it gave the hands some time to explore for game, and the cook some time to gather fresh herbs and other things to break the monotony of a straight beans-and-fry-bread diet.

Prairie chickens, once one of the most common creatures of Montana, are becoming rare due to loss of habitat as farmers convert open space from grazing to cultivating wheat. So I'm thinking most of you probably don't have a prairie chicken available, but a regular chicken or capon will work just the same. All of these ingredients are native to the American West and provide us with a tasty example of how the creative chuck-wagon chef used what was available. The recipe calls for a prairie or fryer chicken but a pre-cooked rotisserie chicken will work as well—just pull the cooked chicken off the bone.

4 QUARTS CHICKEN STOCK

1 LARGE (4- TO 5-POUND)
PRAIRIE CHICKEN OR FRYER
(SUBSTITUTE A ROTISSERIE
CHICKEN)

1/2 CUP OLIVE OIL OR
BACON FAT

4 MEDIUM YELLOW ONIONS,
DICED

1/2 CUP CHOPPED FRESH
GARLIC

1 CUP CANNED GREEN CHILES,
POBLANO CHILES, OR OTHER
MILD GREEN CHILES, DRAINED

4 BAY LEAVES

3 TABLESPOONS DRIED
MEXICAN OREGANO

1/2 TEASPOON CAYENNE PEPPER

2 TABLESPOONS GROUND CUMIN

2 TABLESPOONS SMOKED (OR
REGULAR) PAPRIKA

3 RUSSET POTATOES, DICED
INTO 1/2-INCH CUBES (ABOUT
3 CUPS)

4 CUPS COOKED (OR CANNED
AND DRAINED) PINTO BEANS

2 CUPS COOKED CORN (FROZEN
WORKS FINE)

PLACE THE STOCK IN A LARGE STOCKPOT, and add the chicken. Bring to a boil over high heat, and then reduce the heat to maintain a simmer. Simmer the chicken until it is cooked through, 20 to 30 minutes, and then remove the chicken to a cutting board to cool. Reserve the pot of stock.

Pull the meat off the bones and chop into bite-sized pieces, discarding the skin. (If using a rotisserie chicken, heat the stock, set aside, and pull the meat off the bones into bite-sized pieces, discarding the skin.)

In a large skillet over medium-high heat, add the oil (or bacon fat) and onions, sautéing until transparent, about 5 minutes. Add the garlic, chiles, bay leaves, oregano, cayenne, cumin, paprika, and stir to combine. Transfer the cooked vegetables to the pot of stock, scraping all the browned bits from the skillet. Bring the stock to a boil, and then reduce the heat to medium to keep a simmer. Add the potatoes and pulled chicken and cook until the potatoes are fork-tender, about 20 minutes.

To finish, add the cooked pinto beans and corn and then reduce the heat to a gentle simmer. Continue cooking until the potatoes begin to break down and begin thickening the stew, about 20 minutes.

ROAST PHEASANT WITH TARRAGON VINEGAR

THE VAST WHEAT FIELDS OF CENTRAL AND eastern Montana are famous for huge populations of game birds, mainly pheasants, Hungarian partridge, and sharp-tailed grouse.

We both know a rabid group of bird hunters who spend the whole year living for those three months—from September through November—when they can head out to far-flung places where the largest nearby towns have names such as Harlowtown, Malta, and Plentywood, and they can work their dogs and tramp through huge fields of stubble, stalking pheasants and "Huns."

It is not unknown for these fanatics to spend thousands of dollars on dogs, shotguns, and all of the paraphernalia of bird hunting. Patrick nearly bought into a time-share dog—a chocolate lab—here in Montana; for a mere $1,000 the dog would be available whenever he made his way up here—about four times a year, tops.

As I've confessed, I'm not much of a bird hunter for two reasons: I don't like walking, and I am, without a doubt, the world's worst wing shooter. I am happy to accept a brace of pheasants or any bird from my hunting friends because frankly, I love the idea of great eating without suffering through the work required to put wild birds on the table.

They are always asking me for a recipe and the truth is, as I tell them, that any good chicken recipe will work for pheasants. Here is one of my favorites. This recipe calls for boneless, skin-on split pheasant breasts, generally two pieces per person. If I have the time, I like to use the rest of the carcass and make a pheasant stock, but you can skip this process and use chicken stock. Serve with rice pilaf or polenta.

SERVES 4

- 4 BONELESS, SKIN-ON PHEASANT BREASTS, HALVED
- FINE SALT AND FRESHLY GROUND BLACK PEPPER
- 5 TABLESPOONS OLIVE OIL
- 1/4 CUP (1/2 STICK) UNSALTED BUTTER, DIVIDED
- 5 SHALLOTS, MINCED
- 1 MEDIUM YELLOW ONION, THINLY SLICED
- 1 TABLESPOON ALL-PURPOSE FLOUR
- 1 CUP DRY WHITE WINE
- 1/2 CUP WHITE TARRAGON VINEGAR
- 2 CUPS CHICKEN STOCK (SUBSTITUTE 2 TEASPOONS GOOD-QUALITY CHICKEN BASE PLUS 2 CUPS WATER)
- 1 (14-OUNCE) CAN GOOD-QUALITY DICED TOMATOES, DRAINED
- 1 BUNCH FRESH TARRAGON LEAVES, CHOPPED

PREHEAT THE OVEN TO 325°F. SPRINKLE A generous amount of salt and pepper on the pheasant.

In a deep-sided cast-iron sauté pan, heat the oil and half of the butter over medium-high heat, and when it is hot, add the pheasant skin-side down. Cook until the skin is browned, about 12 minutes.

Set the pheasant aside and add the rest of the butter, then add the shallots and onion and cook until the onion is beginning to lightly caramelize, about 5 to 8 minutes. Add the flour and blend, creating a light roux; cook for about 2 minutes.

Deglaze the pan with the wine, vinegar, and chicken stock and cook until the mix is reduced by half. Stir in the tomatoes and chopped tarragon. Return the pheasant to the pan, skin-side up and roast in the oven for around 20 minutes. Serve hot with extra pan sauce.

DEARBORN RANCH PHEASANT WRAPPED IN BACON AND GRAPE LEAVES

PATRICK AND HIS BUDDIES HAVE HAD THE good fortune of stalking pheasant as guests on the vast and breathtakingly beautiful Dearborn Ranch near Wolf Creek, between Great Falls and Helena. Part of the deal requires the guests to clean and help cook their prey. No problem for my friend Patrick, who cut his galley chops on a crab boat in the Bering Sea. (See his book, *Lost at Sea*.) Anyway, here's how he does it. Pair with Grilled Asparagus (see page 195) and Rice Pilaf (see page 187) or Baked Brown Rice (see page 190). Patrick also recommends drinking a light Pinot Noir or austere Chardonnay.

SERVES 6

5 TABLESPOONS OLIVE OIL

6 BONELESS, SKIN-ON PHEASANT BREASTS, HALVED

5 SHALLOTS, MINCED

1 YELLOW ONION, THINLY SLICED

FINE SALT AND FRESHLY GROUND BLACK PEPPER

1 POUND SMOKED BACON (LIKE APPLEWOOD), THINLY SLICED

1 (14.5-OUNCE) JAR GRAPE LEAVES

PREHEAT OVEN TO 325°F.

Set up a deep-sided cast-iron sauté pan over medium-high heat and heat the olive oil (if you have two pans, it will make the browning go much more quickly). Brown the breasts on both sides in the olive oil, four pieces at a time. Once browned, set them aside and add the shallots and onion to the pan. Stir to lightly caramelize, about 4 minutes, then remove and set aside. Salt and pepper the pheasant, adjusting the seasoning to taste, and then wrap each half in bacon,

about 2 strips per half breast. Lay each wrapped breast on a grape leaf, sprinkle in the shallot and onion mix, and then wrap in the grape leaf. Lay the wrapped pheasant halves seam-side down in a baking dish, packed in tightly but without overlapping.

Roast in oven for 20 minutes, until the juices run clear. The bacon will cook without crisping and provide all the moisture you need.

WILD GOOSE MEDALLIONS

Montana to the golf courses in Florida, this country is overrun with wild geese. But there is a positive side to all of this; they can be very good to eat if prepared properly. Remember, geese or any wild game carry little or no fat, so you must preserve what fat there is by either undercooking or by adding extra fat like bacon, olive oil, or butter. The other alternative is long, slow braising in liquid, which doesn't lend itself to a lot of wild game recipes, including geese.

My solution is to treat goose like a piece of wild game tenderloin. This means I breast it out, disposing of the rest of the carcass, and using only the two pieces of boneless, skinless breast that come from either side of the breastbone.

I remember one fall night at the Continental Divide, my old restaurant in Ennis, when a bunch of Texans brought in some geese they had shot on nearby Ennis Lake. They said that they were coming back for dinner later, and wanted me to "do something" with the geese. A couple of hours later they were back and well into their third glass of Woodford Reserve whiskey when I brought out the fruits of their previous labor on the lake. I didn't say anything, just put down the plates, and said "Here boys, have an appetizer," and walked off.

When I went out to find out how they liked it one declared: "That sure was great beef tenderloin. Now, how are you going to do those damn geese?" I answered, "Guess what boys? Those were the geese!" I don't know if it was the whiskey, the food, or both, but they sure loved the dish. Hopefully, you will too.

Serve the Caramelized Onion and Mustard Sauce (see page 229) or the Red Currant Sauce (see page 246) alongside the finished goose breast. Just remember, this dish is very similar to beef loin so you can use the same side dishes as you would with tenderloin.

SERVES 4

1 CUP OLIVE OIL

5 GARLIC CLOVES, MINCED

2 TABLESPOONS FRESHLY CRACKED BLACK PEPPER

1 TABLESPOON SOY SAUCE

1 TABLESPOON WORCESTERSHIRE SAUCE

2 TEASPOONS SEA SALT

2 SKINLESS, BONELESS GOOSE BREASTS, SEPARATED INTO 4 HALVES (ABOUT 3 POUNDS)

CARAMELIZED ONION AND MUSTARD SAUCE (SEE PAGE 229) OR RED CURRANT SAUCE (SEE PAGE 246), FOR SERVING

IN A RESEALABLE PLASTIC BAG, COMBINE the olive oil, garlic, pepper, soy sauce, Worcestershire, and salt. Marinate the meat in the refrigerator for at least 2 hours and up to 24 hours.

To cook the goose, you can use either a charcoal grill or a pre-heated cast-iron skillet on the stove top. Whatever you use, the cooking process must be hot and fast. Preheat your grill or cast-iron skillet over high heat. Remove the goose from the refrigerator and cook the goose long enough to develop a good crust, no longer than 5 minutes per side for medium-rare (any temperature higher than that will dry out the meat). If you are using a cast-iron skillet, spoon a little of the marinade over the top of the goose. This will cause a flare-up; however, as I've subtly tried to suggest, you should not be afraid of a little flame. Flames help put a crust on the surface of the meat to add flavor and help retain moisture. Serve with the sauce of your choice.

ELK LOIN
WITH BÉARNAISE SAUCE

I HATE BEING COLD. WANDERING AROUND the woods in mid-winter is not my idea of a great way to spend time. Fortunately, I have friends who hunt elk, much to my benefit. One of my favorite game dishes is elk tenderloin that has been marinated and then cooked over a hot grill. Whether elk, beef, bison, venison, or any red meat, a tenderloin (also known as a backstrap) that has been cooked over a hot open fire to a crusty finish begs for a silky smooth sauce like béarnaise, choron, or other egg-based sauces to provide the perfect foil to the grilled meat.

SERVES 4 TO 5

1 CUP OLIVE OIL

1 TABLESPOON GRANULATED GARLIC

3 TABLESPOONS COARSELY GROUND FRESH BLACK PEPPER

2 TABLESPOONS COARSE SEA SALT, PLUS MORE FOR SEASONING

2 POUNDS ELK TENDERLOIN (ALSO KNOWN AS BACK-STRAP)

BÉARNAISE (SEE PAGE 227) OR CHORON (SEE PAGE 227), FOR SERVING

COMBINE THE OLIVE OIL, GARLIC, PEPPER, and salt in a large resealable plastic bag. Add the tenderloin and marinate in the refrigerator for at least 4 hours, but preferably for a day (no longer than 2 days).

Drain the meat, reserving the marinade. Preheat a grill to high heat. Just before you put the meat on the fire, sprinkle the outside with some coarse sea salt, adjusting seasoning to taste. Place the elk directly over the hot fire, close enough to the heat source to allow the marinade on the meat to burst into flame and sear the outside, turning as needed. When you have achieved an outside crust you can move the meat to a cooler spot on the grill to finish cooking, or partially douse the flames with water. The key here is a hot fire to sear and crust the outside of the meat to contain the juices that lie within. When dealing with a large piece of meat, it can be hard to determine the degree of doneness by just poking at it, so I recommend a good meat thermometer; aim for an internal temperature of 115°F. Remove from the fire and allow to rest for about 5 to 10 minutes. The finished meat should reach 120°F to 125°F, but no higher, before serving. Carve into 2-inch slices and serve over a béarnaise sauce or other sauce of your choice.

VENISON CHOPS WITH SAGE BUTTER

THIS IS A VARIATION OF A RECIPE FOR VEAL and lamb chops commonly associated with the cuisine of Milan, and it works very well with venison or antelope. Simplicity is the key. The chops are marinated for just a few minutes in olive oil and lemon. Have the chops cut about an inch thick with the bone attached, and then flatten them with a meat hammer or small sauté pan until they are about a ½-inch thick.

SERVES 4

- 8 (4-OUNCE) BONE-IN VENISON CHOPS
- ¾ CUP OLIVE OIL
- ¼ CUP FRESHLY SQUEEZED LEMON JUICE
- 1 CUP PLAIN BREADCRUMBS
- 1 CUP GRATED PARMESAN CHEESE
- 1 TABLESPOON FRESHLY GROUND BLACK PEPPER

SAGE BUTTER

- 1½ CUPS (3 STICKS) UNSALTED BUTTER, DIVIDED
- 10 FRESH SAGE LEAVES
- FRESHLY SQUEEZED JUICE FROM 1 SMALL LEMON (2 TEASPOONS)
- FINE SALT
- 4 LEMON WEDGES, FOR GARNISH

PLACE THE CHOPS BETWEEN TWO PIECES of plastic wrap and use a small heavy skillet or meat mallet to flatten the chops slightly to a thickness of about ½ inch. Marinate the chops for 30 minutes in the olive oil and lemon juice in a resealable plastic bag.

Stir the breadcrumbs, Parmesan, and pepper together in a shallow dish. Press the top side of each chop into the breadcrumb and cheese mixture firmly to ensure a good coating; only one side of the chop will be breaded.

Heat 2 sticks of the butter in a large sauté pan over medium-high heat. Gently sauté the chops in the butter, cooking the breaded side to a golden brown, then turn and cook the other side for about 30 seconds. (Do not overcook!) Put the cooked chops breaded side up in a low oven to keep warm until they are all finished.

Turn the heat to high and add the sage leaves and the rest of the butter. Add the lemon juice to the pan and cook until the butter has turned brown and is beginning to foam. Add salt to taste. Arrange the chops on a platter or individual plates, pour the sauce over the chops, garnish with lemon wedges, and serve.

NOTE: Sometimes I leave some of the sauce in the hot pan, add a tablespoon of freshly chopped garlic, a stick of extra butter, and ½ cup olive oil. When the mixture has browned, toss in some al dente penne pasta. Sauté the pasta until everything is hot and arrange alongside the chops. Garnish it with fresh sage leaves or chopped, fresh flat-leaf parsley.

SICILIAN-STYLE VENISON TENDERLOIN

THIS IS A VARIATION OF A BISON RECIPE that also appears in this book (see page 143) and was featured by my friend the late A.J. McLane in *Esquire's* "Man at His Best." This is a great way to do any red meat tenderloins: beef, antelope, and even pork or lamb. With venison, I have the best results when I make medallions out of the backstraps or tenderloins. The blend of sweet wine and tomatoes with the salty anchovies and capers evokes the taste of Sicily. Simple, fast, and great! It goes well with penne dressed with toasted garlic, red pepper flakes, and olive oil. Add a crispy green salad, some crusty bread, and a bottle of good Chianti or some other soft and fruity red wine.

SERVES 4

- 2 POUNDS VENISON FROM THE TENDERLOINS, OR BACKSTRAP SLICED INTO 1½-INCH-THICK PIECES
- 6 TABLESPOONS OLIVE OIL, DIVIDED
- 1 TABLESPOON FRESHLY CRACKED BLACK PEPPER
- 3 TABLESPOONS TOMATO PASTE
- 3 TABLESPOONS CAPERS, DRAINED
- 1 TABLESPOON CHOPPED ANCHOVIES OR ANCHOVY PASTE
- 1 CUP SWEET MARSALA

PAT THE VENISON DRY AND THEN TOSS IN 3 tablespoons of the olive oil and the black pepper and marinate for 1 hour.

Preheat a 10- to 12-inch sauté pan or cast-iron skillet over high heat and add the rest of the oil. When the oil is smoking add the venison and allow the hot oil to form a crust. Don't touch the meat for at least 4 minutes and when you turn it, slide a spatula under the meat to preserve the crust. Flip and cook for another 2 minutes on the other side until rare to medium-rare. Remove the meat from the pan and set it aside to keep warm. Add the tomato paste, capers, and anchovies to the pan and deglaze with the wine.

Stir and cook until the volume is reduced by half, about 3 to 5 minutes. Return the venison to the pan, spooning the reduced sauce over the meat. Cook until the meat is reheated and coated with the sauce, and then serve.

VENISON IRON-POT GOULASH

MY FAVORITE TIME OF YEAR IN MONTANA IS the first two weeks in October. Along the rivers, the cottonwoods are covered in leaves of reddish-gold, and the mountainsides are brilliant with the fluorescent yellow of aspen groves.

My friend Hans Dietrich, rabid hunter, retired chef, and definitely a world-class campfire cook, does a goulash for venison that really captures the flavor of fall in Montana. The last time we had it together was camping along the Madison River on a frosty Montana evening. Maybe it was the whiskey in tin cups, the murmur of the river, the smell of the fire, or a combination, but this fragrant and hearty stew gently simmering in an old iron pot along with the glorious setting made me feel, at least there, and at that time, that all was right in the world.

Even if you can't replicate the setting, or the cast-iron pot sitting on the campfire, this is still a great lean and hearty dish. Serve it with a crisp salad, some crusty sourdough bread, and a fruity Pinot Noir.

SERVES 6

- ³/₄ CUP OLIVE OR CANOLA OIL
- 4 POUNDS VENISON, ELK, OR BEEF, CUT IN 1¹/₂-INCH CUBES
- ²/₃ CUP ALL-PURPOSE FLOUR
- 3 BAY LEAVES
- 5 TABLESPOONS GRANULATED GARLIC
- 5 TABLESPOONS DRIED THYME
- 3 TABLESPOONS DRIED OREGANO
- ¹/₂ CUP SWEET PAPRIKA
- 3 TABLESPOONS CARAWAY SEEDS
- 1 TEASPOON CAYENNE PEPPER
- 3 TABLESPOONS GOOD-QUALITY BEEF BASE
- 4 LARGE YELLOW ONIONS, COARSELY CHOPPED
- 3 GREEN BELL PEPPERS, COARSELY CHOPPED
- 3 RED BELL PEPPERS, COARSELY CHOPPED
- 3 LARGE RUSSET POTATOES, CUT IN 1¹/₂-INCH CUBES
- KOSHER SALT AND FRESHLY GROUND BLACK PEPPER
- 1 POUND EGG NOODLES, COOKED AL DENTE ACCORDING TO PACKAGE DIRECTIONS

IN A LARGE HEAVY POT HEAT THE OIL TO smoking over high heat. Add the cubed venison and sear on all sides until it begins to brown. Add the flour and stir, being careful not to let it burn, about 5 minutes. When a roux has formed and turned golden-brown, add the bay leaves, garlic, thyme, oregano, paprika, caraway seeds, cayenne, beef base, and 1 quart of water. Bring to a boil, reduce the heat to medium, and simmer for 1 hour, or until the meat is just becoming tender.

Add the onions, peppers, and potatoes to the pot and simmer for another hour uncovered, or until the vegetables are tender. If the mixture becomes too thick, simply add more water. Season with salt and pepper to taste. When you are ready to serve, ladle the hot goulash over the warm egg noodles in warm bowls. Like most comfort foods this dish gets better with age, so don't be afraid of leftovers.

LBJ'S NO-FAT VENISON CHILI

MY SISTER CHRISTY WORKED IN THE CAPITOL
Hill office of a Democratic senator when Lyndon Baines Johnson was president. She got this recipe from one of the White House cooks who used to go down to LBJ's ranch on the Pedernales River in Texas Hill Country when it was used as his summer residence.

He claimed to have cooked thousands of gallons of this presidential concoction and served it to many a world leader and their minions. Lyndon's doctor had put him on a low-fat diet after a serious heart attack and venison chili was a big part of his new diet. Rumor has it that the main ingredient for this dish, Texas whitetail deer, were laid low by the presidential rifle, shot from the back seat of a 1962 Cadillac convertible.

You can serve with cooked pinto beans, chopped raw onions, shredded Cheddar, cilantro, or whatever extras you might have around.

SERVES 10

- 5 POUNDS GROUND VENISON OR OTHER RED GAME MEAT (SUBSTITUTE VERY LEAN TRIMMED CHUCK), COARSELY GROUND
- 3 LARGE YELLOW ONIONS, CHOPPED
- 10 GARLIC CLOVES, CHOPPED
- 2 TABLESPOONS DRIED OREGANO
- 2 TABLESPOONS GROUND CUMIN
- 5 TABLESPOONS CHILI POWDER
- 1 (28-OUNCE) CAN DICED OR CRUSHED TOMATOES
- HOT SAUCE
- CAYENNE PEPPER
- FINE SALT

HEAT A LARGE DUTCH OVEN OR HEAVY deep skillet over high heat and combine the meat, onions, and garlic in the pan. Cook until the meat has browned and the vegetables are wilted, about 8 minutes. Stir in the oregano, cumin, chili powder, and tomatoes, bring to a boil, then reduce the heat and simmer for at least an hour, stirring occasionally. Add hot sauce, cayenne, and salt if preferred, and adjust seasoning to taste. Refrigerate the chili overnight.

The next day, skim off any congealed fat. Bring the chili to a boil, and it's ready to serve.

VENISON SAUERBRATEN

IT SEEMS AS THOUGH NOBODY LOVES HUNTING as much as the Germans, and my friend Hans personifies this passion. When he comes to Montana during hunting season, he can barely contain himself as we drive down back roads scouting for herds of deer grazing in the hayfields. He dreams of the perfect buck; I dream of the sauerbraten he's going to cook when the hunt is over.

Hans likes to cut up his venison in the European style, boneless and seamed, which means that the shape and size of each piece is defined by the location of muscles and sinews. The typical Montana game processor we take our meats to tends to use meat saws to cut through bones and across the grain. The European method, on the other hand, results in cuts that are not only more versatile but are better-tasting because by removing the bones whole, you avoid having any bone residue left behind, which can impart a bitter and gamy flavor to the meat.

The best cuts for sauerbraten are the large rounds and sirloins from the rear legs, or even a whole leg. Larger cuts lend themselves better to the long braising process. This recipe works equally as well with elk, bison, or moose.

The marinating process should be at least 5 days and I usually like to do it for a week. Believe me, this is the ultimate winter dinner. It should be accompanied with sweet red cabbage, and the traditional side dish of spaetzle or potato dumplings. When I don't want to go to all that trouble, simple egg noodles work just fine.

SERVES 6 TO 8

MARINADE
2 CUPS RED WINE VINEGAR

2 CUPS RED WINE

10 WHOLE GARLIC CLOVES

10 JUNIPER BERRIES (SUBSTITUTE 1 CUP GOOD-QUALITY GIN)

5 BAY LEAVES

1 LARGE CARROT, SLICED

2 LARGE YELLOW ONIONS, SLICED

3 TABLESPOONS FRESHLY CRACKED BLACK PEPPER

1/2 CUP PACKED DARK BROWN SUGAR

2 TABLESPOONS KOSHER SALT

5 TO 6 POUNDS VENISON ROUND ROAST

SAUERBRATEN
1/2 CUP CANOLA OR VEGETABLE OIL, OR MORE IF NECESSARY, DIVIDED

1 LARGE YELLOW ONION, FINELY CHOPPED

2 LARGE CARROTS, FINELY CHOPPED

2 STALKS CELERY, FINELY CHOPPED

3 TABLESPOONS ALL-PURPOSE FLOUR

FINISHING SAUCE
4 TO 6 GINGERSNAPS, PULVERIZED TO CRUMBS IN A FOOD PROCESSOR

FINE SALT AND FRESHLY GROUND BLACK PEPPER

IN A POT, COMBINE THE VINEGAR, WINE, garlic, juniper berries, bay leaves, carrot, onion, pepper, sugar, salt, and 1 cup of water and bring the marinade to a boil. Stir to dissolve the sugar, then remove from the heat and allow it to cool to room temperature. In a nonreactive bowl or a large resealable plastic bag, place the meat in the marinade and allow it to marinate, covered, in the refrigerator for 5 to 7 days. If the meat isn't completely submerged in the liquid, turn it occasionally.

Remove the meat from the marinade (reserving marinade) and dry the outside with paper towels. Preheat a few tablespoons of the oil in a large Dutch oven over high heat. When the oil is very hot, sear the outside of the meat on all sides to get a good crust. Set the meat aside and sauté the onion, carrots, and celery until they are slightly browned, about 5 minutes, then add the flour. Stir the flour into the vegetables and cook it until it has colored and smells nutty, about 4 minutes; be careful not to let the flour burn. (If you burn the flour, just start over with more vegetables as burned flour will impart a bitter taste that cannot be eliminated.) Add 3 cups of the reserved marinade and a cup of water to the mixture. Stir to get all of the cooked bits off the bottom of the pot and return the meat to the pot. The liquid should come three-quarters of the way up the sides of the venison. If it doesn't, add a little more water.

Bring the pot to a boil over medium-high heat, reduce to a slow simmer, then cover and cook for at least two hours. Check occasionally; when done, the meat should be fork-tender. When ready to serve, carefully lift the meat out of the pot to a serving platter, cover, and keep warm in a low oven.

To finish with the sauce, add all of the remaining marinade to the pot and mix it well. Cook over high heat to reduce, and stir when needed to keep it from burning on the bottom. Sometimes, I like to strain the vegetables out of the remaining liquid at this point, although I sometimes choose to puree everything in a blender or with an immersion blender for a thicker gravy (fish out the juniper berries and bay leaves first, and discard). Return the resulting liquid to the pot and stir in the gingersnap crumbs. If the sauce is too thick, thin out with some water. Add salt and pepper, adjusting seasoning to taste. Cut the meat into $1/4$-inch thick slices, across the grain, and serve on warm plates with a generous amount of sauce.

POACHER'S DEER LEG

I DON'T WANT TO SUGGEST THAT I AM ENCOUR- aging the illegal harvesting of wild game. Lots of Montana families, however, depend on deer, elk, and, to a lesser degree, moose and other large mammals, to provide a large percentage of the meat in their diets. Game is cheap, it's there, and it can be really good, if prepared right.

My friend Rod Zullo came up with the title and recipe for this dish. Rod is a great cook who also happens to be a nationally renowned artist and sculptor. He lives in Bozeman, but in the fall and early winter, he holes up in a log cabin in the middle of a big ranch north of Big Timber, doing what he loves to do: hunting birds and stalking big mule deer. Rod and his friends consequently eat a lot of those big deer, and he prepares them in a number of different ways, the most popular being his poacher's deer leg over charcoal. The first time I had it, I thought it was one of the best wild game preparations I had ever eaten. I was, however, curious about the origin of the name of this recipe.

Rod explains it this way: Poachers will typically shoot a deer, usually at night, and very quickly field dress it as quick as possible. They cut off all four legs, leaving the skin on, cut out the backstraps, (the loins), and boogie on out of the scene of the crime. Thus the name, Poacher's Deer Leg, came about because Rod likes to retain the hoof (with about 6 inches of the hide left on) to use as a handle to turn the fairly heavy leg on the grill, without the need of tools. When you think about it, it makes a lot of sense.

SERVES 8 TO 10

HIND QUARTER OF A DEER, ABOUT 10 POUNDS (YIELDS ABOUT 5 POUNDS OF MEAT)

DRY RUB
1 CUP KOSHER SALT

1/2 CUP PACKED LIGHT BROWN SUGAR

1/4 CUP GRANULATED GARLIC

1/4 CUP ONION POWDER

1 CUP SMOKED OR REGULAR PAPRIKA

WET RUB
10 TO 12 GARLIC CLOVES

1 CUP OLIVE OIL

4 CUPS CHOPPED FRESH ROSEMARY

REMOVE THE SKIN OF THE HIND LEG, WITH the exception of the last six inches of hide, leaving the hoof intact. Carefully wash down the leg, removing any blood, hair, and dirt, then dry. Mix together the salt, sugar, garlic, onion powder, and paprika and apply to the meat. Leave it to rest, covered, in the refrigerator for 24 hours.

With a small sharp knife, cut slits all over the leg and insert the garlic cloves. Mix the olive oil and rosemary together to make a paste, then cover the leg with the paste. Let the leg sit for 2 to 3 hours at room temperature before grilling.

Preheat a charcoal or gas grill on high heat. Sear the leg for about 12 minutes per side to seal in the moisture. Use the hoof as a handle to rotate the meat. There is very little fat in venison, so anything you can do to preserve moisture is important.

After searing, reduce the heat to very low (moving the leg to cook over indirect heat if using a charcoal grill) and continue cooking for 2 to 3 hours, until the internal temperature hits 125°F. Let rest for about 10 minutes, then carve and serve.

JEWISH-STYLE ELK BRISKET

ONE OF THE GREAT DISHES OF AMERICAN Jewish cuisine is beef brisket. It's also a great way to do an elk or moose brisket as well. It's the kind of dish that's great to do ahead and it never lets you down. Everyone I know loves tender and juicy slices of slow-cooked red meat smothered in onion gravy. Served with oven-roasted or mashed potatoes, or Potato Dumplings (see page 209), it's always a hit, especially in the winter when the wind coming off the Montana high line up north howls against the windows and threatens to drive snow under the door.

SERVES 4 TO 6

- 1 (4- TO 6-POUND) WHOLE ELK, MOOSE, VENISON, OR BEEF BRISKET, WELL-TRIMMED OF OUTER MEMBRANE (SILVER-SKIN) AND FAT
- ½ CUP CANOLA OR VEGETABLE OIL, DIVIDED
- 4 YELLOW ONIONS, THINLY SLICED
- 10 GARLIC CLOVES
- 2 BAY LEAVES
- 1 TEASPOON SEA SALT
- 1 TABLESPOON FRESHLY GROUND BLACK PEPPER
- 3 TABLESPOONS UNSALTED BUTTER
- 3 TABLESPOONS ALL-PURPOSE FLOUR
- 6 CUPS BEEF STOCK (SUBSTITUTE 3 TABLESPOONS GOOD-QUALITY BEEF BASE PLUS 3 CUPS WATER)

PREHEAT THE OVEN TO 300 F.

For the brisket, heat half of the oil in a braising pan or Dutch oven over high heat. Sear all sides of the meat. When it is well browned, remove the elk and set aside. Add the remaining oil to the hot pan, then the onions, garlic, and bay leaves. Cook for around 5 to 7 minutes until the onions begin to brown, then add the salt and pepper. Turn the heat down to medium and stir in the butter. When it has melted, stir in the flour and cook for an additional 5 minutes to create a roux, stirring constantly. At this point add the beef stock, scraping the brown bits from the bottom of the pan to enrich the braising liquid. Add the brisket to the liquid, cover, and braise in the oven for 2 to 3 hours until the brisket is fork-tender. Check every hour to see if more liquid is needed. During the last half hour of cooking, remove the lid to allow some reduction and thickening of the braising liquid.

Remove the brisket from the Dutch oven and set aside, covered. If you'd like the remaining sauce to be thicker, move it to the stovetop and simmer over high heat to reduce to your liking. If it gets too thick, add a little water to thin out. Return the brisket to the pot and coat with sauce. Serve hot.

CHICKEN

THE VERSATILE BIRD

THE FIRST KNOWN RECORD OF DOMESTIC CHICKENS IN MONTANA WAS WHEN FATHER PIERRE DeSmet founded a mission and settlement among the Salish (Flathead) Indians that later became known as St. Mary's, near the shores of Flathead Lake in western Montana in 1841. That first year he brought in wheat, potatoes, and oats, and by the following year he was able to bring in cattle, pigs, and chickens.

There were a lot of firsts in the tiny settlement, including agriculture, irrigation, and a gristmill used to grind the newly raised grain, but the when the mission began to encounter hard times and the number of converts dwindled, the whole site was purchased by an ex-army officer named John Owen who changed the name to Ft. Owen. The church remains on the site and is a popular tourist destination. Whatever the outcome of the settlement, the chickens remained and flourished, and as a result, many of the chickens raised in Montana today can probably trace their lineage to those hearty forebears. When you think of all of those wagon trains coming west during that period and later, there were a lot of chickens in those wagons.

As far as my own relationship with this venerable bird, I love chicken and when it's done correctly there is nothing better. When I go to a restaurant the first thing I look at on the menu is chicken (provided it is not the ubiquitous boneless, or even worse, skinless, breast that has no flavor or texture). To me the best way to judge a restaurant is by the way they do chicken; it is the best test of a competent cook.

Feeding the Chickens, Eastern Montana, ca. 1922

ARGENTINE GRILLED CHICKEN THIGHS WITH HONEY

I HAVE REFERRED ELSEWHERE TO THE PLANCHA, a cast-iron plate used in traditional Argentine cooking over open wood fires. You can achieve the same result over a gas grill or even your kitchen gas stove if you have the proper ventilation. The plancha can be as simple as a steel plate. Different models have a smooth or ridged surface; generally I use the smooth side in most of my cooking.

This is a great basic recipe that works well with chicken but also for pork chops. (I like to brine chicken and pork because the salt and water cause a chemical reaction that keeps moisture in the meat, (especially when grilling). Serve with smashed potatoes (page 216), or better yet, black beans and rice (see page 188).

SERVES 4

$^1/_2$ CUP KOSHER SALT

6 TO 8 BONELESS, SKINLESS CHICKEN THIGHS

MARINADE

$1^1/_2$ CUPS OLIVE OIL

4 TABLESPOONS CHOPPED FRESH ROSEMARY

4 FRESH GARLIC CLOVES, MINCED

2 TABLESPOONS FRESHLY SQUEEZED LEMON JUICE

KOSHER SALT AND FRESHLY CRACKED BLACK PEPPER

$^1/_2$ CUP WARM HONEY

MIX THE SALT WITH 2 QUARTS OF COLD water until it has dissolved. Put the chicken and the brine in large resealable plastic bags for 2 hours. Drain the chicken, pat dry, and with a meat hammer or small sauté pan, flatten the chicken to an even thickness.

Combine the olive oil, rosemary, garlic, lemon juice, sugar, and salt and pepper in a large bowl. Adjust the amount of salt and pepper to taste. Toss the chicken and marinate in the refrigerator for 2 to 3 hours.

Preheat a cast-iron grill pan over high heat, preferably on a grill directly over the flames.

Spoon some of the marinade on top of each chicken thigh and then lay the chicken, on the hot grill pan. Cook for 5 to 7 minutes to allow a crust to form, but do not let the garlic in the marinade burn. If it looks like it is burning, flip it quickly. Cook the other side for another 5 minutes. (If the chicken needs to cook further, finish it in a preheated 350°F oven: it should be 160°F inside, with the juices running clear.)

Remove the chicken thighs from the pan, drizzle the warm honey over them, and serve hot.

GRILLED CORIANDER CHICKEN BREASTS

WE ARE USED TO THE TASTE OF CILANTRO (also called coriander) in Mexican food, where the leaves are often used to season and garnish a multitude of dishes, but coriander seeds can be ground to produce a pungent and wonderful flavor as well. Here is a simple grilled chicken breast recipe that can be served as a sandwich on toasted pita bread, or as an entrée with stir-fried vegetables and basmati rice. If I am doing these as an entrée I like to use our Curry Butter for finishing (see page 235) to add an extra kick.

You can cook the chicken skinless or with the skin on; I prefer the skin intact. When you are flattening the meat, do so carefully, under plastic wrap, with the skin-side down.

SERVES 4

4 BONELESS CHICKEN BREASTS

MARINADE

1 CUP OLIVE OIL

1 YELLOW ONION, FINELY DICED

1 TABLESPOON SMOKED PAPRIKA

1 TABLESPOON GROUND CORIANDER SEED

1 TABLESPOON GRANULATED GARLIC

1 TABLESPOON FRESHLY GROUND BLACK PEPPER

1 TEASPOON FINE SALT

PLACE EACH CHICKEN BREAST BETWEEN sheets of plastic wrap, skin-side down. Use a heavy meat mallet or small skillet to flatten the chicken breasts to about $3/4$-inch thick.

Combine the olive oil, onion, paprika, coriander, garlic, pepper, and salt, and then pour over the chicken in a resealable plastic bag. Marinate in the refrigerator for 4 hours.

Preheat your grill pan and gas or charcoal grill to medium heat. (If you don't have a grill pan, just grill directly over the flames.) Remove the chicken from the marinade and place skin-side down on the grill. Cook for 4 minutes on each side. The skin should be crisp and the meat thoroughly cooked.

GRILLED JERKED CHICKEN

HERE IS A SPICY, LOW-FAT SUMMER APPETIZER or main course of Jamaican-style jerked, marinated, boneless chicken breasts on skewers. If you opt to go with wooden skewers, remember to soak them for at least an hour before using. I serve this as an appetizer at The Mint, but you can serve it over rice with grilled vegetables as a main course. By the way, this jerk spice recipe goes well with pork, beef, or fish.

SERVES 4

4 BONELESS, SKINLESS CHICKEN BREASTS

JERK SPICE MIX
2 TABLESPOONS GROUND GINGER

2 TABLESPOONS PAPRIKA

1 TABLESPOON GRANULATED GARLIC

1/2 TEASPOON CAYENNE PEPPER

1/2 TEASPOON FRESHLY GROUND BLACK PEPPER

1 TEASPOON GROUND ALLSPICE

1 TEASPOON GROUND NUTMEG

2 TABLESPOONS PACKED DARK BROWN SUGAR

1 TEASPOON FINE SALT

MARINADE
1/2 CUP OLIVE OIL

1/2 CUP SOY SAUCE

CUT THE CHICKEN BREASTS INTO STRIPS about 1/2-inch thick and 3 inches long.

Stir together the ginger, paprika, garlic, cayenne, black pepper, allspice, nutmeg, sugar, and salt. Measure out 3 tablespoons for the marinade, and reserve the remainder for another use.

Combine 3 tablespoons of the jerk spice mix, the olive oil, and the soy sauce in a resealable plastic bag with the chicken. Marinate in the refrigerator for at least 3 to 4 hours or overnight.

Preheat a gas or charcoal grill on high heat with a cast-iron grill pan directly over the flames, if using.

Drain the marinade from the chicken. Thread chicken onto skewers and cook directly over the hot fire for 8 to 10 minutes, turning occasionally until done in the middle. If you skip the skewers, remember to turn the chicken with tongs as it cooks. Serve right away.

GREEK-STYLE ROAST CHICKEN

THERE HAS NEVER, TO MY KNOWLEDGE, BEEN a large Greek population in Montana, but the guy living next door to The Mint is a one-man cultural phenomenon. His name is Kostas Lazarides. He immigrated to the U.S. as a kid, learned English by listening to country music on the radio, and grew to be one of the most successful writers/composers of country songs in history. He's as beloved in Nashville as he is treasured in Montana. Occasionally, he brings his guitar into The Mint, treating appreciative guests with renditions of his greatest hits. He also brings with him a love of Greek food, and has handed over one of his favorite recipes.

SERVES 3 TO 4

1 (4-TO 5-POUND) ROASTING CHICKEN, RINSED AND DRIED

1/2 CUP OLIVE OIL, DIVIDED

1 CUP FRESH OREGANO, COARSELY CHOPPED, OR 1/4 CUP DRIED CRUMBLED OREGANO LEAVES, DIVIDED

FRESHLY SQUEEZED JUICE OF 2 LEMONS, DIVIDED, RINDS RESERVED

FINE SALT AND FRESHLY GROUND BLACK PEPPER

4 MEDIUM RUSSET POTATOES, CUT INTO 1 1/2-INCH CUBES

1/2 CUP CHOPPED FRESH FLAT-LEAF PARSLEY

PREHEAT THE OVEN TO 350°F.

Rub the chicken down with 2 tablespoons of the olive oil and sprinkle with half of the oregano and half of the lemon juice. Salt and pepper the bird, adjusting seasoning to taste. Stuff the cavity with juiced lemon rind for extra flavor. In a large bowl, toss the potatoes with salt and pepper, adjusting seasoning to taste, plus the remaining 6 tablespoons of olive oil, coating them thoroughly. Spread them in a roasting pan and place the chicken directly over the potatoes so the fat will drip over them during cooking.

Cover the pan with foil and cook for around 30 minutes.

To brown the skin, turn the oven to 425°F, remove the foil, and cook uncovered for an additional 20 minutes, or until the chicken and potatoes have become crispy and browned. The internal temperature of the chicken should read 160°F. Tent it with foil and let it rest for 10 minutes before serving.

Carve the chicken and arrange the pieces along with the potatoes on a serving platter. Add the rest of oregano and the lemon juice to the pan juices, stirring with a whisk to get the browned bits on the bottom, and then pour the pan juices over the chicken. Sprinkle the fresh parsley over the chicken and serve.

CAST-IRON ROASTED HALF CHICKEN

ONE OF THE REASONS THAT BONE-IN ROAST chicken isn't seen on many restaurant menus is that it takes a lot of time to prepare. Some try to speed the process by partially roasting a chicken and then setting it aside to finish when it is ordered. That generally results in a dry, tasteless bird fit neither for man nor beast.

I awakened one morning with a heavy snow falling and not much to think about except solving the roast chicken riddle. It was then that I came up with the idea of putting half of a marinated chicken between two preheated cast-iron skillets to see if cooking it from both sides at once to order would produce a fresh-tasting, juicy, and more flavorful bird with a crispy skin. It does.

If you don't have a couple of 10-inch cast-iron skillets in your kitchen, for this dish, it's worth the expense to go out and buy them.

SERVES 2

- ½ CUP KOSHER SALT
- 1 (4 TO 5) POUND ROASTING CHICKEN, SPLIT IN HALF
- 3 TABLESPOONS FRESH ROSEMARY LEAVES, PLUS 1 WHOLE SPRIG
- 1 CUP OLIVE OIL
- FRESHLY SQUEEZED JUICE FROM 1 LEMON, PLUS ADDITIONAL WEDGES FOR GARNISH
- FINE SALT AND FRESHLY GROUND BLACK PEPPER

Dissolve the salt in a gallon of water. Pour over the chicken and brine for at least 3 or up to 24 hours in the refrigerator. Remove it from the water and pat dry.

Combine the rosemary leaves, olive oil, lemon juice, and salt and pepper (adjust seasonings to taste) and thoroughly coat the two chicken halves with the mixture. Allow the chicken to rest for 2 hours at room temperature to absorb the flavors.

At least 30 minutes before cooking, place two 10-inch, seasoned cast-iron skillets in the oven set at 450°F.

When you are ready to begin roasting, carefully place both halves skin-side down, in one of the preheated cast-iron skillets, and place the other skillet on top (right-side up). Return to the hot oven and roast the halves for about 25 minutes or until the internal temperature of the thigh reaches 160°F. The time may vary with the size of the bird, the altitude, or the weather, but 25 to 30 minutes should work.

When the bird is done, very carefully slide a metal spatula under each half and then carefully flip it to be skin-side up on the plate. The skin should be crispy and intact. Pour the pan juices over the bird and garnish with additional lemon wedges and a fresh rosemary sprig.

HERB-ROASTED CHICKEN WITH YAMS, POTATOES, AND KALAMATA OLIVES

SOMETIMES THERE IS NOTHING MORE SATIS- fying than a simple roast chicken: juicy and delicious, the skin crackling with herbs. When you throw a medley of yams and Idaho russets into the mix, you have captured the very essence of comfort food. This is the way I like to do chicken at home.

I find the most efficient and flavorful way to cook this chicken is to roast everything at the same time. The potatoes act as a roasting rack for the chicken, which not only helps the chicken to cook more evenly but bathes the potatoes in juices and fat from the chicken.

My herb of choice is usually fresh rosemary, but thyme or even fresh sage is a good variation.

SERVES 3 TO 4

¹/₂ CUP KOSHER SALT

1 (4- TO 5-POUND) ROASTING CHICKEN

4 BRANCHES FRESH ROSEMARY

FINE SALT AND FRESHLY GROUND BLACK PEPPER

¹/₂ CUP OLIVE OIL, DIVIDED

1 WHOLE GARLIC BULB, PLUS 1 BULB SEPARATED INTO CLOVES, PEELED AND DIVIDED

3 YAMS OR SWEET POTATOES, PEELED AND CUT INTO 2-INCH CUBES

3 RUSSET POTATOES, PEELED AND CUT INTO 2-INCH CUBES

2 CUPS PITTED WHOLE KALA-MATA OLIVES (OPTIONAL)

1 RECIPE COMPOUND BUTTER, CUT INTO DISCS (SEE PAGE 234)

¹/₂ CUP DRY WHITE WINE

DISSOLVE THE SALT IN A GALLON OF COLD water. Brine the chicken in the salted water for 3 to 4 hours in the refrigerator, then drain and pat dry.

Preheat the oven to 375°F.

Strip the leaves from two of the rosemary branches, leaving the other two intact. Place one branch in the cavity along with a good amount of salt and pepper and the whole bulb of garlic. Rub some of the olive oil on the outside of the chicken then sprinkle on half of the rosemary leaves, salt, and pepper. Set aside.

In a large bowl, toss the garlic cloves, yams, potatoes, and olives (if using). Add the remaining olive oil and toss well, coating everything. Place the potato mixture on the bottom of a large roasting pan. Sprinkle with the remaining rosemary leaves and add salt and pepper.

Slide discs of cold butter under the skin of the chicken on both sides of the breast and under the skin of each thigh.

Place the chicken on the potatoes and bake for 1 hour and 45 minutes, until the skin is browned and crisp and the thigh separates easily from the bird; the internal temperature of the thigh will read 155°F. Remove from the oven and cover with a piece of foil. Allow it to rest for 5 to 10 minutes. Carve the chicken into serving portions and put on a warm platter, then arrange the potatoes, yams and olives around it on the platter. Drain some of the fat from the roasting pan (leaving about 2 tablespoons) then, using a spatula, scrape all of the goodies off the bottom of the pan. Set the pan over two burners, add the wine, and bring to a quick simmer. Pour over the chicken and serve.

MOSCA'S CHICKEN Á LA GRANDE

EVERY DECEMBER, WHEN I MAKE MY ANNUAL pilgrimage from Montana to New Orleans to visit my brother Tony, I take the opportunity to revisit my favorite restaurants and catch up on the latest chefs and emerging restaurants.

There are all kinds of stories about Johnny Mosca's, located in a down-at-the-heels, masonite-sided building that looks as if it was moved from a World War II-era subdivision and plunked down in the middle of a swampy section of town near Highway 90, across the river from New Orleans. They opened the restaurant in 1946 and it quickly became the destination of choice for the more notorious members of the New Orleans Italian community, who flocked to the joint to eat crab pasta, baked oysters, and Italian Creole food. There is an urban legend that the swamps and woods surrounding Mosca's became a veritable dumping ground for the various crime families that called the Crescent City home. This may or may not be the case, but all I can say is that if Mosca's Chicken á la Grande were my last meal on earth, I would enjoy the perfect sendoff.

They have a recipe posted on their website, but I think they left out some of the ingredients. Here is my take on this classic. Serve hot over rice pilaf (see page 187), polenta (see page 217) or grits (see page 218).

SERVES 3 TO 4

HOT SAUCE

1 LARGE (4- TO 5-POUND) FRYER CHICKEN, CUT INTO 8 PIECES

2 TABLESPOONS GRANULATED GARLIC

1½ TEASPOONS SMOKED OR HUNGARIAN PAPRIKA

2 TABLESPOONS COARSE SALT

2 TABLESPOONS FRESHLY CRACKED BLACK PEPPER

½ CUP OLIVE OIL, AS NEEDED

3 TABLESPOONS UNSALTED BUTTER

½ CUP CHOPPED FRESH OREGANO

½ CUP CHOPPED FRESH ROSEMARY

12 TO 15 SMALL GARLIC CLOVES, PEELED

½ CUP WHITE WINE

1 CUP CHICKEN STOCK (SUBSTITUTE 1 TEASPOON GOOD-QUALITY CHICKEN BASE PLUS 1 CUP WATER)

RUB A LITTLE HOT SAUCE ON EACH PIECE of chicken. Combine the garlic, paprika and salt, and pepper in a small bowl and then sprinkle over the chicken on all sides, coating it lightly. I usually do this an hour or so ahead and let the chicken sit uncovered at room temperature.

Preheat your oven to 350°F.

Add half of the olive oil and the butter to a large ovenproof skillet and heat over medium-high heat. Cook each piece of chicken in the pan until evenly browned, in batches if needed.

Remove the chicken from the pan, pour off half the remaining fat, and add the fresh oregano, rosemary, and garlic cloves to the pan and sauté for 1 minute. (The oil will pop and sizzle when you add the herbs, so keep at an arm's length.) Add the wine and stock to the pan and stir, scraping the bottom. Arrange the chicken in the sauce and bake covered for 30 minutes.

Raise the oven temperature to 400°F, uncover, and cook for another 10 minutes, or until tender.

SHEEPHERDER-STYLE SMASHED GARLIC CHICKEN

MONTANA USED TO HOST THOUSANDS OF sheep and Basque sheepherders who, in their own ways, played just as big a role in the history of this state as their more famous counterparts, the working cowboys. Most of them kept chickens for themselves because the lambs were too expensive to eat.

There are a number of cuisines—principally Spanish, Basque, and Portuguese—that offer variations on this recipe. If you like garlic, I mean, really like garlic, then this recipe is for you. Try and preserve the skin, as it is an important part of this dish. Do not try to cook the pieces of chicken in anything but a seasoned, cast-iron skillet or a non-stick pan, otherwise the skin will stick and you will lose the essence of this dish, which is the crisp garlic-infused skin.

Usually I will serve the chicken over a bed of herbed rice pilaf (see page 187) with some of the resulting garlicky olive oil or a batch of crispy fresh-cut fries (see page 207) together with the toasted garlic used in the cooking.

SERVES 4

6 TO 8 BONELESS CHICKEN THIGHS

SEA SALT

³/₄ CUP OLIVE OIL OR CLARIFIED BUTTER (SEE PAGE 236)

20 GARLIC CLOVES, SMASHED

1 TABLESPOON RED PEPPER FLAKES

SEASON THE CHICKEN WELL WITH SALT. In a 12- to 14-inch cast-iron skillet or nonstick sauté pan, preheat the oil over medium-high heat. Slowly add the chicken. A splatter screen would probably be a good idea as there will be a lively interaction between the moist chicken skin and hot oil. (Whether you use olive oil or butter is a personal choice. Olive oil is healthier, and offers a more authentic taste, but butter can brown the chicken faster, making for a juicier result.) Turn each piece as needed to brown evenly, about 10 minutes or until the chicken is golden, then add the garlic and red pepper flakes mixing them in among the chicken pieces.

Continue to cook the chicken for about 5 to 7 more minutes or until the garlic has browned, but not burned. The juices from the chicken should run clear. Add salt, adjusting seasoning to taste, then remove the chicken from the pan and serve immediately, spooning some olive oil, garlic, and pepper flakes over each portion. Pop the garlic cloves out of the skin and eat them whole. The cooking will have mellowed them and made them soft.

SIDE DISHES

IN THE CLASSIC TRADITION OF THE OLD WESTERN FLICKS OF THE THIRTIES, FORTIES, and fifties, all the good-guy cowboys had their "sidekicks." These stars of the black-and-white screen were uniformly handsome, purposeful guys who rode tall in the saddle and fought for truth and justice but they never rode alone.

Consider Roy Rogers and Gabby Hayes or The Lone Ranger and Tonto. How about Gene Autry and Pat Butrum or the Cisco Kid and Pancho? The typical sidekick was almost always goofy, some of them were overweight buffoons, others grizzled old codgers with an attitude. But their roles served to give the stars an opportunity to shine.

This is kind of a roundabout way for me to lead the chapter of side dishes and how they can add to and enhance the main dish of any meal. How about roast beef and mashed potatoes or black beans and rice? It's hard to think of one without the other. Don't be afraid to experiment and try different combinations. Frankly some of these side dishes shine on their own, so have at it. They will outfit a fancy table or be right at home at the humblest campfire meal.

CHUCK-WAGON CUISINE

AFTER THE CIVIL WAR, CATTLEMEN SEARCHING FOR NEW AND UNTAPPED SOURCES OF GRASS
realized that the last remaining frontier was the northern Great Plains. The era of the great cattle drives began when Texas ranchers began moving huge herds to the untouched prairies of eastern Montana and Wyoming. Here the grass seemed endless and rangeland was free for the taking. This great wave of cattle soon overwhelmed the feeding grounds of the remaining herds of bison and the home of the Native Americans who had coexisted with them over the eons. It only took twenty years to settle the range, and the development of the barbed wire fence put an end to a way of the open range.

The story of the drives is immortalized in literature, music, and movies with tales of dirty, dangerous work, with the trails littered with bleached remains of Texas longhorns and the lonely, windblown graves of unfortunate drovers.

What the movies don't tell you is, next to the trail boss, the cook was probably the most important member of the crew. The few moments of leisure were usually spent around the chuck wagon. It was the social center of the crew and the cook was the ringmaster. With drives lasting several months, and with virtually no other diversions other than gambling around the fire (if you could stay awake) and the occasional spree in a nearby town, the quality and quantity of the food became the central focus of daily life on the trail. Good food and some variety were essential to maintain good morale among the trail hands.

The cook had his work cut out for him, and, by necessity, he became the master of improvisation. Surrounded by hundreds of heads of cattle too valuable to butcher (unless one broke a leg) the chuck wagon chef had to make do with whatever game and other edibles he could scrounge from the surrounding countryside. Other than the basics of flour, coffee, salt, beans, and sugar, the cook was left to his own foraging abilities. A cook who could locate wild varieties of onion, garlic, peppers, and oregano as well as other indigenous flora and fauna was as revered as any trail boss. On the other hand, a consistently bad cook was no less a scourge than a string of dry water holes or run of bad weather.

Roundup Chuck Wagon, Colorado, ca. 1910

TOASTED GARLIC BREAD WITH A PARMESAN-CHEESE CRUST

OKAY, SO GARLIC BREAD ISN'T A "NATIVE" Montanan dish, but I guarantee that nothing in the world better accompanies a moose or bison stew. It's so simple and so good that it will become one of your standbys.

Any loaf of plain white, run-of-the-mill French bread works great. My dirty secret is that for this recipe, I prefer canned, ground Parmesan from the shelf, not the expensive fresh Parmesan. The cheap stuff forms a better crust.

SERVES 4

1 LOAF FRENCH BREAD

1/2 CUP (1 STICK) SALTED BUTTER

1/2 CUP OLIVE OIL

4 GARLIC CLOVES, PEELED AND SMASHED

1 CUP GROUND PARMESAN CHEESE

1/2 CUP CHOPPED FRESH FLAT-LEAF PARSLEY (OPTIONAL)

PREHEAT THE OVEN TO 350°F.

While the oven is heating, slice the loaf in half lengthwise and then cut the halves into even slices about 2 inches thick.

In a sauté pan heat the butter and olive oil over medium heat until melted, then add the garlic. Sauté until it becomes light golden brown, then remove the garlic from the pan. Dip the cut side of the bread slices into the garlic-infused butter and oil to saturate well, then place the bread cut side up on a rimmed baking tray. Bake the bread until it is lightly toasted then remove the bread from the oven. Preheat the broiler to low.

Stir the Parmesan and parsley together in a small bowl. Sprinkle the cheese and parsley mixture over the bread, generously coating each slice. Place the bread under the broiler, watching it carefully until the cheese begins to brown. Remove from the heat and serve immediately. Ideally, the bread should be oily and crunchy, with a crusty, cheesy top.

RICE PILAF

A GOOD RICE PILAF HAS A SOLID PLACE ON ANY menu. As a side dish it can go with just about anything. By adding and mixing different ingredients you can customize its role in any number of different cuisines.

The truth is that just about every dish has already been done at one time or another. I have spent my long career in food, learning from, working for and with some very talented chefs, following and modifying the ideas of others and ideas obtained from books, articles, and recently the Internet, and lots of experiments, not all of which turned out the way I wanted. Like any profession, cooking is not a static thing, you can always learn something new, and when you cease to learn, you are in big trouble.

This is a roundabout way of saying that when I needed to do a simple but great dish like rice pilaf, I went to one of my heroes: the late and certainly great Julia Child. When Julia and Simone Beck published their monumental work *Mastering the Art of French Cooking* in 1961 most of the content was traditional French food. What the authors did was to make a theretofore complicated process into something every home cook could master.

Don't be afraid to experiment with different herbs and spices to accompany different cuisines. For example; add some chopped garlic and a little chili powder when you sauté the onions to give it a southwestern flavor. I also like to add a little lime juice and chopped garlic to give it a Cuban or Jamaican twist. Use your imagination.

SERVES 6

¼ CUP (½ STICK) UNSALTED BUTTER OR OLIVE OIL

3 MEDIUM YELLOW ONIONS, DICED

1 TABLESPOON DRIED HERB OF YOUR CHOICE (PATRICK LIKES HERBES DE PROVENCE)

1½ CUPS LONG-GRAIN WHITE RICE

3 CUPS CHICKEN, BEEF, SEAFOOD, OR VEGETABLE STOCK

FINE SALT AND FRESHLY GROUND BLACK PEPPER

PREHEAT THE OVEN TO 375 F.

In a 10-inch sauté pan, heat the butter over medium heat. Cook the onions and herbs for 5 minutes, or until translucent. Add the rice and cook until the grains appear opaque and smell nutty, about 5 minutes.

In a lidded, ovenproof saucepan, bring the stock to a boil then add the cooked onions and rice. Cover and cook in the oven for 18 to 20 minutes. Remove the pan from the oven to see if the rice is done and all the liquid has been absorbed: tilt the pan and lift the rice with a wide spoon to check for remaining liquid at the bottom. (Do not stir until the rice is finished.) If you see a few teaspoons' worth of liquid, cover the pan and return it to the oven for another 2 minutes. When the rice is slightly al dente, fluff with a fork and serve.

BLACK BEANS AND RICE

THIS ISN'T SOMETHING ONE WOULD THINK of in a book on red meat, but it goes so well with some of the recipes in this book that it would have been criminally negligent of me not to include my version of this Latin comfort food. I am a fan of the Cuban-style black beans, which uses a sofrito, a combination of onions and green peppers fried in olive oil and added toward the end of the cooking process. I like mine a little spicier than the average Cuban recipe so I add a tablespoon of red pepper flakes at the end.

SERVES 6 TO 8

1 POUND DRIED BLACK BEANS

2 QUARTS CHICKEN STOCK (SUBSTITUTE $^1/_2$ CUP GOOD-QUALITY CHICKEN BASE PLUS 2 QUARTS WATER)

$^3/_4$ CUPS OLIVE OIL

3 LARGE YELLOW ONIONS, DICED

3 GREEN BELL PEPPERS, DICED

3 TABLESPOONS GRANULATED GARLIC

2 TABLESPOONS DRIED OREGANO

1 TABLESPOON DRIED THYME

1 TABLESPOON CHILI POWDER

2 TABLESPOONS WHITE VINEGAR

2 TABLESPOONS GRANULATED SUGAR

SEA SALT

FRESHLY GROUND BLACK PEPPER OR RED PEPPER FLAKES

COOKED LONG-GRAIN WHITE RICE, FOR SERVING

SOAK THE BEANS OVERNIGHT IN WATER to cover by 5 to 6 inches, and sort for stones or "floaters" to remove and discard. Rinse the beans and drain. When you are ready to cook, bring a large stockpot of water to a boil and add the beans. Reduce to a simmer, and cook uncovered for 45 minutes to 1 hour, or until the beans are partially cooked but still firm to the tooth. Skim off any scum that has accumulated. Drain the beans, rinse the pot, and add the chicken stock and beans. Bring to a boil, reduce the heat to a simmer, and cook uncovered.

While the beans are cooking, add the olive oil to a pan and sauté the onions, green peppers, garlic, oregano, thyme, and chili powder over medium-high heat until the vegetables are transparent.

Add the vegetable mixture to the beans and cook until the beans are tender, 30 to 45 minutes, testing frequently. Add vinegar, sugar, salt, and pepper, adjusting seasoning to taste, and serve alongside or over white rice. (This is an excellent addition to Vaca Frita, see page 98.)

CUBAN-STYLE RICE

THIS IS A SIMPLER BUT NO LESS ZESTY relative of the Latin-style black beans recipe. I like it with any blackened fish or meat.

SERVES 4

¾ CUP OLIVE OIL

2 CUPS LONG-GRAIN WHITE RICE

2 GARLIC CLOVES, MINCED

2 TABLESPOONS FRESHLY SQUEEZED LIME JUICE

HEAT THE OIL OVER HIGH HEAT IN A saucepan, add the rice, and stir, coating the grains of rice with oil until they turn a chalky white, about 5 minutes. This indicates that the surface starch has been cooked away, and the rice is ready to be steamed. Add the garlic, lime juice, and 4 cups of water. Bring to a boil, reduce the heat and simmer, tightly covered, for 20 to 25 minutes. The rice should be firm, and not sticky. When the liquid has been fully absorbed, fluff the rice and serve hot.

BAKED BROWN RICE

THIS IS PATRICK'S MORE CONSIDERED APPROACH to traditional rice dishes done on the stovetop. The combination of a tightly closed iron skillet, high heat, and spices makes for a savory sidekick to just about anything else you want to throw on the plate. You can also throw just about anything into the pot, including mushrooms, bell peppers, or green olives. This makes a great accompaniment for chicken, wild fowl, fish, or pork.

SERVES 4

1 TABLESPOON UNSALTED BUTTER

2 TABLESPOONS OLIVE OIL

1 WHITE ONION, FINELY DICED

1 1/2 CUPS BROWN RICE

4 STRANDS SAFFRON

3 CUPS CHICKEN, BEEF, OR VEGETABLE STOCK

1 TABLESPOON GROUND THYME

1 TABLESPOON GROUND CUMIN

1 SPRING ONION, SLICED INTO COINS, OR 3 SCALLIONS, SLICED

1/2 CUP FINELY CHOPPED FRESH FLAT-LEAF PARSLEY (OPTIONAL)

PREHEAT OVEN TO 350°F.

In a cast-iron skillet on stovetop, heat the butter and oil over medium heat. When the butter has melted into the oil, add the white onion, stirring occasionally until the onion turns translucent, about 3 minutes. Then add the rice, stirring until the rice glistens with oil.

Meanwhile, drop saffron threads into a 1/4 cup hot water. Heat the saffron water in the microwave for 3 minutes, until boiling.

Add the saffron liquid, stock, thyme, cumin, and spring onion into the rice. Stir, cover the pot, and place it in the oven, baking for 40 minutes. Remove, behold the steamy rice, sprinkle with parsley, and serve immediately.

ANDOUILLE AND CRANBERRY CORNBREAD STUFFING

HAVING LIVED AND WORKED IN NEW ORLEANS, my psyche is indelibly marked with its food and culture. Whenever a special occasion rolls around I inevitably resort to recipes and ideas that are influenced by my exposure to those two great cuisines for which the region is famous: Creole and Cajun.

The first time I tried a variation of this recipe was Thanksgiving. My wife and I were living on the second floor of a 120-year-old house in Mid-City, overlooking a beautiful garden full of banana trees and all varieties of exotic flowers and shrubs. As we ate dinner with friends, the sights and gentle murmurs of other families in the neighborhood came drifting through the open French doors, the whole scene enhanced by the wonderful smells of the garden below.

Today, as I write this, a few days before Thanksgiving in Montana, the snow is drifting across my living room window and as the temperature plunges, my recollections of that time still warms my spirit. I rouse myself from my torpor to begin the task of dicing green peppers and onions for one of my favorite holiday rituals, the preparation of cornbread stuffing. Don't ever be afraid of making too much. This stuffing has an almost mysterious way of disappearing.

SERVES 6 TO 8

4 LINKS ANDOUILLE OR POLISH SAUSAGE, DICED

3 GREEN BELL PEPPERS, DICED

4 RIBS CELERY, DICED

2 LARGE YELLOW ONIONS, DICED

1/4 CUP DRIED THYME

4 CUPS DRIED CRANBERRIES

5 CUPS CHICKEN STOCK, PLUS MORE AS NEEDED (SUBSTITUTE 5 TABLESPOONS GOOD-QUALITY CHICKEN BASE PLUS 5 CUPS WATER)

10 CUPS DRY, CRUMBLED CORNBREAD (FROM TWO 9 X 13-INCH PANS)

2 EGGS, LIGHTLY BEATEN

1/2 TEASPOON CAYENNE PEPPER

2 TABLESPOONS FRESHLY GROUND BLACK PEPPER

1 CUP CHOPPED PAN-ROASTED PECANS (SEE PAGE 237)

PREHEAT THE OVEN TO 350°F.

Heat a very large skillet over medium-high heat. Sauté the sausage until some of the fat is rendered, about 10 minutes. Remove the sausage from the pan and set aside. Add bell peppers, celery, onions, and thyme, and continue to sauté until the vegetables are soft, about 10 minutes.

Add the cranberries and chicken stock and bring to a boil. Add the cornbread gradually, tossing until all of the stock is absorbed. The mixture should be moist but not overly so, and not too compacted. Add a bit more if the mixture is too crumbly.

Fold in the cooked sausage, eggs, cayenne, and black pepper, working them evenly throughout the mixture.

Grease a roasting pan or other large pan for the stuffing. Spread the stuffing evenly in the pan, cover with foil, and bake for about 45 minutes. Uncover and sprinkle the pecans over the top. Bake for another 20 minutes at 425°F, or until a thick golden crust forms on top. You can assemble the stuffing up to 24 hours ahead of time and refrigerate, covered with foil; bake it just before serving.

CURRIED COLESLAW

I USED TO LIKE MY COLESLAW TRADITIONAL, meaning heavy and creamy. During the last few years I've gotten away from traditional dressing and into lighter, zestier renditions of this classic barbecue sidekick. I came up with this recipe when I was on a low-sugar, high-protein diet and I liked it so much I use it all the time now.

SERVES 10 TO 12

³/4 CUP OLIVE OIL

¹/3 CUP CIDER VINEGAR

1 TABLESPOON CURRY POWDER

¹/2 TEASPOON GROUND CUMIN

¹/2 TEASPOON RED PEPPER FLAKES

6 TABLESPOONS GRANULATED SUGAR

1 POUND COLESLAW MIX OR A MIX OF SHREDDED GREEN CABBAGE, CARROTS, AND RED CABBAGE

IN A LARGE BOWL BLEND ALL OF THE OIL, vinegar, curry powder, cumin, red pepper flakes, and sugar. Add the cabbage mix and toss to blend. Refrigerate for about an hour before serving.

SAUTEED MUSHROOMS
WITH OLIVES AND THYME

THIS MUSHROOM DISH IS A GOOD ACCOMP- animent for most red meats. We use it particularly to enhance the flavor of our locally raised rack of lamb from Big Timber, Montana. It's a great way to add a hint of flavor to lamb chops without doing a formal sauce. Be sure the oil is hot but not burning, and don't turn the mushrooms until they have had a chance to achieve a dark golden color.

SERVES 4

¹/₂ CUP OLIVE OIL (SUBSTITUTE DUCK FAT, GOOSE FAT, OR CLARIFIED BUTTER)

1 POUND WHITE OR CREMINI MUSHROOMS, HALVED

6 KALAMATA OLIVES, PITTED AND DICED

3 GARLIC CLOVES, DICED

2 TABLESPOONS CHOPPED FRESH THYME OR ROSEMARY

2 TABLESPOONS BALSAMIC VINEGAR

ADD THE OIL TO A SAUTÉ PAN SET OVER high heat. Just before it begins to smoke, add the mushrooms. Cook without stirring for at least 2 to 3 minutes, until they're golden and crusty on the bottoms. Stir and add the olives, garlic, and thyme. Cook for 3 minutes, or until the garlic is soft and the herbs are wilted, then add the vinegar and toss to coat. Serve hot.

GRILLED ASPARAGUS

WHENEVER SPRING ROLLS AROUND (I USE the phrase warily because in Montana, it can snow in July), my mind turns to trout fishing and grilled asparagus. In certain parts of southwestern Montana especially, wild asparagus grows along the roadside and everyone has his or her favorite place to harvest. Asparagus must be picked before it turns from a sprout to a large and fairly tall bush. One secret to identifying likely spots for asparagus is to cruise the back roads in the summer and early fall looking for mature, lacy-leaved plants that have grown to about four or five feet. Mark them well because that's where you'll want to return the following spring, when the sprouts are poking their little heads through the brush or snow. Of course the easy way is to buy them in the store while they are cheap and plentiful. No matter how you find them, there isn't anything better. Look for asparagus with well-developed, taut green heads. Anything ragged or turning black is over the hill.

SERVES 4

1 POUND ASPARAGUS

PINCH OF BAKING SODA

1 CUP OLIVE OIL

2 TABLESPOONS
   LEMON PEPPER

BREAK OFF THE TOUGH BOTTOM PART OF the stems of the asparagus—the last inch or two of the stalk. Prepare an ice bath (ice and cold water). Bring a stockpot of water to a boil, add a pinch of baking soda, and cook the asparagus for about 30 seconds or until the stalks turn bright green. Remove the asparagus from the heat and immediately plunge them into the cold water to stop the cooking process. (This process is called parboiling.) Drain and pat the asparagus dry.

Spread them on a cookie sheet and toss with the olive oil and lemon pepper.

Heat a gas or charcoal grill to high heat. If you have it, set a cast-iron plate or griddle directly over the flames and preheat. Cook the asparagus for around 5 minutes, allowing the heat to slightly blacken the asparagus, but without overcooking it. It should still have plenty of snap.

GRILLED SWEET CORN ON THE COB WITH LIME BUTTER

IF I HAD TO CHOOSE MY LAST MEAL ON EARTH, my unhesitating choice would be fried chicken and an ear of perfectly cooked sweet white corn. Make that 6 to 8 ears.

This recipe sums up my philosophy when it comes to food. Keep it simple with the best ingredients you can find. Never over-complicate and always let the essence of the dish shine through. In Montana the corn season lasts about two weeks in late summer. The corn season in the U.S. is typically about two months, from the middle of July to the middle of September, depending on where you are. Don't even think of buying fresh corn outside of this time frame. The perfect ear of corn is straight from the field. And the sooner you cook an ear, the better, because as soon as it is picked the sugar starts converting to starch and the texture changes, leaving you with a tough and tasteless piece of junk.

When you are looking at fresh corn in the store, first look at the husk: it should be dark green and have been kept as moist as possible. Second, peel back the husk and look at the kernels. Once again, there should be good moisture and the kernel should pop when you press it. Third, if you really want to determine if this is the corn for you, take a bite if possible. The sweetness should burst on your taste buds.

You have two choices when it comes to grilling corn: husk on or husk off. Either way works if it is done right. Both require a hot fire. The cooking itself can be done directly over the flames.

SERVES 6

1 POUND UNSALTED BUTTER, AT ROOM TEMPERATURE

FRESHLY SQUEEZED JUICE FROM 3 LIMES

1 TABLESPOON KOSHER SALT, PLUS MORE AS NEEDED

1 TABLESPOON FRESHLY GROUND BLACK PEPPER, PLUS MORE AS NEEDED

12 EARS FRESH CORN

OLIVE OIL

BEAT THE BUTTER WITH THE LIME JUICE, salt, and pepper until it is light and fluffy, and no liquid remains in the bowl. Roll the butter into a cylindrical shape inside waxed paper or foil, and then refrigerate until hard. (This butter is excellent on steak, chicken, or roasted potatoes as well.)

Preheat the grill on medium heat. The first cooking method, and the one I use most, is with the husks off. Shuck the corn and remove the silks, keeping the ears submerged in water until you're ready to cook. Rub the ears all over with olive oil, salt, and pepper. Place the corn directly over the flames. Roll the ears around until some of the kernels have charred on all sides, about 5 minutes. The inside should still be a little under-cooked and crunchy.

If you'd like to cook your corn in the husk, soak the ears in water for about 20 minutes, placing a heavy plate on top to keep them submerged. Pull back the husks just enough to remove the silks, then pull them back to cover the kernels. Place the corn directly over the flames, cooking them for around 5 minutes rolling occasionally to cook evenly. Pull back the husks to check done-ness: the kernels should be juicy and crisp.

Remove the corn and serve hot with slices of lime butter, salt, and pepper.

CORN MACQUE CHOU

THIS IS ONE MY FAVORITE DISHES USING LEFT-over roasted corn. It is a Cajun dish very roughly translated from French, "mock cabbage" even though there is no cabbage in the dish. In John Besh's great book, *My New Orleans*, he claims that the name originated with the Choctaws, Louisiana's original residents, who called the dish Matache, which means "spotted." As far as I know, there are only two places to find it done right, though. One is in southern Louisiana. The other is here at The Mint. It is essentially a corn and tomato stew, although there are plenty of interpretations.

Some versions call for peeled shrimp, crabmeat, or both. If you want to use shrimp, sauté them briefly in the beginning, remove them from the heat, then return them to the pan for the last 5 minutes. If you use crab, add it with the vegetables and leave it in to cook. A more substantial seafood version can also be served as an unusual appetizer.

SERVES 8

1/2 CUP (1 STICK) UNSALTED BUTTER

10 EARS (OR ABOUT 8 CUPS) ROASTED CORN, CUT OFF THE COB (YOU CAN ALSO USE FROZEN CORN IF NECESSARY)

1 YELLOW ONION, DICED

1 GREEN OR RED BELL PEPPER, DICED

1 CUP HEAVY WHIPPING CREAM OR HALF-AND-HALF

1 CAN DICED TOMATOES, DRAINED

PINCH OF CAYENNE PEPPER

FINE SALT

1/3 CUP CHOPPED FRESH FLAT-LEAF PARSLEY (OPTIONAL)

MELT THE BUTTER IN A LARGE SAUTÉ PAN over medium-high heat and sauté the corn, onion, and peppers until the onions are translucent, about 5 or 6 minutes. Add the cream, tomatoes, and cayenne. Reduce the cream for about 5 minutes, then taste for salt, adding as needed. Sprinkle the parsley over the dish for added color and serve.

STEAKHOUSE SPINACH

ANY RESTAURANT THAT CALLS ITSELF A STEAK-house must carry baked, creamed spinach. We think ours can hold its own with anyone else's. We actually have parents who bring in their children to expose them to healthy vegetables, like spinach, that can taste really good! After all, how can you go wrong with lots of milk, butter, and cheese?

In case you think we're being one-sided in our indulgence here, we also have another spinach recipe (see page 203) that positively reeks (lots of garlic) of healthy ingredients.

This dish freezes well, so don't be afraid of leftovers. If you want to do a smaller quantity, beginning with, say, a one-pound package of spinach, you can adjust the other amounts down accordingly to good effect. Besides steak, you can serve this with baked chicken and fish recipes. Try a variation with half spinach, half steamed and chopped Swiss chard (or other hearty green), and a panko topping.

SERVES 4

- ¹/₂ CUP (1 STICK) UNSALTED BUTTER
- 1 CUP ALL-PURPOSE FLOUR
- 1 MEDIUM YELLOW ONION, SLICED
- 2 QUARTS WHOLE MILK
- 3 TABLESPOONS CHICKEN BASE
- 1 TEASPOON GROUND WHITE PEPPER
- 1 TEASPOON GROUND NUTMEG
- 3 TABLESPOONS FRESH BASIL
- 3 (1-POUND) PACKAGES FROZEN SPINACH, THAWED AND DRAINED
- 1 CUP GRATED PARMESAN CHEESE, PLUS MORE AS NEEDED

PREHEAT THE OVEN TO 350°F.

Start by making a roux with the butter and flour: melt the butter in a large skillet over medium heat, and then stir in the flour. Allow it to cook for 1 or 2 minutes, stirring constantly, then, slowly blend in the onion, milk, chicken base, pepper, nutmeg, and basil, making a flavored béchamel sauce. Cook until the mixture is thickened and reduced slightly, about 7 minutes.

In the meantime, press the thawed spinach in a colander to remove as much water as possible.

Stir in the spinach and continue to cook until the sauce has thickened. Before serving, transfer the mixture into a large casserole dish, or divide among 4 ramekins, and sprinkle the Parmesan over the top. Bake until the spinach begins to bubble and the top begins to brown, about 20 minutes.

FLASH-COOKED SPINACH WITH GARLIC AND BALSAMIC VINEGAR

AFTER ALL OF THE BUTTER, CHEESE, AND MILK in the Steakhouse Spinach recipe (see page 200), this is a super-healthy alternative that uses fresh spinach. This dish cannot be cooked ahead of time and is best prepared immediately before serving.

Remember that a pile of fresh spinach may look like a lot, but reduces to a small amount when cooked.

SERVES 4

- ½ CUP OLIVE OIL
- 3 GARLIC CLOVES, MINCED
- 1 TEASPOON RED PEPPER FLAKES
- 3 TABLESPOONS BALSAMIC VINEGAR
- 2 POUNDS FRESH SPINACH LEAVES
- FINE SALT AND FRESHLY GROUND BLACK PEPPER

HEAT THE OIL IN A CAST-IRON SKILLET OVER medium-high heat. Throw in the garlic and pepper flakes, followed by the vinegar. Swirl around the pan with a wooden spoon until the garlic takes on a nutty brown color, about 10 seconds.

Add the spinach, shaking the skillet or tossing the spinach with tongs until it has wilted and most of the moisture has evaporated. Add salt and pepper to taste, and serve immediately.

SWEET AND SOUR RED CABBAGE (ROTKOHL)

CABBAGE WAS BIG AMONG THE IMMIGRANTS who came to Butte during the boom mining years. Irish, Poles, Welsh, and even the Chinese all had their versions of some kind of cabbage dish. But the predominant version might have been the dish the German miners brought to Butte for a taste of home. That taste came with a steaming plate of sauerbraten und rotkohl. Pretty soon a number of taverns and saloons featured this dish, and the German version of beef stew crossed ethnic and cultural lines. Decades later, my friend Hans Dietrich makes his own version with a Bavarian twist. This is the perfect winter accompaniment to just about anything, particularly pork and beef. This recipe is sufficient for 8 to 12 but it freezes well and once you taste it you'll pray for leftovers.

You will notice that I call for juniper berries. When I first looked around, none of the neighborhood stores carried them. Then my wife Mary hatched a brilliant idea: it was Christmastime and, spying the wreath hanging on our front door, she discovered that juniper berries had been added for decoration. So, we began picking them right off our front door. We picked about a year's worth. So, look for berries in your next holiday wreath; just be sure it hasn't been sprayed with any chemicals.

SERVES 8 TO 12

4 BAY LEAVES

10 JUNIPER BERRIES

10 WHOLE CLOVES

2 SMALL, DENSE HEADS DARK RED CABBAGE, CORED AND THINLY SLICED

2 SWEET RED APPLES (FUJI, GALA, OR DELICIOUS), CORED AND SLICED

4 RED ONIONS, THINLY SLICED

FRESHLY SQUEEZED JUICE FROM 2 LEMONS

$^3/_4$ CUP GRANULATED SUGAR

1 QUART APPLE JUICE

1 CUP RED WINE VINEGAR

$^1/_4$ CUP BACON FAT, MELTED, OR $^1/_4$ CUP CHOPPED, CRUMBLED BACON

2 TABLESPOONS CORNSTARCH

FINE SALT AND FRESHLY GROUND BLACK PEPPER

IN A SAUCEPAN, COMBINE THE BAY LEAVES, juniper berries, cloves, and 2 cups of water. Bring to the barest simmer and cook uncovered for an hour, until the liquid is significantly reduced. Strain the remaining liquid into a large bowl and cool slightly. Add the cabbage, apples, onions, lemon juice, sugar, and apple juice to the bowl and marinate in the refrigerator for at least 24 hours.

Transfer the contents of the bowl to a stockpot and bring to a boil. Reduce the heat and simmer the mixture until soft, about 30 minutes, then add the red wine vinegar and bacon fat. Simmer a few more minutes.

Stir the cornstarch in $^1/_2$ cup of water to dissolve. Stir into the cabbage to thicken slightly, simmer a few more minutes, and then add salt and pepper, adjusting seasoning to taste. Serve hot. Leftovers can be stored in the refrigerator for a week or frozen for months.

ROASTED ROOT VEGETABLES

DURING THE HARD MONTANA WINTER, THIS dish comes to the table preceded by the pungent aroma of what we survivalists know as ambrosia. Almost any "cellar roots" will do, but this is a care package developed by Patrick and sent to us from "always warm and sunny" California.

SERVES 4

2 RED ONIONS, DICED INTO LARGE PIECES

1 LARGE GARNET YAM, PEELED AND DICED INTO LARGE PIECES

1 POUND RED POTATOES, DICED

12 OUNCES FINGERLING POTATOES, DICED

3 PARSNIPS, PEELED AND DICED INTO LARGE PIECES

1/2 CUP OLIVE OIL

2 TABLESPOONS DRIED CUMIN

1 TABLESPOON PAPRIKA

3 TABLESPOONS CHOPPED FRESH ROSEMARY

FINE SALT AND FRESHLY GROUND BLACK PEPPER

FRESHLY SQUEEZED JUICE FROM 2 LEMONS

1/2 CUP CHOPPED FRESH FLAT-LEAF PARSLEY

PREHEAT OVEN TO 400°F.

Toss the onions, yam, red and fingerling potatoes, and parsnips into a resealable plastic bag. Add olive oil, cumin, paprika, rosemary, salt, and pepper, adjusting seasoning to taste. Vigorously shake the bag to mix contents. When it appears the vegetables are evenly coated, spread them on a large rimmed baking tray in a single layer.

Place the vegetables in the oven and cook for 35 minutes, turning once about halfway through. They should be browned on the edges. Arrange the vegetables on a platter. Sprinkle with lemon juice and chopped parsley and serve. Any leftovers will make a great breakfast accompaniment to poached eggs.

THE ULTIMATE FRENCH FRIES

MY FIRST KITCHEN JOB WAS ON THE VEGETABLE station at the Louis XVI in New Orleans. Chef Daniel Bonnot, a transplanted Parisian, took his pommes frites very seriously and, if they weren't done to his satisfaction, he became dangerously irritated. There were rumors to the effect that apprentices who couldn't do French fries correctly were themselves plunged into the hot oil, cooked to a desired crispness, and served as cracklings to an unsuspecting dining room. Needless to say, we learned to do it the way he wanted.

When I opened The Mint, one of the critical menu decisions was the size, shape, and texture of the fries. After a lot of trial and error, we have finally developed something akin to the street food of France and Belgium. I think even Daniel would approve!

The secret is in the kind of potato, the size (not too thick, not too thin) and shape, and also the way it is cooked and served. Older potatoes are much better: freshly dug potatoes have a high moisture content, which is hard to crisp properly when frying. We use locally grown russet potatoes, cut into pencil thickness and cooked twice. We differ from the French tradition in that we like to leave the skin on.

SERVES 4

4 LARGE RUSSET POTATOES (ABOUT 3 POUNDS), THE OLDER THE BETTER

VEGETABLE OIL, PEANUT, CANOLA OR BEST OF ALL, LARD, AS NEEDED

FINE SEA SALT

WASH THE POTATOES THOROUGHLY AND PAT them dry. Cut them lengthwise into fries about the thickness of a pencil and set aside to dry for about 15 minutes. They may begin to brown but that won't affect the fries.

Heat a Dutch oven or a large heavy pot with oil to a depth of 3 inches to 350°F. Use a frying thermometer to monitor the temperature while you're cooking. Carefully add the potatoes in small batches, being careful not to let the oil boil over. The purpose of the first frying is to partially cook and remove some of the moisture, which helps keep them crisp. Cook until limp, but not brown. Drain the cooked potatoes on paper towels and allow them to cool to room temperature.

When the fries are cool, raise the temperature so that the oil reaches 360°F. Add the potatoes, being careful not to crowd them. Cook the potatoes until they appear to float, and they have a lovely golden-brown color. Drain on paper towels, sprinkle lightly with sea salt, and serve immediately. You can hold them very briefly in a 200°F oven while you finish frying all the potatoes, but not for long, as they will quickly become limp. Remember the texture is just as important as the taste.

MASHED POTATOES

THIS IS MY FAVORITE "MOM-INSPIRED" recipe for classic mashed potatoes, with some excellent variations. The nice thing about mashed potatoes is that you can put darn near anything in them and they still taste great, so don't be afraid to experiment. There are variations on the basic recipe below.

SERVES 4

- 4 TO 6 RUSSET POTATOES (ABOUT 3 POUNDS), PEELED OR NOT, DEPENDING ON YOUR PREFERENCE (I LIKE YUKON OR MONTANA RUSSETS)
- 1 TO 1$\frac{1}{2}$ CUPS WHOLE MILK OR HALF-AND-HALF, AS NEEDED, HEATED AND KEPT WARM
- 3 TABLESPOONS UNSALTED BUTTER, CUT IN SMALL PIECES, AT ROOM TEMPERATURE (SUBSTITUTE OLIVE OIL)
- FINE SALT AND FRESHLY GROUND BLACK PEPPER

CUT THE POTATOES INTO 1-INCH PIECES AND cover with salted water in a large stockpot. Bring to a boil, and then cook until they are fork-tender, about 15 to 20 minutes. Drain the potatoes and place them in a warm bowl. Add half of the milk, and mash with a masher, potato ricer, or a large serving fork and spoon. (This can also be done in an electric mixer with the paddle attachment on low speed; but don't overbeat.) While mashing the potatoes, add more milk as needed to make them creamier. Be sure to leave a few lumps so everyone will know you did them from scratch, although the taste is the true measure of real mashed potatoes. Stir in the butter and add the salt and pepper, adjusting the seasoning to taste. Serve them immediately. If you are lucky you may have some leftovers.

VARIATIONS:

GARLIC MASHED POTATOES: Every bistro is doing garlic mashed potatoes these days, and for good reason: they're not only great, but also easy. Place 4 to 6 peeled garlic cloves in a small bowl or mug and cover with water. Microwave for 8 minutes, checking during the process to be sure there is enough liquid to cover. They should be soft with a mellow flavor from the cooking. Blend the garlic and the remaining cooking liquid with the potatoes while mashing.

CHILI AND GARLIC MASHED POTATOES: Follow the procedure for the garlic mashed potatoes, and stir in 2 to 3 tablespoons of mild chili powder.

CURRIED GARLIC MASHED POTATOES: Similar to the chili and garlic potatoes, except here substitute 2 to 3 tablespoons of curry powder for the chili powder.

MASHED POTATOES WITH WHITE CHEDDAR AND CHIVES: Follow the same procedure as the classic mashed potatoes, but melt 1 cup of shredded white cheddar with 1 cup of the milk in the microwave. Blend in the melted cheese with the potatoes while mashing, and add 1/3 cup chopped fresh chives. If needed, add another splash of milk. If you wish you can substitute fresh chopped rosemary or thyme.

POTATO DUMPLINGS (KLOSSE)

WHY WOULD I INCLUDE GERMAN COMFORT FOOD in a book about western food? Because a significant number of Germans settled in Butte at the turn of the nineteenth century to work in the mines, and they loved to hunt. So they adapted this classic preparation from their homeland to accompany wild game from the area.

There is a myth in this country that German food is heavy and tasteless. But while working in Germany as a consulting chef for a global manufacturer of home appliances, I found that my initial impressions of that great cuisine were misplaced. Working in Germany gave me the chance to dine in some of the finest restaurants in the Rhine Valley where nouvelle and traditional German cuisine has been carried to new heights.

I have included one of my favorite recipes for potato dumplings from my former daughter-in law Marianna Fiewager Donch, who served them to me when I visited her family farm located in the beautiful Hundsruck district near the Rhine River.

This is a simple process. Make plenty, as these dumplings will keep in a refrigerator for a week and can become habit-forming. These are particularly good with Venison Sauerbraten (see page 165) or Jewish-Style Elk Brisket (see page 169).

SERVES 8

- 2 LARGE RUSSET POTATOES (ABOUT 1½ POUNDS)
- 2 CUPS ALL-PURPOSE FLOUR
- FINE SALT AND FRESHLY GROUND BLACK PEPPER
- 1 TEASPOON GROUND NUTMEG (OPTIONAL)
- 2 EGGS, LIGHTLY BEATEN, PLUS MORE AS NEEDED

PEEL THE POTATOES, AND THEN PLACE THEM in a saucepan and cover with water. Bring to a boil and cook 10 to 12 minutes, or until they are easily pierced with a fork. Drain and push the potatoes through a ricer, or, using a large fork, break them down into crumbly pieces the size of rice. Put the potato mix in a large bowl and allow to cool to room temperature.

Add the flour, salt, pepper, and nutmeg (if using) to the potatoes and mix well. Add the eggs and combine to form a dough. If the dough is too dry, add a few additional teaspoons of a beaten egg at a time, or if too wet, add some extra flour. Don't overwork the dough. Shape into 2-inch balls and set on a rimmed baking sheet.

Bring a large pot of water to a rolling boil. Add the dumplings to the water in batches without crowding. Cook the dumplings for around 15 minutes, or until they float to the surface and stay there. You may want to taste one occasionally for doneness. You can keep the dumplings covered in a low oven until ready to serve.

POTATOES AU GRATIN

THIS IS NOT SOMETHING YOU WOULD FIND ON your typical Montana steakhouse menu, but any book with as much red meat as this one would not be complete without at least one recipe for potatoes au gratin. Every region and, it seems, every cook in France has a favorite recipe. The common ingredients are some combination of potatoes with cheese and milk or cream. My favorite came from my mentor and friend Chef Daniel Bonnot of New Orleans. Daniel says that this simple and straightforward gratin typifies the best in Parisian cuisine. I agree.

SERVES 6

3 POUNDS RUSSET POTATOES, PEELED AND SLICED ¼-INCH THICK

3 CUPS WHOLE MILK

2 BAY LEAVES

4 GARLIC CLOVES, MINCED

FINE SALT

¼ CUP (½ STICK) UNSALTED BUTTER

2 CUPS GRATED CHEESE, PREFERABLY GRUYÈRE (SUBSTITUTE SWISS IF NEEDED), DIVIDED

1 CUP HEAVY CREAM, DIVIDED

1 TEASPOON FRESHLY GROUND NUTMEG (OPTIONAL), DIVIDED

PREHEAT OVEN TO 400°F.

Combine the sliced potatoes in a large saucepan with the milk, bay leaves, garlic, and salt, adjusting seasoning to taste. Bring to a boil and cook until the potatoes are tender, but not overcooked, about 10 minutes.

Using a slotted spoon, transfer half of the potatoes to a gratin or casserole pan that has been greased generously with the butter. Sprinkle with half the cheese, drizzle half the cream over them, and top with a sprinkle of salt and half the nutmeg. Add the rest of the potatoes and then the remaining cheese, cream, nutmeg, and a final sprinkle of salt. Dot the top with any remaining butter.

Bake for an hour, or until the top is crisp and golden. Serve hot. They will keep warm under foil for a while, but they are better fresh out of the oven.

PUGET POTATO SALAD

AS THE NAME SUGGESTS, THIS CLASSIC OF a classic grew up on the banks of Puget Sound in the Pacific Northwest. More specifically, it comes from Patrick in collaboration with his mother Joanne Dillon, a Bainbridge Island native, who previously collaborated with her mother when preparing this generational side dish (Patrick swears it goes back at least three generations with some sideways permutations) for a traditional family Fourth of July picnic dinner. It can easily scale upward to feed more hungry people: increase by 1 potato and 1 hard-boiled egg per person, adjusting the other ingredients accordingly.

SERVES 6

- 8 MEDIUM RED POTATOES (ABOUT 3$^1/_2$ POUNDS)
- 8 HARD-BOILED EGGS, PEELED AND CHOPPED
- 4 DILL PICKLE SPEARS, COARSELY CHOPPED
- 1 LARGE BUNCH SCALLIONS, CHOPPED (THE WHITES WITH JUST A BIT OF GREEN)
- 3 TO 4 TABLESPOONS MAYONNAISE, OR MORE TO TASTE
- 1$^1/_2$ TABLESPOONS SOUR CREAM, OR MORE TO TASTE
- 3 TABLESPOONS YELLOW MUSTARD, OR MORE TO TASTE
- 2 TABLESPOONS PICKLE JUICE
- 2 TEASPOONS SEASONING SALT (SUCH AS LAWRY'S)
- FINE SALT AND FRESHLY GROUND BLACK PEPPER

COVER THE POTATOES WITH WATER IN A large pot and bring to boil. Cook for 15 to 20 minutes, or until they are very soft but not falling apart.

In a large mixing bowl, combine the eggs, pickles, scallions, mayonnaise, sour cream, and mustard. Whip with a fork until pale yellow and creamy. Add additional mayonnaise, sour cream, and mustard, if desired.

Drain the potatoes and rinse in cold water. Set aside to cool. When cool enough to handle, peel and dice roughly. Add to the sauce mix. Stir in pickle juice and seasoning salt, adjusting seasoning to taste. Cover the bowl in plastic wrap and refrigerate for at least 24 hours. Taste just before serving and add salt and pepper.

ROASTED POTATOES
WITH KALAMATA OLIVES, ROSEMARY, AND GARLIC

ROASTED POTATOES AND RED MEAT ARE natural partners. This is my favorite way to roast potatoes. The kalamata olives flavor the olive oil and the potatoes as they cook, and they attain a crisp, salty texture like bacon bits. Always make more than you will need because you'll be just as happy with the leftovers.

SERVES 4

- $^3/_4$ CUP OLIVE OIL
- 1 CUP PITTED KALAMATA OLIVES, HALVED
- 2 POUNDS SMALL RED POTATOES, HALVED OR QUARTERED, WITH SKIN ON
- 15 TO 20 GARLIC CLOVES, PEELED
- $^1/_2$ CUP FRESH ROSEMARY LEAVES
- FINE SALT AND COARSELY GROUND BLACK PEPPER

PREHEAT OVEN TO 425°F.

Pour the oil in large roasting pan to coat it thoroughly, and then add the olives and potatoes. Sprinkle with the garlic, and toss the potatoes to coat with oil.

Cook for 1 to 1$^1/_4$ hours or until potatoes are tender and browned all over. The secret to great roasted potatoes is not to turn them for at least half an hour. They must have the time to develop a good brown crust before they are stirred. When you do turn them, use a metal spatula to get under the crusty bits. Remove from oven and add salt and pepper, adjusting seasoning to taste.

SMASHED BROWNS

WHEN YOU COOK ENOUGH ROASTED POTATOES with Kalamata Olives, Rosemary, and Garlic to make Smashed Browns with the leftovers, you'll see: this dish is even better than the original. I like to grind extra pepper and Parmesan over the top. It's an awesome side either way.

SERVES 4

½ TO ¾ CUP OLIVE OIL OR BUTTER, OR AS NEEDED

4 CUPS LEFTOVER ROASTED POTATOES WITH KALAMATA OLIVES, ROSEMARY, AND GARLIC (PAGE 215)

FINE SALT AND FRESHLY GROUND BLACK PEPPER TO TASTE

GRATED PARMESAN CHEESE, AS NEEDED

PREHEAT HALF OF THE OIL IN A LARGE cast-iron skillet or sauté pan on medium-high heat. Cover your kitchen work surface with a piece of waxed paper or plastic wrap larger than your pan. Mound the potatoes on top of the wax paper and press them down with your hand to shape the potatoes in a rough approximation of the pan. Place another piece of waxed paper over the potatoes and using a heavy pan, smash the potatoes into a cake 1½ to 2 inches high.

When the oil has begun to smoke but not burn, use a spatula to carefully slide the potatoes into the hot oil. Reduce the heat to medium and cover. This will allow the interior of the cake to heat while crisping the bottom. Cook for 10 minutes. Using a spatula, carefully raise one side of the cake to check on the degree of crispness.

(You can cut up the potatoes in the pan like a pie and serve in wedges at this point, or brown the other side too.) Carefully slide the spatula under the cake, dislodging any parts of the cake that may be sticking to the bottom without breaking it. Using a couple of pot holders, place the lid over the pan and turn it the whole pan upside down so the cake ends up on the lid crisp-side up. Place the pan back on the burner at medium-high and add the rest of the oil.

When the oil is hot, slide the cake, crisp-side up, into the hot oil. Reduce the heat and cook uncovered for 7 to 10 minutes, until browned on the bottom side. Season with salt and pepper and sprinkle with Parmesan. Cut into wedges and serve.

SOFT POLENTA WITH HERBS

HISTORICALLY, CORNMEAL WAS A MAINSTAY of the Native American diet. It was also a staple in rustic Italian kitchens. This goes great with a big steak, and is a nice change from potatoes.

SERVES 4 TO 6

2 TABLESPOONS OLIVE OIL

1 YELLOW ONION, FINELY DICED

6 GARLIC CLOVES, CHOPPED

5 CUPS CHICKEN STOCK (SUBSTITUTE 5 TABLESPOONS GOOD-QUALITY CHICKEN BASE PLUS 5 CUPS WATER)

1 CUP HALF-AND-HALF

2 CUPS COARSE-GROUND YELLOW CORNMEAL (SOMETIMES CALLED POLENTA OR GRITS)

$^{1}/_{2}$ CUP GRATED PARMESAN CHEESE

1 CUP CHOPPED FRESH BASIL, THYME, OR ROSEMARY, OR A COMBINATION

FINE SALT AND FRESHLY GROUND BLACK PEPPER

OVER MEDIUM HEAT IN A SAUCE POT, ADD the olive oil and sauté the onions and garlic until transparent, about 5 minutes. Stir in the chicken stock and half-and-half, bring to a boil, and then reduce to medium heat. Gradually stir in the cornmeal to keep it from clumping, and continue to stir as it begins to absorb some of the liquid. Cook for around 15 minutes, stirring constantly to prevent it from sticking or burning. Add water as necessary, if it becomes too thick— it should have the same consistency of loose mashed potatoes.

Add the cheese and herbs and continue to stir. Add salt and pepper, adjusting seasoning to taste. The polenta should be uniformly creamy. Serve immediately. (Alternatively, pour into a baking pan and refrigerate until solid. Cut into squares and pan-fry in butter on both sides before serving.)

SOUTHERN-STYLE GRITS

USUALLY THESE ARE MADE FROM GROUND white corn, but any type of cornmeal coarsely ground will work. Eat them for breakfast with eggs and bacon.

2 CUPS WHOLE MILK

2 CUPS STONE-GROUND WHITE GRITS

1 CUP SHREDDED SHARP CHEDDAR CHEESE

1 CUP SHREDDED MEDIUM CHEDDAR CHEESE

FINE SALT AND FRESHLY GROUND BLACK PEPPER

BRING 5 CUPS OF WATER TO A BOIL IN A saucepan. Add the milk and reduce the heat to medium-low. Add the grits gradually, stirring to keep them from clumping. Continually stir the grits as they cook for 15 minutes, until they are creamy and thick. Stir in the cheeses and season to taste. If the grits are too thick, thin with a little milk. Serve immediately.

CORNMEAL MUSH

IN THE EARLY DAYS, MANY OF THE NATIVE American tribes in Montana, particularly the plains dwellers, would supplement their meat-based diet with various tubers and wild legumes. Because of their nomadic lifestyle, there was little crop cultivation as we know it, but when crops were grown it was usually corn.

Corn could be used in a number of ways: from pemmican (an early trail mix of dried game meat, wild berries, and corn) to stews thickened with cornmeal. This cornmeal mush was served either fresh from the pot, or cooled and cut into squares to be eaten later. Sometimes it was sweetened with wild berries or honey, and later, with the advent of trade, unrefined sugar.

SERVES 4

1/2 CUP DRIED CRANBERRIES OR DRIED CHERRIES

1 CUP CORNMEAL

PINCH OF SALT

BUTTER (OPTIONAL)

HONEY OR MAPLE SYRUP (OPTIONAL)

BRING 4 CUPS OF WATER TO A BOIL IN A saucepan and then reduce the heat to a simmer. Add the dried cranberries and cook for 5 minutes, until they soften and plump up. Add the cornmeal very slowly and whisk to prevent lumps from forming. Continue whisking to achieve a thick, creamy consistency. Add salt to taste.

When the mush is the same consistency of finished risotto, serve immediately. Alternatively, cool down completely in a square baking dish, then cut into squares. When you are ready to serve, fry the squares of mush in butter (or even bacon fat) and serve with honey or syrup.

POLENTA, GRITS, AND CORNMEAL MUSH

WHETHER IT'S PREPARED WITH FRESH HERBS, CHEESE, MUSHROOMS, STOCK, MILK, SUGAR, OR ANY OF A number of other ingredients, ground corn has earned universal appeal for thousands of years. From the cornmeal mush bubbling in a cooking pot in front of a Crow lodge along the Big Horn River in Montana to the polenta served in a Roman trattoria to the cheese grits of the American South, cornmeal dishes have their niche. Generally anything labeled grits, polenta, or ground cornmeal will work just fine.

TWO-POT PINTO BEANS WITH PORK SHOULDER

THIS IS A COWBOY VERSION OF BLACK BEANS and rice. This dish literally begs to be served on tin plates, beside a crystalline mountain stream high up in the Spanish Peaks, at the end of a late summer trail ride. In fact, it was. I came across this recipe in an old book that was used by the folks at Karst's Camp, one of several of the old-style dude ranches that flourished between Bozeman and Yellowstone Park during the "golden age" of dude ranching from the 1930s to around 1960. In its heyday, Karst's Camp was located on the beautiful Gallatin river, but today, only the name remains.

At the ranch, the cooks would assemble and cook all the ingredients in a large Dutch oven. This would then be hauled by horseback up the mountain to that night's campsite where they would finish the cooking over an open fire just in time to serve the hungry riders. This was usually accompanied by freshly made sourdough rolls also baked in a Dutch oven, and a crisp iceberg lettuce salad. After dinner everyone sat around the campfire fire as the night fell over the peaks and the digestive process set in.

One trick that I have learned over the years is that if you "twice cook" any kind of dry beans you can avoid a lot of the sounds and aromas normally associated with their consumption. It seems as though the first cooking removes certain enzymes, which cause flatulence, and by draining, adding fresh water, and continuing the cooking process, you can pretty much eliminate the requirement of sleeping in separate tents.

The smoky flavor of the meat complements the rich flavor of the fresh green chile and chipotle peppers. Serve with rice, grilled smoked sausage, and jalapeño corn bread.

SERVES 10 TO 12

2 POUNDS PINTO BEANS, SOAKED OVERNIGHT IN WATER TO COVER

5 BAY LEAVES

1/2 CUP FRESH CHOPPED OREGANO

5 TABLESPOONS GOOD-QUALITY CHICKEN BASE

1/2 (8-OUNCE) CAN CHIPOTLE PEPPERS IN ADOBO SAUCE, CHOPPED

1/2 CUP TOMATO PASTE

1/2 CUP OLIVE OIL (OR SUBSTITUTE LARD, AS THE RANCHERS DID), DIVIDED

3 POUNDS SMOKED BONELESS PORK SHOULDER OR HAM, CUT INTO 1 1/2-INCH CUBES

3 FRESH ANCHO OR NEW MEXICO GREEN CHILE PEPPERS, SEEDED AND COARSELY DICED OR 1 (4-OUNCE) CAN GREEN CHILES

3 RED OR GREEN BELL PEPPERS, CORED, SEEDED, AND DICED

3 LARGE YELLOW ONIONS, COARSELY DICED

FINE SALT AND FRESHLY GROUND BLACK PEPPER

DRAIN AND RINSE THE SOAKED BEANS. COVER WITH FRESH WATER AND BRING THE BEANS TO A BOIL, THEN TURN OFF THE heat and allow them to sit for about 20 minutes. Drain the beans in a colander, return to pan and cover with fresh water by 4 to 5 inches. Then bring to a boil. Once boiling, reduce the heat to simmer. Add the bay leaves, oregano, chicken base, chipotles, and tomato paste and continue to simmer for 20 to 30 minutes.

In another large pot or Dutch oven, heat about half of the olive oil over high heat. Sauté the pork until it is evenly browned on all sides, about 10 minutes, then add to the pot of beans. Reserve the pot you used for the pork and return it to the heat.

Add more oil if needed, then sauté the chiles, bell peppers, and yellow onions until slightly transparent, about 5 minutes, and add to the pot of beans. Simmer until the meat is tender, about 2 hours, and add salt and pepper, adjusting seasoning to taste. Serve right away or allow the mixture to cool down and refrigerate overnight. Skim off any accumulated fat from the top, and then reheat. The flavor gets deeper with age.

A SUPPORTING CAST
OF RUBS, SAUCES, DRESSINGS, AND DIPS

PAN-SEARING CAN BE TRACED TO A MONGOL WARRIOR SOMEWHERE ON THE STEPPES of Central Asia more than a thousand years ago. The meat was likely mutton and the cooking implement was his metal shield. During the colonial period of South America, cooking and searing of meat on a hot metal surface was instrumental to the cuisine, particularly in Argentina where, even today, the plancha or cast-iron griddle plays a major role for grass-fed beef from the pampas.

I first experienced cooking with cast iron when I was apprenticing at the Louis XVI restaurant in New Orleans in 1980. Local chef Paul Prudhomme was becoming famous for his revival of Cajun cuisine. He also was one of the first chefs to use a cast-iron skillet to sear fish. Paul's technique was to brush the fish fillets with butter, coat the fish with a spice mixture he had developed, and then place the fish on a very hot cast-iron skillet. The hot surface would cauterize the outside of the fish, mellowing the taste of the spice mixture, and creating a crusty surface that not only added texture, but also had the additional effect of sealing the moisture inside the fish.

Meat, however, really is an even better medium for this kind of cooking. I like to call it contact cooking because the searing effect of the hot metal gives a whole new dimension to grilling meats.

At home, the best way to cook like this is to remove the grate from your backyard gas grill and place the cast-iron skillet directly on top of the burners. Preheat your grill on the highest setting for around 15 minutes, or until a small piece of butter dropped directly on the surface bursts into flames.

In this chapter, I'm including recipes for rubs and flavorings that directly enhance flame-roasted meats, or that serve as sidekicks to help dress the meat.

BASIC BLACKENING MIX

WHAT DOES A RECIPE WITH ORIGINS IN New Orleans have to do with Montana? For one thing, New Orleans chef Paul Prudhomme's wife Kay is from Miles City, Montana, down near the Custer battlefield, and secondly, the whole technique of blackening has a lot of applications to the food Montanans like to eat. Here is the basic mix that I use, although I have added my own innovations. Don't be afraid to add your own.

MAKES ABOUT 1 CUP

1/2 CUP HUNGARIAN PAPRIKA

2 TABLESPOONS GRANULATED GARLIC

2 TABLESPOONS ONION POWDER

1 TABLESPOON DRIED THYME

1 TABLESPOON DRIED OREGANO

1 TABLESPOON FRESHLY GROUND BLACK PEPPER

1 TEASPOON CAYENNE PEPPER

1 1/2 TABLESPOONS FINE SALT

BLEND TOGETHER AND STORE IN A JAR IN THE PANTRY. IT WILL KEEP FOR ABOUT 3 MONTHS. After that you're better off starting fresh.

THREE LAMB AND GAME RUBS

HERE ARE THREE RUBS THAT I FIRST USED at the Continental Divide and brought with me to The Mint. These flavors give lamb dishes a new and exotic twist. I usually cut the meat from lamb shoulders or boneless legs into 1½-inch cubes, grill them on a skewer, and serve with rice, couscous, or other ethnic side dishes. The yields below should season up to three pounds of meat. Rub generously over the meat and store any extra rub in the refrigerator. Be sure to season the meat at least 24 hours before using to maximize the flavor. By the way, these rubs work equally well with chicken, pork, antelope, and venison. They should last for months in your freezer.

CURRY SPICE RUB

MAKES 1 CUP

1 TABLESPOON GROUND CUMIN

1 TABLESPOON CURRY POWDER

1 TABLESPOON SMOKED PAPRIKA

1 TABLESPOON PACKED DARK BROWN SUGAR

1 TABLESPOON GRANULATED GARLIC

½ CUP RED WINE VINEGAR

¼ CUP VEGETABLE OIL

Stir together with a fork and use right away, or refrigerate for up to a month.

CHILI ORANGE SPICE RUB

MAKES ½ CUP

1 TABLESPOON CHILI POWDER

1 TEASPOON GROUND CUMIN

1 TEASPOON SMOKED PAPRIKA

1 TEASPOON GROUND CORIANDER

1 TEASPOON GRANULATED GARLIC

½ TEASPOON CAYENNE PEPPER

2 TABLESPOONS CHOPPED FRESH CILANTRO

2 TABLESPOONS FROZEN CONCENTRATED ORANGE JUICE, THAWED

1 TABLESPOON FRESHLY SQUEEZED LIME JUICE

Stir together with a fork and use right away, or refrigerate for up to a month.

THAI SPICE RUB

MAKES ¾ CUP

4 GARLIC CLOVES, MINCED

2 TABLESPOONS CHOPPED FRESH CILANTRO

3 TABLESPOONS DARK SOY SAUCE

3 TABLESPOONS ASIAN FISH SAUCE (OPTIONAL)

1 TABLESPOON CHOPPED GINGER

½ TEASPOON CAYENNE PEPPER

2 TABLESPOONS VEGETABLE OIL

Stir together with a fork and use right away, or refrigerate for up to a month.

THREE CLASSIC SAUCES

GRANTED, THESE SAUCES, LIKE THE FRENCH, can be difficult, but once you master them, you will discover why they have been around for so long, and why they will continue to stick around long after today's fashionable sauces will have been forgotten. The best thing about hollandaise sauce (and beurre blanc for that matter, on page 228) is that you can make so many variations of the same sauce with a simple addition of flavoring ingredients. You merely have to master one to make all.

Hollandaise is the mother of all French sauces. It, along with its relatives Béarnaise and Choron, are particularly great with red meat and salmon. The Choron sauce is also very nice with lamb.

HOLLANDAISE

MAKES 1 CUP

4 EGG YOLKS
2 STICKS (1 CUP) UNSALTED BUTTER, MELTED
FINE SALT
WHITE PEPPER
1 TO 2 TABLESPOONS FRESHLY SQUEEZED LEMON JUICE

SET UP A SMALL METAL BOWL THAT FITS TIGHTLY OVER A saucepan with an inch or two of water in it. Heat the water until it simmers. Add the yolks to the bowl and set it over the simmering water. Using a whisk, whip the yolks constantly until they begin to thicken and cook slightly from the heat of the hot water. When you can see the bottom of the bowl with each stroke of the whisk, start to drizzle the butter very slowly into the yolks, constantly stirring to emulsify. When you have incorporated all of the butter, add the salt, white pepper, and lemon juice to adjust the flavor. If the sauce gets too thick, add a little lemon juice to thin it out.

You can hold hollandaise for a short time, but it is best to use it as soon as possible.

BÉARNAISE

4 EGG YOLKS

2 STICKS (1 CUP) PLUS 1 TEASPOON UNSALTED
   BUTTER, MELTED AND DIVIDED

1¹/₂ TABLESPOONS MINCED SHALLOTS

1 TEASPOON FRESH (OR ¹/₂ TEASPOON DRIED) TARRAGON

¹/₄ CUP RED WINE VINEGAR

¹/₄ TEASPOON FINE SALT

¹/₂ TEASPOON FRESHLY CRACKED
   BLACK PEPPER

FOLLOW HOLLANDAISE INSTRUCTIONS TO HEAT THE EGG
yolks and to incorporate the 2 sticks of butter, whisking to emulsify. Heat the remaining 1 teaspoon of melted butter in a skillet and sauté the shallot and the fresh tarragon until the shallots are wilted. Add the vinegar, and reduce by about half. Allow to cool slightly before whisking the shallots and reduced vinegar into the sauce. Season with the salt and pepper.

CHORON

4 EGG YOLKS

2 STICKS (1 CUP) PLUS 1 TEASPOON UNSALTED BUTTER,
   MELTED AND DIVIDED

1¹/₂ TABLESPOONS MINCED SHALLOTS OR SCALLIONS
   (WHITE AND GREEN PARTS)

1 TEASPOON FRESH (OR ¹/₂ TEASPOON DRIED) TARRAGON

¹/₄ CUP RED WINE VINEGAR

¹/₄ TEASPOON FINE SALT

¹/₂ TEASPOON FRESHLY CRACKED BLACK PEPPER

1 TABLESPOON TOMATO PASTE

FOLLOW THE BÉARNAISE SAUCE INSTRUCTIONS TO THE
last step, and stir in the tomato paste with the salt and pepper.

BASIC BEURRE BLANC

IF I COULD CHOOSE ONLY ONE SAUCE, THIS might be the one. Beurre blanc (which means "white butter") and its variations can be used with most seafood as well as chicken, veal, and certain vegetables, such as fresh green beans. I especially like it on fresh wild asparagus that grows by the roadsides in southwestern Montana in April and May. It works well with two seasonal fish, fresh halibut and salmon. It is a versatile sauce, because with the addition of a few extra ingredients you can customize it to fit a specific dish. I prefer to incorporate a small amount of heavy cream to help stabilize the sauce and prevent it from breaking.

MAKES 1 CUP

½ CUP DRY WHITE WINE

1 TABLESPOON FRESHLY SQUEEZED LEMON JUICE

¼ CUP HEAVY WHIPPING CREAM

2 TABLESPOONS CHOPPED FRESH SHALLOTS (SUBSTITUTE THE WHITE PART OF SCALLIONS)

2 CUPS (4 STICKS) UNSALTED BUTTER, CUT INTO WALNUT-SIZED PIECES, VERY COLD

FINE SALT

COMBINE THE WHITE WINE, LEMON JUICE, cream, and shallots in a saucepan over medium-high heat. Bring to a simmer and reduce the contents by about half, until a thick slurry has formed. Slowly whisk in the butter, several pieces at a time, until all has been incorporated into the mix. You should end up with a creamy and smooth sauce. Add salt and any other flavorings at this time, adjusting seasonings to taste, and serve immediately.

VARIATIONS:

SHRIMP BEURRE BLANC: Heat ½ cup of shrimp stock (simmer 12 ounces of shrimp in their shells in a cup of water for 20 minutes, then strain) in a small saucepan over high heat to reduce by half. Add the stock in with the white wine, lemon juice, cream, and shallots, then proceed with the basic beurre blanc sauce.

TOMATO TARRAGON BEURRE BLANC: Stir in oven-roasted and chopped tomatoes and tarragon with the salt.

HERB BEURRE BLANC: Stir in chopped fresh rosemary and thyme with the salt.

CAJUN TARTAR SAUCE

WE CAME UP WITH THIS SAUCE A FEW YEARS ago and it has become a popular accompaniment with our fried catfish. It has a bit more of a bite than your basic tartar sauce but you can control the heat to your liking with more or less hot sauce. You can make your own mayo (see page 242) or, if you go with the store-bought kind, I like Hellman's® or Best Foods®. I also happen to love the habañero sauce from Tabasco. You can use this sauce for just about any fish; we like it with grouper, halibut, catfish, and walleye fillets.

MAKES 3 CUPS

2¹/₂ CUPS MAYONNAISE

³/₄ CUP SWEET PICKLE RELISH

2 TABLESPOONS SMOKED OR HUNGARIAN PAPRIKA

¹/₄ CUP FRESHLY SQUEEZED LEMON JUICE

¹/₂ TEASPOON CAYENNE PEPPER OR 1 TEASPOON HOT SAUCE (LIKE TABASCO HABAÑERO SAUCE)

¹/₄ CUP CAPERS (OPTIONAL)

MIX EVERYTHING TOGETHER THOROUGHLY. USE IMMEDI-ately or store in a covered jar in the refrigerator for up to a couple of weeks.

CARAMELIZED ONION AND MUSTARD SAUCE

I PRIMARILY USE THIS SAUCE FOR FLANK steak but it works just as well with pork chops or any meat grilled over the fire. The sweetness from the onions add a nice flavor: be sure that they get lots of color. This is also a great sauce for grilled fresh salmon. Don't be afraid to use this with grilled chicken. You can even apply it to spareribs.

MAKES ABOUT 3 CUPS

¹/₄ CUP (¹/₂ STICK) UNSALTED BUTTER

2 LARGE SWEET ONIONS, DICED

2 TABLESPOONS PACKED LIGHT BROWN SUGAR

1 CUP DIJON MUSTARD

¹/₂ CUP CHOPPED FRESH TARRAGON

1 CUP WHITE WINE

2 TO 3 TABLESPOONS FRESHLY CRACKED BLACK PEPPER

MELT THE BUTTER IN A SAUTÉ PAN AND ADD THE ONIONS and brown sugar. Cook over medium heat until the sugar has melted and the onions are caramelized, but not burned, about 5 minutes. Add the mustard, tarragon, wine, and pepper and cook until the mixture has reached the consistency of a relish. Serve warm or at room temperature.

CHIMICHURRI SAUCE

ARGENTINES LIKE TO REFER TO THEIR nation as the beef capital of the world. I know plenty of Montana ranchers who take serious exception to their claim. But one thing that we all have to concede is that the chimichurri sauce they use on their grilled beef and lamb has no equal.

My first experience with this legendary condiment came from one of our regulars at The Mint, Tim Crawford, a well-traveled hunter and fisherman, who told me about being hooked on a wonderful herb and garlic concoction he had on a trip to Patagonia. I had him describe the tastes and that night, threw together an approximation of chimichurri that more or less matched Tim's memory. Thus began my own obsession with finding the perfect balance of garlic, herbs, and olive oil. Gradually the following recipe evolved and became so popular that it is now on the menu at the restaurant.

The variation on the main recipe comes from my friend Virginia Wax who grew up in Argentina, an incredible cook in her own right. She tells of a favorite uncle whose own recipe was such a fixture at the table that it was always made in the same bottle, time after time, year after year. When the sauce ran low, he would merely add more, never allowing the bottle to become empty, and thus, of course never changing or washing the bottle: rather like a sourdough starter that resides in the same container for years. I thought this was a great story and a prime example of the reverence with which Argentines treat their national treasure. Virginia was quick to point out that every region, and even every family, has its own version.

MAKES ABOUT 3 CUPS

- ½ CUP RED WINE VINEGAR
- 1 PACKED CUP FRESH PARSLEY, LARGER STEMS REMOVED
- 1 PACKED CUP FRESH OREGANO, LARGER STEMS REMOVED
- 15 GARLIC CLOVES, DICED
- 1 TABLESPOON RED PEPPER FLAKES
- 1 TEASPOON FINE SALT
- FRESHLY SQUEEZED JUICE FROM A QUARTER OF A LEMON
- 2 TO 3 CUPS OLIVE OIL

COMBINE THE VINEGAR, PARSLEY, OREGANO, garlic, pepper flakes, salt, and lemon juice in a food processor and drizzle in 2 cups of the olive oil. Pulse until the garlic and parsley are chunky but definitely not pureed. If you want a looser sauce, add more olive oil. Store in the refrigerator for at least an hour to let the flavors meld, and let the sauce come to room temperature before serving. You can add more olive oil if you want to drizzle over meat, or keep in more of a paste form to enjoy on the plate.

VARIATION:

VIRGINIA WAX'S CHIMICHURRI SAUCE FOR LAMB: Follow the same recipe as above, adding ½ cup of fresh rosemary to the herbs and substituting balsamic vinegar for the red wine vinegar. You might need a bit more lemon juice to brighten up the flavor.

PERUVIAN GREEN SAUCE

ANOTHER GREAT SAUCE FROM SOUTH AMERICA that I have fallen in love with is Peruvian green sauce, which, as the name indicates, is indigenous to Peru. Like chimichurri, Peruvian green sauce has many variations and local interpretations, but I utilize a simple version as an accompaniment for steaks and fish. At The Mint we especially love this sauce with seared salmon. The richness of wild-caught sockeye or king salmon is the perfect foil for this South American gem.

MAKES 2 CUPS

1 CUP OLIVE OIL, DIVIDED

1/2 CUP RICE OR WHITE WINE VINEGAR

2 CUPS FRESH CILANTRO LEAVES

1 CUP FRESH FLAT-LEAF PARSLEY

5 SCALLIONS (WHITE AND GREEN PARTS)

1 JALAPEÑO, SEEDED AND COARSELY CHOPPED

6 GARLIC CLOVES, COARSELY CHOPPED

1/4 CUP SUGAR IN THE RAW (OR UNREFINED ORGANIC SUGAR)

1 TABLESPOON SEA SALT

COMBINE HALF THE OLIVE OIL AND THE vinegar in a food processor and pulse in the cilantro, parsley, scallions, jalapeño, and garlic. When you have a thick paste, add the sugar and salt slowly, tasting frequently. It should be fairly balanced: not too sweet, not too salty. Add the rest of the olive oil and refrigerate for at least an hour to let the flavors meld, and let the sauce come to room temperature before serving.

NOTE: In Peru this sauce is often mixed with mayonnaise for use in salads and on sandwiches. So keep this option in mind. You are going to like this one.

COMPOUND BUTTERS

COMPOUND BUTTERS WORK WELL WITH MEAT and fish dishes. At The Mint we serve the Maître d'Hôtel butter with our bison tenderloin. Compound butters are easy to make and they offer a great way to enhance the flavors of broiled meats. When you are ready to use it, merely slice into ¾-inch rounds and place it over the hot entrée. The warmth of the meat causes the butter to melt, forming an instant sauce.

These butters can be frozen until needed, and at The Mint, we usually have two to four variations of this versatile sauce ready to be thawed and used when needed.

The technique is the same, only the ingredients differ. If you use unsalted butter, add a tablespoon of salt per pound.

MAITRE D'HOTEL BUTTER

MAKES 1 POUND

2 CUPS (4 STICKS) SALTED BUTTER, AT ROOM TEMPERATURE
½ CUP FRESHLY SQUEEZED LEMON JUICE
3 TABLESPOONS CHOPPED FRESH FLAT-LEAF PARSLEY
1 TABLESPOON FRESHLY CRACKED BLACK PEPPER

WHIP THE BUTTER WITH A WHISK OR THE PADDLE ATTACH- ment of an electric mixer until it is fluffy. Blend in the lemon juice, parsley, salt and pepper. Shape the butter into long cylinders using waxed paper or parchment paper. Refrigerate the finished butter until firm.

DIJON BUTTER

MAKES 1 POUND

2 CUPS (4 STICKS) SALTED BUTTER, AT ROOM TEMPERATURE
1 TABLESPOON CHOPPED FRESH GARLIC CLOVES
½ TEASPOON FRESHLY SQUEEZED LEMON JUICE
2 TABLESPOONS DIJON MUSTARD
2 TABLESPOONS CHOPPED FRESH FLAT-LEAF PARSLEY
1 TEASPOON FRESHLY GROUND BLACK PEPPER

WHIP THE BUTTER WITH A WHISK OR THE PADDLE ATTACH- ment of an electric mixer until it is fluffy. Blend in the garlic, lemon juice, mustard, parsley, and pepper. Shape the butter into long cylinders using waxed paper or parchment paper. Refrigerate the finished butter until firm.

CURRY BUTTER

MAKES 1 POUND

2 CUPS (4 STICKS) SALTED BUTTER, AT ROOM TEMPERATURE
1 TABLESPOON CURRY POWDER
3 GARLIC CLOVES, FINELY CHOPPED
2 TABLESPOONS CHOPPED FRESH FLAT-LEAF PARSLEY

Whip the butter with a whisk or the paddle attachment of an electric mixer until it is fluffy. Blend in the curry powder, garlic, and parsley. Shape the butter into long cylinders using waxed paper or parchment paper. Refrigerate the finished butter until firm.

ROSEMARY BUTTER

MAKES 1 POUND

2 CUPS (4 STICKS) SALTED BUTTER, AT ROOM TEMPERATURE
1/2 CUP CHOPPED FRESH ROSEMARY
2 TABLESPOONS FRESHLY GROUND BLACK PEPPER

Whip the butter with a whisk or the paddle attachment of an electric mixer until it is fluffy. Blend in the rosemary and pepper. Shape the butter into long cylinders using waxed paper or parchment paper. Refrigerate the finished butter until firm.

TARRAGON BUTTER

MAKES 1 POUND

2 CUPS (4 STICKS) SALTED BUTTER, AT ROOM TEMPERATURE
1/2 CUP FRESH CHOPPED TARRAGON
2 TABLESPOONS FRESHLY GROUND BLACK PEPPER

Whip the butter with a whisk or the paddle attachment of an electric mixer until it is fluffy. Blend in the tarragon and pepper. Shape the butter into long cylinders using waxed paper or parchment paper. Refrigerate the finished butter until firm.

BLUE CHEESE BUTTER

MAKES 1 POUND

2 CUPS (4 STICKS) SALTED BUTTER, AT ROOM TEMPERATURE
1 CUP CRUMBLED BLUE CHEESE, AT ROOM TEMPERATURE
2 TABLESPOONS FRESHLY CRACKED BLACK PEPPER

Whip the butter with a whisk or the paddle attachment of an electric mixer until it is fluffy. Blend in the blue cheese and pepper. Shape the butter into long cylinders using waxed paper or parchment paper. Refrigerate the finished butter until firm.

CLARIFIED BUTTER

CLARIFIED BUTTER (ALSO CALLED GHEE, AND used in Indian cooking) is simply butter that has been melted and strained to eliminate the solids. Clarified butter has a much higher smoke point and is essentially butter reduced to pure fat. It allows you to sauté meat, fish, and vegetables at a higher heat and it imparts a great buttery taste without smoking or burning.

Most restaurants of any consequence always have a pot of clarified butter on the line. Any leftover butter can be refrigerated or frozen if necessary.

MAKES 3¹/₂ CUPS

4 CUPS (8 STICKS) UNSALTED BUTTER

PLACE THE BUTTER IN A 2-QUART POT OR LARGER SAUCE pan over medium to low heat. Allow the butter to heat and separate. The solids will eventually sink to the bottom. Carefully pour the fat into a clean, dry container, leaving behind the solids. Discard the solids and store the clarified butter in the refrigerator.

MINT-STYLE SESAME DRESSING

BILL SMITH, A VETERAN OF DUDE RANCH kitchens, was our chef in the mid-nineties and his sesame dressing recipe became an instant classic. Its tangy flavor is great on all kinds of salads. We also recommend using it as a marinade and even as a sauce for cold Asian noodles.

MAKES ABOUT 1¹/₂ CUPS

¹/₄ CUP SESAME SEEDS, TOASTED
¹/₄ CUP HONEY
¹/₂ CUP SOY SAUCE
¹/₄ CUP PACKED DARK BROWN SUGAR
¹/₂ TEASPOON GROUND GINGER
¹/₄ TEASPOON CAYENNE PEPPER
³/₄ TEASPOON FRESHLY GROUND BLACK PEPPER
¹/₄ TABLESPOON GRANULATED GARLIC
1 TABLESPOON DIJON MUSTARD
¹/₂ CUP RICE VINEGAR
³/₄ CUP CANOLA OIL
¹/₄ CUP SESAME OIL

In a food processor or blender, blend everything except the canola and sesame oils until smooth. Gradually add the canola and sesame oils with the motor running and process until emulsified. Refrigerate until ready to use. If the dressing is too thick, thin it with a little water.

CONTINENTAL DIVIDE CAJUN HOUSE DRESSING

I WAS DRIVING FROM MONTANA TO NEW ORL-eans one winter and had just come through a harrowing experience: a snowstorm between Dallas and Shreveport that was far worse than anything I had experienced in Montana. South of Shreveport the sun started to shine, the temperature climbed, and, almost magically, the snow disappeared. Just below Natchitoches (the home of Lasyone's meat pies, see page 103) and relieved to be out of danger, I jubilantly drove through an area of large pecan groves, and had an inspiration—Cajun pecan dressing.

This turned out to be the most requested of all our recipes at the Continental Divide, where it was our house dressing. We serve it at The Mint and I'm happy to admit, it's like an addiction for our regulars. The salad is good with red bell peppers, red onions, and more of the pecans.

MAKES 2 CUPS

PAN-ROASTED PECANS

$^1/_2$ CUP (1 STICK) UNSALTED BUTTER

3 CUPS WHOLE OR SPLIT PECANS

1 TEASPOON SEA SALT

1 TEASPOON CAYENNE PEPPER

DRESSING

$^1/_3$ CUP HONEY

$^1/_3$ CUP WHOLE-GRAIN BROWN MUSTARD

1 CUP VEGETABLE OR OLIVE OIL

$^1/_3$ CUP RED WINE VINEGAR

$^1/_2$ TEASPOON CAYENNE PEPPER

$^3/_4$ TEASPOON SEA SALT

FOR THE ROASTED PECANS, MELT THE BUT-ter in a sauté pan on high heat. Add the pecans and cook until they are well browned but not burned, tossing frequently. Just before removing from the heat, sprinkle them with the salt and cayenne, adjusting seasonings to taste. You'll have to experiment to achieve the level of heat that you desire. Drain on paper towels and set aside. Allow the nuts to cool. (This makes more than you need for the dressing, but you won't have trouble finding ways to use them elsewhere.)

In a food processor, add the honey, $^1/_3$ cup of the pecans, and mustard, and blend well. Slowly blend in the oil, then $^3/_4$ cup of water and the red wine vinegar. Add the cayenne and salt, adjusting seasonings to taste. Be sure that the consistency is creamy. If the mixture breaks, you can usually bring it back by adding ice cubes one at a time.

CRACKED BLACK PEPPER AND RASPBERRY SAUCE

THROUGHOUT MONTANA YOU CAN FIND THE remains of old homesteads and abandoned cabins, each with its own raspberry patch planted no doubt with visions of the wonderful pies and jams to help offset difficult frontier lives. The heartier strains of these berries thrive in the short dry summers typical of the high plains. Native American tribes that inhabited or hunted the territory relied on this prolific berry to make pemmican, a kind of jerky and dried fruit trail food that they often also used as a naturopathic remedy for all kinds of ailments.

I confess that I prefer to purchase a large jar of raspberry jam than pick raspberries in the wilds while being supervised by the ghost of some old settler. In any event, using raspberry jam as the base for a sauce opens up options for salmon (as with the Seared Salmon with Cajun Rub and Raspberry Sauce on page 54), as well as wild game and even beef. In this case I want to focus on my favorite sauce for fresh wild-caught salmon.

MAKES 1⅓ CUPS

- 2 TABLESPOONS UNSALTED BUTTER
- 1 SMALL YELLOW ONION, FINELY DICED
- 1 CUP BEEF STOCK (SUBSTITUTE 1 TABLESPOON GOOD-QUALITY BEEF BASE PLUS 1 CUP WATER)
- 1 CUP RASPBERRY JAM (SEEDLESS IF YOU PREFER)
- 2 TABLESPOONS FRESHLY CRACKED BLACK PEPPER
- FINE SALT

MELT THE BUTTER IN A SAUTÉ PAN OVER medium-high heat and sauté the onion until slightly caramelized, about 10 minutes. Add the stock and reduce to half its volume. Stir in the jam and pepper and reduce to a syrupy consistency, about 10 minutes, then add salt, adjusting seasoning to taste. Serve warm.

GARLIC MUSTARD SAUCE

THIS SAUCE IS GREAT FOR GRILLED BEEF and game, as well as pork and lamb. It has the character and texture to hold up to the strong flavors of meats cooked over an open fire.

I first ran into a variation of this sauce in a James Beard book on outdoor cooking, and I have modified it over the years. It keeps in the refrigerator, and gets better with age.

MAKES ABOUT 1½ CUPS

2 MEDIUM YELLOW ONIONS, FINELY DICED

6 GARLIC CLOVES, FINELY DICED

2 TABLESPOONS OLIVE OIL

½ CUP DIJON MUSTARD

2 CUPS RED WINE

¼ CUP WORCESTERSHIRE SAUCE

¼ CUP FRESHLY CRACKED BLACK PEPPER

2 TABLESPOONS GOOD-QUALITY BEEF BASE

SEA SALT

IN A SAUCEPAN OVER MEDIUM HEAT, SAUTÉ the onions and garlic in the oil until they are translucent. Add the mustard, wine, Worcestershire, pepper, beef base, and 1 cup of water and cook over high heat until the mixture has been reduced to a thin paste. There should be enough salt, but if you need more, add a little sea salt, adjusting seasoning to taste.

Store any leftover sauce in the refrigerator and use when needed. It's great served hot on most meats or cold on a roast beef sandwich.

PERFECT MAYONNAISE

THERE WAS A LONG PERIOD WHEN I DIDN'T eat mayonnaise because everyone said that eggs and oil were bad for you; but that was then and this is now. The latest studies say that eggs are not as bad as everyone was saying. In fact, they are now acknowledged as a good source of protein, and, when you use olive or canola oil, mayonnaise can actually be of some nutritional benefit. I take this news seriously because I am a mayonnaise addict.

There are three basic techniques to make your own mayonnaise. The first, and the most traditional, is by hand with a whisk; the second uses a blender; and the third uses a food processor. I have tried all three ways, and I think the food processor method is not only the fastest, but also the most foolproof. It seems to have a longer shelf life, and doesn't break down as hand-whisked mayonnaise tends to do.

I normally blend canola and olive oils, which produces a balanced flavor and texture. Olive oil tends to make the flavor heavier, reflecting the fruity characteristics of the oil. Canola has very little flavor and has a definite lightening effect. For example, if I'm going to do a cold aioli, which is merely garlic-infused mayonnaise, then I will use a higher percentage of olive oil in the mix. Speaking of infused sauces, mayonnaise lends itself to all kinds of variations by adding herbs, spices, and other ingredients. I have listed some of the more popular variations after the basic recipe. This recipe holds well, so you can prepare a double batch if the urge overtakes you.

MAKES 2 CUPS

1 EGG

2 EGG YOLKS

1 TEASPOON DIJON MUSTARD

1/2 TEASPOON SEA SALT

2 TABLESPOONS FRESHLY SQUEEZED LEMON JUICE OR WHITE VINEGAR (OR 1 TABLESPOON OF EACH)

1 TEASPOON WHITE PEPPER

1 CUP OLIVE OIL

1 CUP CANOLA OIL

COMBINE THE EGG, YOLKS, MUSTARD, SALT, lemon juice, and pepper in a food processor and pulse it until the ingredients are well mixed. Then turn on to full speed for about 15 seconds. With the machine running, slowly drizzle the oils into the mixture a few drops at a time until you have added about half a cup. The mixture should be showing some cohesion. With the machine running continue adding the rest of the oils. Check for thickness. If the mayonnaise is too thick, add a tablespoon of water until it reaches the desired thickness.

If the mixture breaks and doesn't come together, pour the broken mayonnaise into a bowl and set aside. Start again with another egg yolk and a teaspoon of mustard. Begin the mixing process again and slowly reincorporate the broken mixture as you would the oil. Chances are that you added the oil too quickly the first time. Once you get the hang of it you won't have a problem doing it perfectly every time. The mayonnaise can be refrigerated for 3 to 5 days.

VARIATIONS:

AIOLI: Stir in 3 minced garlic cloves.

CHILI MAYO: Stir in 1 tablespoon chili powder, 1/2 teaspoon cumin, and 1/4 teaspoon cayenne pepper.

SPICY CHILI MAYO: Stir in 2 teaspoons Asian chili-garlic paste.

CURRY MAYO: Add 2 tablespoons curry powder and 1/2 teaspoon cumin.

BASIC MARINARA SAUCE

MARINARA SAUCE IS ONE OF THE BASICS OF Italian cooking. This ubiquitous and venerated standard of Italian cuisine was said to have originated in Naples and traditionally incorporated mussels, squid, and various other types of fish or shellfish, hence the name "Marinara".

I always keep some in the freezer for a quick batch of pasta on demand and though I normally use it as-is, I will often add capers, anchovies, or red pepper flakes, when I want something different.

MAKES 1 QUART

1 CUP GOOD-QUALITY OLIVE OIL

1 SMALL YELLOW ONION, DICED

$^{1}/_{4}$ CUP FINELY CHOPPED FRESH GARLIC
   (FROM ABOUT 8 CLOVES)

2 (15-OUNCE) CANS DICED TOMATOES

$^{1}/_{2}$ CUP CHOPPED FRESH BASIL

1 /4 CUP CHOPPED FRESH OREGANO

1 TEASPOON GRANULATED SUGAR

1 TEASPOON FINE SEA SALT

IN A 2-QUART SAUCE PAN PREHEAT THE OLIVE OIL OVER medium heat, around 3 to 5 minutes. Add the garlic and onions. Cook for 5 minutes, or until the garlic and onions are soft and translucent. Add the tomatoes, basil, oregano, and sugar, turn the heat down to low and simmer for around 30 minutes. Add the salt and taste for seasonings.

HORSERADISH SAUCE

I LIKE IT HOT. BUT EVEN MILD, HORSERADISH sauce sets off the flavor of roast and corned beef.

MAKES 4 CUPS

1 CUP PREPARED, GRATED HORSERADISH

1 CUP MAYONNAISE

2 CUPS SOUR CREAM

1 TEASPOON SALT

BLEND TOGETHER THOROUGHLY, CHILL, AND SERVE.

SPAGHETTI SAUCE

NO DISCUSSION OF SAUCES WOULD BE COMPLETE without something funky and meaty to throw on spaghetti. You know, the kind of stuff you find in those ubiquitous neighborhood Italian restaurants, what in New Orleans they call "red gravy" or even the kind of stuff your best friend's mom used to make when you were kids.

Any ground meat—beef, pork, veal, whatever is at hand and in any combination—will work equally well. By the time I add as much garlic and hot pepper flakes as I like, the variety of meat doesn't really matter. I like to use wild game, which I grind with no added fat, (other than the olive oil) because I can eat tons of the stuff without a lot of guilt. This recipe makes a great sauce even without ground meat. You can also use meatballs or even Italian sausage.

I normally use a lot more garlic and red pepper than is specified in this recipe. I toned it down for general consumption, but don't hesitate to add as much as you want. I always make a bigger batch than I need because like all comfort food, it gets better with age, and it gives me a warm feeling knowing that I will always have some in the freezer.

SERVES 6 TO 8

2 TABLESPOONS OLIVE OIL

2 LARGE YELLOW ONIONS, DICED

5 GARLIC CLOVES, MINCED

2 POUNDS LEAN GROUND MEAT (BISON, VENISON, OR ELK WORK AS WELL AS BEEF, PORK, OR VEAL)

1 (14.5-OUNCE) CAN TOMATO SAUCE

2 (28-OUNCE) CANS WHOLE PLUM TOMATOES WITH JUICE

1/2 (6-OUNCE) CAN TOMATO PASTE

1 CUP BEEF STOCK (SUBSTITUTE 1 TABLESPOON GOOD-QUALITY BEEF BASE PLUS 1 CUP OF WATER)

1/3 CUP FENNEL SEEDS, CRUSHED WITH A MORTAR AND PESTLE (OPTIONAL, BUT RECOMMENDED)

15 LARGE PITTED PIMENTO-STUFFED SPANISH OLIVES, SLICED (OPTIONAL, BUT RECOMMENDED)

1/3 CUP GRANULATED SUGAR

3 TABLESPOONS CHOPPED FRESH OREGANO

1 TABLESPOON CHOPPED FRESH BASIL

2 BAY LEAVES, BROKEN IN HALF

1 TABLESPOON RED PEPPER FLAKES

KOSHER SALT AND FRESHLY GROUND BLACK PEPPER

LINGUINI OR SPAGHETTI, COOKED TO AL DENTE, FOR SERVING

IN A 12- OR 14-INCH HEAVY SAUCEPAN, HEAT the oil over medium-high heat. When the oil pops at the addition of a drop of water, add the onions and garlic. Stir with a wooden spoon, cooking until they are translucent. Then add the ground meat and cook until brown, about 10 minutes. When the meat looks just toasty, stir in the tomato sauce, whole tomatoes with juice, tomato paste, and stock. Bring to a gentle boil. Then add the fennel seeds, olives, sugar, oregano, basil, bay leaves, and red pepper flakes.

Cover and simmer on low heat for 35 to 40 minutes. Taste and season with salt and pepper. Serve generously over pasta.

NEW ORLEANS RED-MEAT GRAVY

MY BROTHER TONY IS A NEW ORLEANS RACE-track announcer, restaurant waiter, opera singer, movie actor, great amateur chef, and lover of wine. His big tomato-mushroom-meat sauce is in a class by itself. I'm always giving him a hard time about his obsession with following a recipe. He uses the same ingredients and follows the same steps, each and every time. And his dish predictably turns out great every single time.

Pasta of any shape will work well with this recipe. I tend to like buccatini or penne, but this stuff is so good you can eat it straight out of the pot with a hunk of good bread and a bottle of soft Italian red.

SERVES 12 TO 14

1 CUP OLIVE OIL

3 POUNDS FLANK OR ROUND STEAK (BEEF, BISON, OR ELK ALL WORK WELL), CUT INTO BITE-SIZED PIECES

1/2 CUP (1 STICK) UNSALTED BUTTER

1/4 CUP CHOPPED FRESH GARLIC (FROM ABOUT 10 LARGE CLOVES)

2 LARGE YELLOW ONIONS, DICED

2 STALKS CELERY, CHOPPED

2 CUPS BEEF STOCK (SUBSTITUTE 2 TEASPOONS GOOD-QUALITY BEEF BASE PLUS 2 CUPS WATER)

3 CUPS DRY RED WINE

4 (14.5-OUNCE) CANS CHOPPED TOMATOES WITH JUICE

2 (6-OUNCE) CANS TOMATO PASTE

2 TABLESPOONS CHOPPED FRESH ROSEMARY LEAVES

4 BAY LEAVES

2 CUPS COARSELY CHOPPED PORCINI OR PORTOBELLO MUSHROOMS (SUBSTITUTE 1 CUP DRIED PORCINI MUSHROOMS, REHYDRATED FOR 20 MINUTES IN HOT WATER)

3 TABLESPOONS FRESHLY CRACKED BLACK PEPPER

FINE SALT

LINGUINI OR OTHER PASTA, COOKED TO AL DENTE, FOR SERVING

HEAT THE OIL IN A LARGE POT OVER MEDIUM-high heat and add the meat. Cook until browned, about 20 to 30 minutes. Pour off and discard the rendered fat and set the meat aside.

Add the butter to the pan and melt over medium-high heat. Cook the garlic, onions, and celery until soft, stirring occasionally, about 7 minutes. Add the stock, wine, tomatoes, tomato paste, rosemary, bay leaves, and 1 1/2 cups of water. Return the meat to the pot. Bring to a boil, and then reduce the heat to maintain a light simmer. Cook uncovered for an hour, stirring occasionally.

Add the mushrooms to the sauce and cook for another 10 to 15 minutes. Add the pepper and salt, if needed, adjustig seasoning to taste. Serve generously with pasta.

RED CURRANT SAUCE

THIS IS A CLASSIC PREPARATION FOR VENISON.
So classic in fact that it is often overlooked today. It's also good with grilled beef and even salmon.

1 TABLESPOON UNSALTED BUTTER
1 TABLESPOON CHOPPED SHALLOTS
1 TABLESPOON FRESHLY CRACKED BLACK PEPPER
¼ CUP RED CURRANT JELLY
½ CUP PORT
1 CUP DEMI-GLACE OR 1 QUART OF BEEF STOCK REDUCED TO 1 CUP

HEAT THE BUTTER OVER MEDIUM HEAT. SAUTÉ THE SHALLOTS
and pepper until the shallots are softened, about 3 minutes. Stir in the red currant jelly. Deglaze the pan with the port and add the demi-glace. Stir until the sauce is blended, then reduce to a semi-thick consistency. Thin with a little water if it reduces too much, and serve hot.

SALSA CRIOLLA, ARGENTINE-STYLE

PAIRED WITH CHIMICHURRI, THIS WONDERFUL
mixture of chopped fresh tomatoes and spices raises the experience of eating grilled meat to another level. I was first introduced to salsa criolla by Elena D'Autremont, an elegant transplant from Argentina, at a streamside asado, or cookout, that she and her husband Chuck threw on their ranch on the upper Ruby River in southwestern Montana. After cooking a roast over a hot cottonwood fire accompanied by mollejas—veal sweetbreads marinated in olive oil and grilled— she brought out this wonderful salsa to accompany the meat.

MAKES 3 TO 4 CUPS

5 RIPE MEDIUM TO LARGE TOMATOES, CORED AND DICED
1 YELLOW ONION, FINELY DICED
1 GREEN BELL PEPPER, SEEDED, CORED, AND DICED
2 TABLESPOON RED WINE VINEGAR
½ CUP OLIVE OIL
1 FRESH SERRANO OR JALAPEÑO PEPPER, SEEDED AND FINELY DICED
SEA SALT

TOSS EVERYTHING TOGETHER AND SALT AS NEEDED. SET ASIDE
to meld for 30 minutes at room temperature and serve on the side of any grilled meat.

ROSEMARY SHALLOT SAUCE FOR LAMB

THIS PAN SAUCE CAN BE MADE QUICKLY IF you have the right ingredients, particularly chicken glace. The most common types of glaces are chicken, beef, and veal. The French restaurants where I worked kept some on hand for sauces that were referred to as "á la minute," a sauce prepared for each dish as it was served, rather than something more elaborate prepared ahead of time. Glace (pronounced "glas-SAY") is merely a stock (in this case chicken stock) that has been reduced to the consistency of thin syrup. This process concentrates and intensifies the flavor to the point where a small amount added to other flavorings—usually wine and herbs—produces a rich and satisfying sauce that elevates a dish to a whole other level.

To make a glace, start out with a quart of stock and reduce it to one cup. When I make a batch I freeze it in ice cube trays and store the cubes in the freezer until needed. When you pull it out of the freezer, the consistency should be hard but slightly rubbery, like a hockey puck. Then it's a simple matter of plopping one of these pucks into our sauce and stir as it melts.

MAKES 1 CUP

2 TABLESPOONS UNSALTED BUTTER

3 MEDIUM SHALLOTS, FINELY DICED

3 TABLESPOONS DICED FRESH ROSEMARY

2 TABLESPOONS FRESHLY CRACKED BLACK PEPPER

1 CUP RED WINE

1/3 CUP MINT JELLY

1/3 CUP CHICKEN GLACE

FINE SALT

IN A SAUTÉ PAN OR SMALL SAUCEPAN, MELT the butter over medium heat, add the shallots, rosemary, and cracked pepper and cook until the shallots begin to caramelize, about 3 minutes. Add the red wine, jelly, and glace and cook, stirring constantly, until the mixture is reduced to approximately 1 cup. The sauce should become syrupy, and coat the back of a spoon. If it gets too thick, thin it with a little more wine. Adjust seasoning to taste.

BOOT HEEL COMEBACK BARBECUE SAUCE

IN THE EARLY DAYS AT OUR CONTINENTAL
Divide restaurant, we set up a big grill out front on Main Street in Ennis, Montana, for the annual Fourth of July rodeo. The town was always packed with well-imbibed celebrants, cowboys, ranchers, tourists, and Montanans both well-heeled and some not so. We would sell unbelievable amounts of quartered and halved roast chickens all generously slathered in my grandfather's famous Boot Heel Comeback Barbecue Sauce.

My father claims that his father, Roy Bentley, whom I never met, was somewhat of a rounder, a real character who lived most of his life in the "Boot Heel" area of Southeast Missouri. I know very little about him since my father didn't really talk about him. The story, as I got it, was that Roy loved barbecue and saloons and that his career as a local pit master of great renown allowed him to have the best of both of those worlds.

The story went on to say that a lot of people, in the predominantly Baptist community of New Madrid, Missouri, where Roy resided, were of two minds. On one hand they detested the evils of strong drink and on the other they loved good barbecue. I like to think that in the end, things kind of balanced out, and given the legacy of this tasty concoction, grandpa Roy went to his eternal rest a little bit on the plus side.

MAKES ABOUT 1 GALLON

3 CUPS CIDER VINEGAR
3 CUPS MOLASSES
5 CUPS KETCHUP
3 CUPS ORANGE JUICE
1/4 CUP CURRY POWDER
1/4 CUP CHILI POWDER
1/4 CUP GRANULATED GARLIC
1/4 CUP ONION POWDER
1 TABLESPOON LIQUID SMOKE (OPTIONAL)
DASH OF ALLSPICE

COMBINE EVERYTHING IN A SAUCEPAN, bring to a boil, and then simmer for 20 minutes, until thickened to your liking. This a great sauce for beef, pork, chicken, lamb, and just about anything that can be cooked on a barbecue pit. It freezes just fine.

THE MINT'S CRANBERRY SAUCE

THIS RECIPE IS SURPRISINGLY VERSATILE because by taking the basic recipe and changing or adding ingredients you can use it for a whole lot more than the family turkey. But even the basic recipe is a great accompaniment to stuffed pork chops, grilled salmon, or anything else you can imagine.

I tend to keep it on the tart side but you can make it sweeter or even tarter depending on your taste and preference. This is a pretty big batch because it freezes well and because fresh cranberries are usually only available around the holidays.

MAKES 2 PINTS

¹/₂ STICK (¹/₄ CUP) UNSALTED BUTTER

1 CUP PEELED AND FINELY DICED FRESH GINGER

1 (12-OUNCE) CAN FROZEN ORANGE JUICE CONCENTRATE, THAWED

1 CUP PACKED DARK BROWN SUGAR

1 TABLESPOON VANILLA

3 WHOLE CLOVES

3 POUNDS FRESH CRANBERRIES

1 TEASPOON FINE SALT, OR TO TASTE

2 (4-OUNCE) CANS MANDARIN ORANGE SLICES, DRAINED (OPTIONAL)

MELT THE BUTTER IN A LARGE SAUCEPAN and add the ginger. Cook for 5 minutes, or until soft. Add the orange juice, brown sugar, vanilla, cloves, and a cup of water, and bring to a boil. Add the cranberries, and then reduce the heat to medium and cook, stirring occasionally, for approximately 30 minutes. Most of the berries should have broken down and the volume should have been reduced by a quarter to a third; the sauce should be thick. Remove from the heat and add the salt and oranges (if using), and transfer to another container to cool. The sauce can be kept in the refrigerator for a week to 10 days, or frozen indefinitely.

VARIATION:

Turn the cranberry sauce into a warm sauce for beef or grilled salmon by sautéing a diced onion in 2 tablespoons of butter until the onions are transparent. Stir in 2 cups of the cranberry sauce, a tablespoon of Worcestershire sauce, a teaspoon of freshly ground black pepper, and a teaspoon of salt. Cook until heated through, then serve.

DESSERTS

I HAVE NEVER BEEN VERY GOOD AT DESSERTS. I DON'T HAVE THE PERSONALITY OF A GOOD PASTRY chef, which includes patience and precision. Anyone who knows me can tell you: those are virtues I simply don't possess. Sure, I've been known to do the occasional pecan pie on Thanksgiving when overwhelmed by a craving, or throw together a batch of chocolate chip cookies, but all in all desserts are not my strength.

Yet, when we were writing this book, we wanted to include a small chapter of dessert all-stars: the best dishes you can have in your repertoire, no more, no less. Fortunately, my former executive chef at The Mint, Jordan Boutry, does everything very well, including desserts. He graciously wrote the recipes for The Mint's bestselling desserts. These will serve you well as you cook through the book: in fact, I'd go so far as to say you won't ever need another dessert recipe outside of this chapter.

MOLTEN CHOCOLATE CAKES WITH STRAWBERRY PURÉE

SERVES 6

3/4 CUP (1 1/2 STICKS) UNSALTED BUTTER

7 OUNCES DARK CHOCOLATE, CHOPPED INTO SMALL PIECES

4 EGGS

5 EGG YOLKS

1 CUP ALL-PURPOSE FLOUR

1 1/2 CUPS CONFECTIONERS' SUGAR, SIFTED

STRAWBERRY PURÉE

1 PINT FRESH STRAWBERRIES, HULLED AND CHOPPED

1/2 CUP BURGUNDY

1/4 CUP GRANULATED SUGAR

1 TABLESPOON FRESHLY SQUEEZED LEMON JUICE

1 TABLESPOON UNSALTED BUTTER

HUCKLEBERRY ICE CREAM (SEE PAGE 254)

CONFECTIONERS' SUGAR, FOR SERVING

PREHEAT THE OVEN TO 400°F. BUTTER 6 LARGE MUFFIN TINS or 4-ounce ramekins.

Combine the butter and chocolate in the top part of a double boiler or in a heat-safe mixing bowl that fits over a pan of simmering water. Stir occasionally as they melt together.

Whisk together the eggs and egg yolks until they are pale yellow. Temper the eggs with the melted chocolate by spooning in a little of the hot chocolate while constantly whisking to keep the eggs from scrambling. Pour the rest of the melted chocolate into the eggs and whisk to combine.

Sift the flour and confectioners' sugar together and then add to the liquid ingredients and mix thoroughly. Pour the batter evenly among the muffin cups or ramekins.

Bake for 10 to 15 minutes. Check constantly after 10 minutes, pulling them out when still gooey and not yet set in the center.

Let the cakes cool for 10 minutes before removing from the muffin tins with a butter knife, being careful not to puncture the melty centers.

Meanwhile, make the strawberry purée by simmering all the ingredients together for 15 minutes, until the strawberries soften and break down. Puree in a food processor until smooth. Allow to cool.

Dust the tops with confectioners' sugar. Serve the warm chocolate cakes with a scoop of huckleberry ice cream drizzled with strawberry purée. Serve warm.

HUCKLEBERRY ICE CREAM

MAKES 1½ QUARTS

2½ CUPS HALF-AND-HALF

1 CUP WHIPPING CREAM

1 CUP MINUS 2 TABLESPOONS GRANULATED SUGAR

1 VANILLA BEAN, SPLIT AND SCRAPED

2 EGG YOLKS

1 CUP FRESH HUCKLEBERRIES
(SUBSTITUTE FRESH BLUEBERRIES)

COMBINE THE HALF-AND-HALF, WHIPPING CREAM, SUGAR, and vanilla bean seeds and pod in a large saucepan and place over medium heat. Stirring occasionally, bring the mixture to 170°F. Remove from heat and allow to cool slightly. Temper the eggs in a mixing bowl with a couple of ladles of hot cream: whisk them vigorously to avoid temperature shock. Pour the warmed eggs into cream. Strain the ice cream base through a fine-mesh sieve into a lidded container and refrigerate overnight.

Lightly pulse the berries in the food processor to chop.

Freeze the ice cream base in an ice cream maker according to manufacturer's instructions. Once the ice cream is three-quarters of the way frozen add the berries and continue churning unil done. Scrape into a lidded container and freeze until firm.

SNICKERS PIE

SERVES 10

PEANUT BUTTER BROWNIE CRUST

10 TABLESPOONS (1¼ STICKS) UNSALTED BUTTER

4 OUNCES DARK CHOCOLATE, CHOPPED

2 EGGS

¾ CUP GRANULATED SUGAR

¼ TEASPOON SEA SALT

1 TABLESPOON VANILLA

¼ CUP PEANUT BUTTER

⅞ CUP ALL-PURPOSE FLOUR

½ CUP GRAHAM CRACKER CRUMBS

ICE CREAM FILLING

1 (HALF-GALLON) CARTON SNICKERS ICE CREAM

2 HEATH CANDY BARS, FINELY CHOPPED

1 PINT MARSHMALLOW FLUFF

CARAMEL SAUCE

CHOCOLATE SAUCE

1 LARGE SNICKERS BAR, ROUGHLY CHOPPED

FOR THE BROWNIE CRUST, BUTTER AN 8X8-INCH GLASS baking dish. Preheat the oven to 400°F.

Combine the butter and chocolate in the top part of a double boiler or in a heat-safe mixing bowl that fits over a pan of simmering water. Stir occasionally as they melt together.

Stir together the eggs, sugar, salt, vanilla, and peanut butter in a bowl. Add a little of the hot melted chocolate mixture to temper the egg mixture, and then stir in the remaining melted chocolate. Add the flour and mix lightly until just incorporated. Pour into the prepared baking dish.

Bake for 45 minutes, or until a toothpick inserted in the center comes out dry. Cool completely. Rough chop the brownies and combine with the graham cracker crumbs in a medium bowl. Mash together, and then press into bottom of greased 10-inch springform pan.

For the ice cream filling, let the ice cream sit out for 10 minutes to come to room temperature. In an electric mixer fitted with the paddle attachment, whip together the ice cream, Heath bars, and marshmallow fluff for 5 to 10 minutes. Spoon the filling into the prepared crust and smooth the top with a spatula. Freeze overnight.

Release the sides of the springform pan, and then cut the pie with a knife dipped into hot water. Serve each slice with caramel sauce, chocolate sauce, and Snickers pieces.

FLATHEAD CHERRY WHITE-CHOCOLATE CRÈME BRÛLÉE

SERVES 8

SUGARED CHERRIES

1 PINT FRESH FLATHEAD OR OTHER FRESH CHERRIES, STEMS ON

$^1/_2$ CUP SIMPLE SYRUP

$^1/_2$ CUP GRANULATED SUGAR

CHERRY COMPOTE

2 PINTS FLATHEAD CHERRIES (SUBSTITUTE ANY FRESH CHERRIES, OR 10 OUNCES FROZEN CHERRIES), PITTED

1 TABLESPOON FRESHLY SQUEEZED LEMON JUICE

$^1/_2$ CUP CABERNET SAUVIGNON

$^1/_2$ CUP GRANULATED SUGAR

CRÈME BRÛLÉE

3 CUPS HEAVY CREAM

$^1/_2$ CUP WHITE BAKING CHOCOLATE

1 CUP HALF-AND-HALF

1 VANILLA BEAN, SPLIT LENGTHWISE AND SCRAPED

8 EGG YOLKS

1 CUP GRANULATED SUGAR, DIVIDED

FOR THE SUGARED CHERRIES, DIP THE CHERRIES ries in the simple syrup, then roll in granulated sugar. Set aside to dry.

For the cherry compote, simmer all ingredients in a small saucepan for 15 minutes. Cool in the refrigerator completely.

For the crème brûlée, heat the cream, white chocolate, half-and-half, and vanilla bean pod and seeds together in pot over medium heat until it begins to simmer. Stir constantly to keep it from scalding.

Meanwhile, whisk the yolks and $^1/_2$ cup of the sugar together in a mixing bowl vigorously until very light and pale yellow. Slowly incorporate half of the cream mixture into the eggs to temper. Add the rest of cream to the warmed eggs and mix thoroughly. Cool in the refrigerator completely.

Preheat the oven to 325°F. Heat a kettle of water to boiling.

Divide the cherry compote among eight 6-ounce ramekins. Ladle the crème brûlée batter on top of the compote.

Set the ramekins on top of a cloth napkin or kitchen towel spread inside of a large baking dish. (This will keep the ramekins from coming in contact with high heat from the pan.) Carefully pour the hot water into the baking dish around the ramekins to make a bain marie (it distributes heat more evenly). Cover the baking dish with foil. Bake for 45 to 55 minutes. You will know that they are done when they have a solid jiggle when shaken (like Jell-O). Remove the ramekins from the pan and place in the fridge for 2 hours.

After chilling the ramekins, sprinkle the top of each crème brûlée with 1 tablespoon of the remaining sugar. Using a blow torch, lightly caramelize the tops of the brûlées; the sugar should melt and form a crust, about 20 to 30 seconds. Place a couple of sugared cherries on top and serve.

HUCKLEBERRY CRISP

SERVES 8

CRISP TOPPING

$^1/_2$ CUP SLIVERED ALMONDS, TOASTED AND COOLED

$1^1/_2$ CUPS ROLLED OATS

2 CUPS ALL-PURPOSE FLOUR

1 CUP PACKED LIGHT BROWN SUGAR

$^1/_4$ CUP GRANULATED SUGAR

1 TABLESPOON GROUND CINNAMON

$1^1/_2$ TEASPOONS GROUND NUTMEG

1 CUP (2 STICKS) UNSALTED BUTTER

HUCKLEBERRY FILLING

12 CUPS FRESH HUCKLEBERRIES
  (SUBSTITUTE BLUEBERRIES)

$^1/_4$ CUP ($^1/_2$ STICK) UNSALTED BUTTER, MELTED

1 CUP GRANULATED SUGAR

$^1/_2$ CUP PORT

WHIPPED CREAM

2 CUPS HEAVY WHIPPING CREAM

$^1/_2$ CUP CONFECTIONERS' SUGAR

1 VANILLA BEAN, SEEDS SCRAPED OUT

VANILLA ICE CREAM, FOR SERVING
  (OPTIONAL, IN PLACE OF WHIPPED CREAM)

FOR THE CRISP TOPPING, COMBINE THE ALMONDS, OATS, flour, both sugars, cinnamon, and nutmeg in an electric mixer with a paddle attachment. Stir to incorporate.

Cube the butter and slowly beat in. Mix for 5 minutes on medium speed. The mixture should hold together when gathered in your hand. Refrigerate the topping while you prepare the filling.

Preheat the oven to 375°F.

For the huckleberry filling, toss together the huckleberries, butter, sugar, and port in a large bowl, and then divide among eight 6-ounce ramekins (one large baking dish). Crumble the topping evenly over the filling and bake for 30 to 40 minutes, or until the filling is bubbling over the crisp topping.

For the whipped cream, combine the cream, sugar, and vanilla bean seeds in the bowl of an electric mixer fitted with the whisk attachment. Beat on high speed until soft peaks form, about 4 minutes. Serve the warm crisp with whipped cream, or ice cream if you prefer.

ACKNOWLEDGMENTS

A LOT OF PEOPLE HELPED ME GET THIS BOOK FROM INSIDE MY HEAD TO THE FINISHED PRODUCT SO ABLY PRODUCED BY the crew at Running Press.

First of all, my beautiful and long-suffering wife, Mary Timmer Bentley and our dog Pal, both of whom had to put up with my loud, numerous, and always profane tirades against technology, deadlines and all of the other issues facing a would-be author of advancing age and an ADD personality.

Next, my friend and mentor, the late and absolutely great A. J. McClane, who for over four decades, published numerous books on cooking and the outdoors. He was a true sportsman and a classic gentleman of the old school.

On the literary side, my co-author Patrick Dillon whose quick wit and sharp pen helped overcome seemingly insurmountable challenges. Our agent, Andrew Stuart who somehow saw the merit in all of this and connected us with the incredible team at Running Press, particularly our editor Kristen Green Wiewora and the book's designer Amanda Richmond, two pros whose creative talent and patience is particularly noteworthy. Also to Lynn Donaldson, whose food and landscape photos illuminate many of these pages. Thanks to my friend Peter Bartlo of Manhattan, Montana, who lent us his beautiful ranch for some great photo shots.

Special thanks to our Belgrade neighbor, Debi Moro and her exceptional antique store Montana Camp, for making her premises and props available during our photo shoots.

I want to make a special mention to Steve Jackson, Curator of Photographs at the Museum of the Rockies in Bozeman, Montana, for his very much-appreciated assistance in locating all of the historical photographs in this book.

Finally, to all of my friends and customers from the Mint who lent their support and encouragement over the years, may you live and eat well always.

—JAY BENTLEY

JAY AND I CONCEIVED OF THIS COOKBOOK A FEW YEARS BACK WHILE BLISSFULLY TENDING AN OUTDOOR GRILL BESIDE a mountain lake in an early autumn snowfall in central Montana. We had already logged plenty of good times together: fly-fishing, wise-cracking, sharing our disdain of politics and our love of mountain streams and rolling pasture lands framed by serrated peaks. But most of all we shared a love for unadorned roadhouse fare and local ingredients: honest food.

From this mutual passion the naïve idea for *Open Range* was hatched. I say naïve because, as we were about to discover, producing a cookbook is a yin and yang collision: the "no detail too small" exactitude of a science lab with the primal desire to let fly with our sensory indulgences. In the end, it's the details that win the day. Thanks to our irrepressible agent Andrew Stuart and subsequently to Kristen Green Wiewora, our editor, who steered both of us with the resolve of any Montana herd dog, we're proud to place our essays and recipes into your kitchen custody.

Cooking is an act of love and so we also thank the multitude of volunteer tasters, chief among them our wives Mary and Anne, Jay's customers at the Mint, as well as our dinner guests in San Francisco and Sonoma County wine country. The latter, of course, had no idea they were performing their roles as canaries in my kitchen coalmine.

I also join Jay in praising local ranchers, herders, farmers, foragers, and vendors upon whose labor we have drawn heavily.

Also, as you turn these pages (and as Jay has given them their rightful due), give your regards to Amanda Richmond, whose creative energy burns hot and bright in our book design. Likewise Lynn Donaldson, Jay's Montana neighbor, whose intimate knowledge of Big Sky terrain and camera talent captured the indelible beauty that makes *Open Range* much more than a cookbook. Thank you, too, cousin Seonaid Campbell, a Montana writer and film producer who helped us "discover" Lynn.

Finally, I pay tribute to "old trusty," my four-burner, dual-oven, dual-broiler, refurbished O'Keefe & Merritt vintage gas range. We've been partners a long time. To many more years cooking for people we love and may you continue long after I'm gone.

—PATRICK DILLON

INDEX

Note: Page references in *italics* indicate recipe photographs.

PHOTOGRAPHY CREDITS

All photography by Lynn Donaldson, unless noted here.

PAGE 13: Top: Hunting Camp, Gallatin Canyon, Montana, ca. 1915.
Photographer: Schlechten Bros., from the Schlechten Collection,
© Museum of the Rockies, Catalog Number: x80.6.3028
Bottom: Packing in Camp Supplies, Mill Creek, Montana, August 1940
Photographer: John C. Haberstroh, from the John C. Haberstroh
Collection, © Museum of the Rockies, Catalog Number: 87.92.384

PAGE 14: Baker, Lamme and Tudor Group Picnic, Caldwell Ranch,
Cherry Creek, Montana, July 4, ca. 1900.
Photographer: Maurice Lamme, from the Maurice Lamme Collection
Rights: Copyright Museum of the Rockies, Catalog Number: x81.25.42

PAGE 15: Clockwise from Top: John Harvat Jr. Cooking Breakfast,
Tom Minor Basin, Montana, September 1925.
Photographer: John C. Haberstroh, from the John C. Haberstroh
Collection, © Museum of the Rockies, Catalog Number: 87.92.520

Twilight View of Lambing Camp, Strickland Creek, Paradise Valley,
Montana, July 1939.
Photographer: John C. Haberstroh, from the John C. Haberstroh
Collection, © Museum of the Rockies, Catalog Number: 87.92.452

Norris Spangler and Lamb, Harvat Flats, Near Livingston, Montana,
May 4, 1939.
Photographer: John C. Haberstroh, from the John C. Haberstroh
Collection, © Museum of the Rockies, Catalog Number: 87.92.672

PAGE 45: Top: Catch of Fish from Yellowstone River, Bozeman,
Montana, ca. 1900s.
Photographer: Unknown Photographer, from the McGill
Collection, © Museum of the Rockies, Catalog Number: x83.13.1705

PAGE 74: Cowhands on Frank Hazelbaker's Ranch, Dillon, Montana,
ca. 1935.
© Museum of the Rockies, Catalog Number: x83.13.334

PAGE 114: Edwin Harvat in Corral, Harvat Ranch, Livingston,
Montana, January 1937.
Photographer: John C. Haberstroh, from the John C. Haberstroh
Collection, © Museum of the Rockies, Catalog Number: 87.92.86

PAGE 115: Carl Jarrett watching the Flock, Harvat Ranch, Livingston,
Montana, June 1940.
Photographer: John C. Haberstroh, from the John C. Haberstroh
Collection. © Museum of the Rockies, Catalog Number: 87.92.612

PAGE 120: © Willow Spring Ranch

PAGE 151: Top: Hunting Camp, Gallatin Canyon, Montana,
ca. 1915.
Photographer: Schlechten Bros., from the Schlechten Collection,
© Museum of the Rockies, Catalog Number: x80.6.3028
Bottom: After a Day's Hunt, Karst's Ranch, Gallatin Canyon, Montana,
ca. 1915.
Photographer: Schlechten Bros., from the Schlechten Collection,
© Museum of the Rockies, Catalog Number: 97.19.12

PAGE 171: Feeding the Chickens, Eastern Montana, ca. 1922.
© Museum of the Rockies, Catalog Number: 84.33.46

PAGE 185: Roundup Chuck Wagon, Colorado, ca. 1910.
© Museum of the Rockies, Catalog Number: x85.2.821